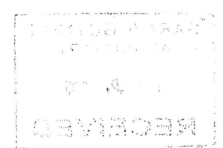

HISTORICAL
ATLAS
—OF THE—
ISLAMIC
WORLD

HISTORICAL
ATLAS
OF THE
ISLAMIC
WORLD

David Nicolle

MERCURY BOOKS
LONDON

HISTORICAL ATLAS OF THE ISLAMIC WORLD

Published in 2004 by Mercury Books
20 Bloomsbury Street,
London WC1B 3JH

You can find Facts On File on the World Wide Web at:
http://www.factsonfile.com

Project editor: Warren Lapworth
Maps and design: Roger Kean
Illustrations: Oliver Frey
Four-colour separation: Proskanz, Ludlow, England

ISBN: 1-904668-17-8

Printed in China by Sun Fung Offset Binding Co., Ltd.

Frontispiece:
Gur Amir Mausoleum of Timur-i Lenk, Samarkand, Uzbekistan, early 15th century AD. *Islamic architecture and applied decoration reached its artistic pinnacle under the Timurid dynasty.*

Title page: One of the great centers of Islamic influence during the medieval period, Cairo—"Mother of the World"— seen today from the city wall, north of the Mosque of Hakim.

Right: The minaret of Vabkent, Uzbekistan

Contents

Introduction

Rarely has Islamic culture been so at the forefront of popular consciousness in the Western world as it is today. At the same time, sadly, much of what the general public believe they know about Islam is incorrect, and is based on widespread myths or prejudices. Some of these myths are, of course, all too often reinforced by the activities of a fanatical few who claim to act in the name of Islam. In most cases their actions run totally counter to the fundamental principles of a noble religion which preaches toleration, peace, justice, love, and the sanctity of human life and human dignity.

The current interest in Islam would alone justify the publication of a book such as this. At the same time, however, the religion, culture, civilization, and arts of Islam are so rich and fascinating in their own right that they deserve to be better known, not only by non-Muslims but also by many Muslims. Many of the latter have a surprisingly narrow and inaccurate appreciation of several aspects of their own cultural history.

For example, there is a widespread belief among both Muslims and non-Muslims that the Faith of Islam emerged in a backward, primitive, and isolated part of the early medieval world: Arabia. However, recent archaeological and historical research has shown that ancient Arabia, or at least the most densely populated parts of the peninsula, were "primitive" only in terms of their religious beliefs. Even this can be overstated since Judaism and Christianity both had significant numbers of adherents within Arabia, as did Persian Zoroastrianism, while the religions of India may have had influence if not followers.

In other respects pre-Islamic Arabia formed a vital part of the ancient world, being closely linked to its western, northern, eastern, and southern neighbors through culture and trade.

The fact that the so-called "Golden Age" of early Islamic civilization played a vital role in the preservation, extension, and transfer of ancient Greek as well as other classical sciences to late medieval and renaissance Europe is generally accepted and widely repeated. But quite how this was done is much less well understood.

The fact that most parts of what are now the Islamic world were converted peacefully by missionaries, who were often at the same time merchants, is again rarely appreciated. The Western public too often regards Islam as a religion spread by force, whereas forcible conversion is, in fact, specifically banned by Islamic law.

One final point must be made. This book focuses on

Islamic history from the time of the Prophet Mohammed until the start of the 16th century AD. Strictly speaking, however, Muslims would maintain that the faith of Islam was the first of all religions, rather than being one of the last to emerge. It was, according to an Islamic interpretation of religious history, the faith of Adam and Eve, meaning in modern terms that it is the "natural" *din* or religion of mankind, and indeed of the newborn child before he or she comes under the influence of parents and society. Muslims maintain that this "original" and most ancient faith was either corrupted or forgotten by early civilizations, some of which went further astray than others. The Prophet Mohammed brought his followers "back to Islam."

Through Mohammed, God or Allah (as the sole deity is called in Arabic) gave humanity the Koran, which Muslims regard as the uncorrupted Word of God. This was to be God's final revelation, while Mohammed was the Seal of the Prophets, meaning he would be the last of those innumerable prophets or messengers whom God had sent to mankind since the dawn of creation.

Kazan

Astrakhan

Samarkand

Kashgar

Nishapur

Aleppo Tabriz

Damasucs Baghdad

TIBET

Lahore

Delhi

Medina

INDIA

Mecca

ARABIA

ARABIAN SEA

Aden

Socotra

Andaman Islands

Nicobar Islands

INDIAN OCEAN

Mogadishu

Maldive Islands

Malacca

Ternate — Tidore
Borneo   Banda

Seychelle Islands

Sumatra

Zanzibar

Macassar

Gomoros Islands

Java

AUSTRALIA

The Islamic world from the 7th–15th centuries AD

- Islamic territory at the death of the Prophet Mohammed, AD 632
- Islamic territory in the 9th century, but lost by 1500
- Islamic territory in the 9th century, and still Islamic by 1500
- Islamic territory gained from the 9th to 15th centuries

A BRIEF SELECTION OF USEFUL ARABIC TERMS

Ahl al-Bayt – descendents of the Prophet Mohammed
Ahl al-Dhimma – "protected people," e.g. People of the Book
atabeg – "father figure" or advisor
barid – government postal service
beylik – small Turkish state
da'i – missionary
diwan – government ministry
diwan al-jaysh – army ministry
furusiyah – military exercises
ghaza – struggle
ghulam – slave-recruited soldier
Haj – the annual Muslim pilgrimage to Mecca
hamam – communal bath
haram – sacred area
harim – family quarters in a palace or residential building
Hegira/Hijra – Mohammed's migration to Medina
Imam – spiritual leader
'itaqah – certificate of freedom
Jahilya – "Age of Ignorance" before Islam
jizya – tax from non-Muslims
Jund – regional structure of Islamic armies
kashan – type of pottery
kumiss – alcoholic drink
kuttub – students
litham – veil worn by desert nomads
majolica – type of ceramic
mamluk – slave recruited soldier
maydan – training ground
minai – varied colors on pottery
musta'a'riba – "those who became Arabs"
nayib al-qala'a – commander of fortress
nayib al-sultana – viceroy
nazir al-juyish – officer
niyabas – territorial units
qibla – orientation of prayer
quwwad – regimental officers
ribat – Islamic frontier outpost
shadd al-dawawin – senior officer
shadd al-muhimmat – aid to Sultan
Shahnamah – Persian epic poem
shurta – police force
sufism – Islamic mysticism
suras – chapters of the Koran
tabaqah – military school
tekke – religious meeting place
thughur – military frontier province
wadi – seasonal river
wali – government official
wilaya – territorial unit

CHAPTER ONE

Arabia from Paganism to Islam

The land of the Prophet, between two empires

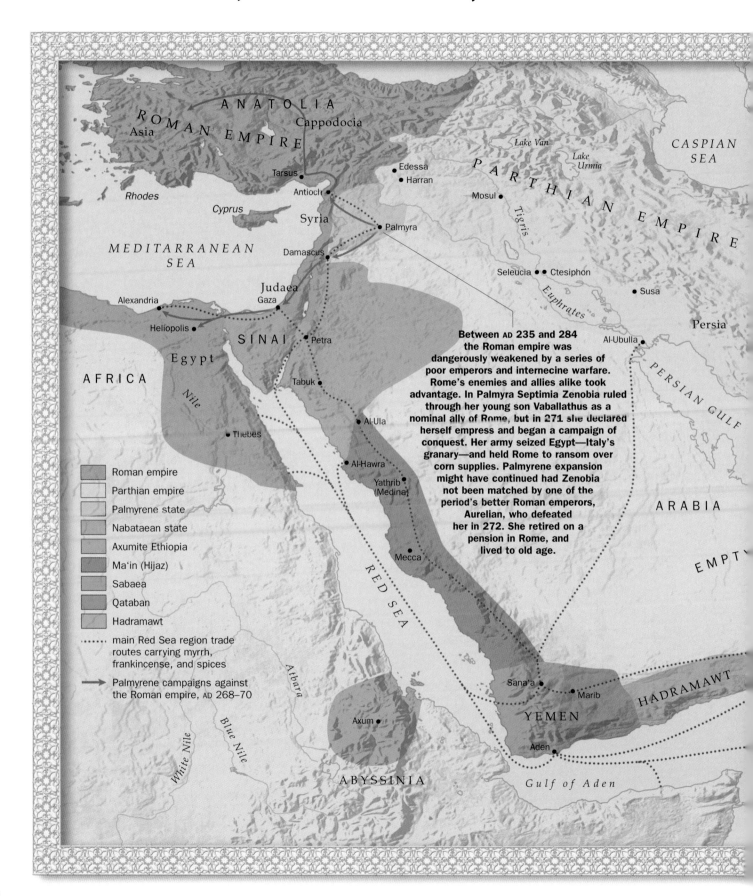

Between AD 235 and 284 the Roman empire was dangerously weakened by a series of poor emperors and internecine warfare. Rome's enemies and allies alike took advantage. In Palmyra Septimia Zenobia ruled through her young son Vaballathus as a nominal ally of Rome, but in 271 she declared herself empress and began a campaign of conquest. Her army seized Egypt—Italy's granary—and held Rome to ransom over corn supplies. Palmyrene expansion might have continued had Zenobia not been matched by one of the period's better Roman emperors, Aurelian, who defeated her in 272. She retired on a pension in Rome, and lived to old age.

Roman empire
Parthian empire
Palmyrene state
Nabataean state
Axumite Ethiopia
Ma'in (Hijaz)
Sabaea
Qataban
Hadramawt

······ main Red Sea region trade routes carrying myrrh, frankincense, and spices

→ Palmyrene campaigns against the Roman empire, AD 268–70

In AD 224–26 the Parthian empire, weakened by decades of war with the Roman empire, was overthrown by the sub-king of Persia, Ardashir I (r.220–40), who founded the Sassanian dynasty. The Sassanids pursued a more aggressive foreign policy than the Parthians. In 244, the king Shapur I (r.240–72) defeated and killed the Roman emperor Philip in battle and captured the emperor Valerian in 260. Sassanian power lasted for more than 400 years until it fell to the forces of Islam.

Gulf of Oman

Sohar

OMAN

UARTER

Salalah

ARABIAN SEA

Socotra

Ancient Arabia was the homeland of the Semitic peoples who, throughout recorded history, spread northward from the Arabian peninsula into what is known as the Fertile Crescent. Here they and their descendants, speaking a variety of related Semitic languages, developed a series of ancient civilizations. During the sixth century BC, however, it seemed as if Semitic energies were temporarily exhausted, and other peoples rose to dominance in the Middle East.

The new empires that rose and fell were dominated by non-Semitic peoples including Persians or other Iranians from the east, and Greeks or Romans from the west. By the first century AD the Middle East and most neighboring regions were dominated by two such empires. The eastern half formed part of the Parthian empire, centered on Iran, but having its economic and cultural heartland in Semitic Iraq.

The western half had long been incorporated into the Greco-Roman world, by then represented by the Roman empire. This region had its cultural and economic centers in Italy and Greece, including what is today western Turkey. Yet it also had a third economic, cultural, and religious powerhouse in one of its eastern frontier provinces; namely Semitic Syria. Bilad al-Sham, as it came to be known by Arabic speakers, comprised today's Syria, Lebanon, Jordan, Palestine-Israel, and part of southern Turkey.

Seemingly despised by Greek and Latin purists of the empire's two other centers, Syria nevertheless played an increasingly important role in the cultural, economic, and political life of the Roman empire. Here, beneath a veneer of Greco-Roman civilization, Christian, Jewish, and so-called pagan Semites had never lost contact with their indigenous cultural heritage. With the coming of the Muslim Arabs in the seventh century AD, the Greco-Roman veneer, which was itself now deeply influenced by Semitic culture including Christianity, was rapidly marginalized. The Semitic world had, in fact, reasserted itself.

SUM OF MANY PARTS

In reality, of course, a millennium of powerful Greco-Roman influence had left an indelible imprint on Syria, Egypt, Turkey, and many other lands which subsequently became Muslim or indeed Arab. During those centuries Greco-Roman civilization had also deeply influenced neighboring Iran and the Arabian peninsula. This was despite the fact that, apart from some disastrous Roman attempts to conquer the peninsula, Arabia had never been ruled by Alexander the Great, his Hellenistic Greek successors, or the Romans. Trade, culture, art, and religion had drawn Arabia into the orbit of Greco-Roman civilization, not Rome's legions.

A parallel process can be seen in Arabia's relationship with its other superpower neighbor, Iran. Here the Parthian empire, that emerged on the central Asian frontiers of the Iranian world in the third century BC, had been replaced by the Persian-Iranian empire of the Sassanians in the third century AD. This would survive as a great power until, to the astonishment of contemporaries and indeed many modern historians, it collapsed when challenged by remarkably small Muslim Arab armies in the seventh century AD.

Western historians have traditionally been preoccupied with the relationship between the Greco-Roman world and Arabia before the sudden emergence of the Arabs as a major factor in world affairs. Yet the influence of the Sassanid empire on pre-Islamic Arabia, and the relationship between Arabia and Sassanian-ruled Iraq, have tended to be neglected. In fact, these relationships were just as important as the one between Arabia and the Mediterranean world. Indeed, Iran would eventually provide the model for many aspects of medieval Islamic civilization.

Merchants and Farmers

Despite the impression frequently given, pre-Islamic Arabia was not inhabited solely by nomads who raided their settled neighbors whenever they had an opportunity. In reality the regions south of the Fertile Crescent were home to a remarkable variety of cultures.

Earlier Arabian cultures were based on differing ways of life, economic and socio-political systems, and—even as late as the sixth century AD—different languages. Northern Arabia, including the deserts of what are now Syria, Iraq, and Jordan, was neighbor to those "great powers" that dominated coastal Syria, Anatolia, and Iraq.

It was, in fact, only the harshness of their landscape that enabled the Aramaic and Arab inhabitants of these regions to maintain their independence. Occasionally they were conquered, but more often they

Right: Carving of a camel-rider from Dura Europos in Syria.

survived as clients or allies of the Roman or Persian empires. In return, the peoples of northern Arabia kept the trade routes open, were respectful to whichever empire they associated themselves with, and confined themselves to raiding each other, the rival empire, or its clients.

The peoples of northern Arabia led and protected merchant caravans between the infrequent sources of water. They also dominated desert warfare. Put simply, these desert peoples, whether they came from complex states based on cultivated oases with great cities or from simple tribes, were useful to their imperial neighbors.

At the same time the desert peoples counted among their number not only warriors, farmers, and herdsmen, but also merchants. Some of these clearly grew rich and, like their rulers, were patrons of art, architecture, and literature. Furthermore, merchants were the most knowledgeable people concerning distant lands, and as such they were probably the source of much of the geographical information preserved in Greek and Roman writings.

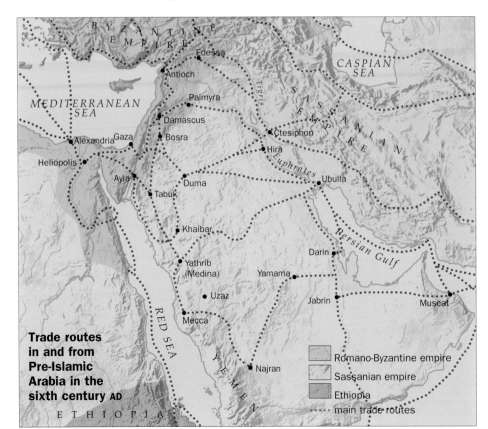

Trade routes in and from Pre-Islamic Arabia in the sixth century AD

Romano-Byzantine empire

Sassanian empire

Ethiopia

····· main trade routes

STUFF OF LEGEND

Among the desert states that maintained a precarious independence in northern Arabia and the Syrian desert were those of the Nabataeans, with their astonishing capital at Petra in Jordan. Most of what remains of Nabataean architecture comprises of rock-cut temples and tombs, such as those which led to Petra being described as the "rose-red city half as old as time."

The Nabataeans were not, of course, alone as patrons of sophisticated desert civilization. Palmyra, in the deserts of Syria, was also

Top: A Nabataean rock-cut tomb at Madain Saleh, Saudi Arabia.

Below: Golden in the sunset, the ruins of Palmyra in Syria sprawl amid the surrounding oasis.

Bottom: The ruins of Hatra in Iraq.

based on oases and trade routes. At first glance, this city was similar to those found in Greece or Rome, but closer inspection shows several distinctive features, the most obvious of which are the tower-tombs. Such monuments, and memories of the wealthy desert peoples who created them, featured prominently in later Arab legend.

On the eastern side of the desert, in what is now Iraq, other desert states emerged whose relationships with the Persian empires mirrored those of Petra and Palmyra with Rome. They included Hatra, whose vast ruins can still be seen in northwestern Iraq.

The Bedouin

Some historians have suggested that the nomadization of Arabia is a relatively recent phenomenon, in terms of the long history of the Middle East. However, most archaeologists believe that these Bedouin people have been a feature of Arabia for thousands of years.

Right: Ancient petraglyphs in Wadi Aday, Oman, depict riders and inscriptions.

Below: Bedouin tend sheep on a plain between Sukhne and the river Euphrates in Syria.

Most of what we know of the ancient Bedouin inevitably comes from the records of their settled neighbors, and as a result the nomads rarely appear in a sympathetic light. The study of early nomadic cultures is difficult because such societies left little for archaeologists to investigate. Nevertheless it is clear that the nomadic and semi-nomadic or transhumant Bedouin had dynamic cultures which were in no sense unchanging. This was true of their arts and languages and even more so of their social or political structures. The tribes and tribal confederations that existed in the fifth century AD were not the same as those seen some centuries earlier.

Tribal organization was based on families or clans that grew or dwindled according to political, economic, ecological, and other circumstances. Similar changes characterized the relationships between tribes, many of which had—or claimed—kinship with one another. The powerful supported the weak to build alliances, while the weak sought protection from the strong.

Yet the relationships between Arabian tribes was as volatile as those between neighboring states. Political tension between the pre-Islamic tribes often reflected interference by the Roman and Sassanian empires. These empires wanted to extend their influence or hegemony over a

strategically and economically important region, since Arabia stood at the hub of inter-regional trade. In return the Arab tribes tried to use great power rivalry to further their own local interests.

Over the years these political maneuverings led to the emergence of two major but internally quarrelsome associations of Arab tribes. One group was widely regarded as being "southerners," or so-called Yemeni tribes, though several actually dominated territory in the center and north of Arabia. The other group were considered to be "northerners," although they were again found in other parts of the peninsula.

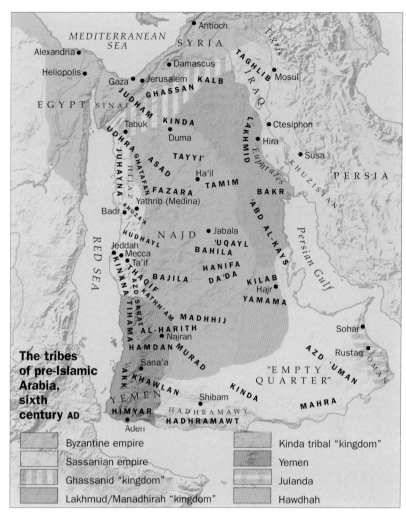

The tribes of pre-Islamic Arabia, sixth century AD

	Byzantine empire		Kinda tribal "kingdom"
	Sassanian empire		Yemen
	Ghassanid "kingdom"		Julanda
	Lakhmud/Manadhirah "kingdom"		Hawdhah

SOURCE OF PRIDE

The camel-riding Bedouin warrior of popular imagination was neither sufficiently well-armed nor did he have the social organization to form strong armies. Instead he generally played the part of a mere auxiliary, prone to looting and likely to go home when conditions became unfavorable.

Nevertheless the Bedouin enjoyed a special place in pre-Islamic Arab culture, being widely regarded as the embodiment of Arab virtues in contrast to the soft and corrupt inhabitants of the neighboring empires. The Bedouin's language, poetry, legends, and code of individual honor were a source of pride among other Arab-speaking peoples, be they semi-nomadic, urban, or even farmers who tended date groves in the oases.

This pride in a real or adopted tribal identity would survive long after the coming

of Islam, despite the fact that the tribal structure on which it was based would undergo fundamental changes during the first two centuries of Islamic history.

A 6th-century AD *Coptic carving from Egypt of a horseman leading a camel.*

13

A Land of Poets

The peoples of Arabia were famous for their oral traditions long before the Koran was written. Kinda rulers and the tribal aristocracy are believed to have been patrons of the rich tradition of Arab oral poetry.

The tribal confederation known as the Kinda passed information from generation to generation solely through memorization, since the written word had not yet become commonplace in the region. The Kinda created a kingdom that survived, in one form or another, for five centuries. Its territory covered most of what is now central Saudi Arabia, from Yemen in the south to the pro-Byzantine and pro-Sassanian tribal kingdoms in the north. The Kinda did not, however, dominate coastal regions bordering the Red Sea in the west, nor did they control any of the Persian Gulf coast to the east.

Nevertheless the landlocked tribal kingdom of the Kinda and their subordinate or allied tribes was powerful enough to play a major role in Middle Eastern affairs.

A noble family is seen feasting in this 1st–5th century AD *wall painting from Qaryat al-Faw in Saudi Arabia.*

Within its territory were several small towns as well as numerous oases inhabited by farming and merchant communities. Its capital was probably at Dhat Kahl, which has been identified as the modern site of Qaryat al-Faw in southwestern Saudi Arabia.

Qaryat al-Faw was an important location at a junction of trade routes. It held a regular trade fair, and irrigated agriculture added to its wealth. Among the ruins of Qaryat al-Faw is a remarkable fortified marketplace which looks rather like a Roman legionary fort. Wall paintings and other artifacts found here show that the Kinda, or at least their ruling elite, were sophisticated and cultured as well as rich. They imported luxuries from the Mediterranean world and elsewhere, while their costume, artistic tastes, and way of life were also influenced by Yemen, Iran, and even India.

Nevertheless the general impression of Kinda civilization shows that, in many ways, this tribal Arab people remained true to much more ancient Semitic traditions.

A LIVING TRADITION

The bulk of ancient Arabic verses was not written down until after Islam introduced widespread literacy to Arabia. Yet traditional Arabian society was one in which poetry was held in extremely high esteem, being handed down from generation to generation by word of mouth.

There is good reason to believe that the poetry that was eventually written down in the seventh to ninth centuries AD was virtually identical to the words which pre-Islamic Arab poets had devised hundreds of years earlier. This living tradition enabled many medieval and indeed some modern Muslims to memorize the entire Koran, a feat that seems incredible to today's Western societies.

Of course the Kinda elite were not alone in their role as patrons of poets. Almost every man or woman of status wished to do the same. In return the wealthy patron could hope for his or her fame to be immortalized by the poets.

Many members of the Arab elite were themselves poets. One of the greatest pre-Islamic Arab poets, Imru'l-Qays, was the son of a king of Kinda. Deprived of his inheritance when a usurper murdered his father and seized the throne, Imru'l-Qays traveled to visit the Roman emperor in the company of another poet-king named Samaw'al, searching for support.

Unfortunately Imru'l-Qays is said to have fallen in love with the emperor's daughter, and as a result the Roman emperor had him killed. Samaw'al, however, remained true to his promise of support for Imr'l-Qays and, when subsequently challenged by the usurper king of Kinda, Samaw'al sacrificed the life of his son rather than betray a trust.

This epic tale probably contains elements of historical truth, but more importantly, it reflects the cultural and ethical values of the society which produced such poets. These demanded that a man remain true to his promise and that he should be willing to travel far to achieve fame or justice. Furthermore these poems emphasized romantic love between men and women at a time when other civilizations regarded relations between men and women mostly as a means of consolidating property, producing children, and controlling sexual appetites.

A bronze statuette of a pagan goddess, dated 1st–5th century AD, found at Qaryat al-Faw.

The fortified "inner market" and unfortified "outer market" at Qaryat al-Faw

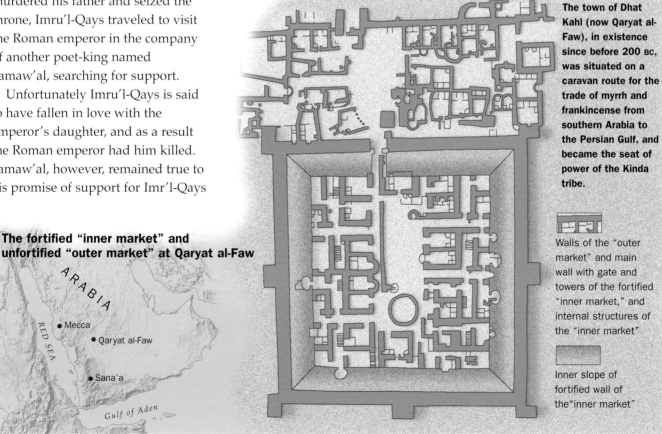

ARABIA

RED SEA

• Mecca

• Qaryat al-Faw

• Sana'a

Gulf of Aden

The town of Dhat Kahl (now Qaryat al-Faw), in existence since before 200 BC, was situated on a caravan route for the trade of myrrh and frankincense from southern Arabia to the Persian Gulf, and became the seat of power of the Kinda tribe.

Walls of the "outer market" and main wall with gate and towers of the fortified "inner market," and internal structures of the "inner market"

Inner slope of fortified wall of the "inner market"

The Land of Sheba

Southern Arabia was different from the rest of the peninsula. There had been the rise and fall of several sophisticated urban civilizations in the region, while today the Qara still maintain a pre-Islamic language and ideals.

Scenes of commerce and trade on a 2nd-century AD alabaster stele found at Saba, Yemen.

Most southern civilizations had thrived on long-distance trade through Yemen or along its coasts from India and Africa to the mighty empires of the ancient Middle East. Its dominant languages were Semitic, although there were significant communities who spoke languages that belonged to the Hamitic or African linguistic family.

Many aspects of southern Arabian civilization were very distinctive, yet Yemen maintained close trading links with distant civilizations. As a result features of Greco-Roman, Persian, and Indian culture can also be found along with artifacts from distant lands. These trade goods were imported by a wealthy urban population with a taste for foreign luxuries.

At the same time the civilizations of Yemen fell into two categories. Those on the coast were well known to merchants from Egypt, Greece, India, and even China, yet they were not necessarily the wealthiest. Some of the most remarkable southern Arabian states were on the other side of the mountains, centered on cultivated valleys whose seasonal streams ran not into the sea but into the desert. However, before they evaporated in marshes and salt flats, these streams sustained sophisticated irrigated or terraced agriculture. In several places their waters were contained by great dams, one of which, the Marib Dam, was so famous that its supposed breaking is thought to have caused the decline in south Arabian civilization.

In addition to having their own culture, art, architecture, language, and presumably a now lost literature, pre-Islamic Yemeni civilizations also had their own religions. They, like the ancient paganisms of the Middle East, had priests and perhaps scholars who, given south Arabia's moon cult, may have preserved a corpus of astronomical knowledge comparable to that of ancient Mesopotamia. Here it is worth

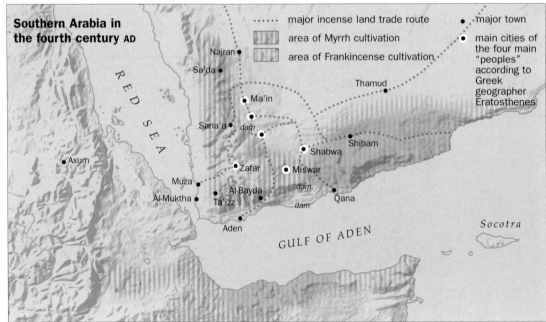

Southern Arabia in the fourth century AD

······ major incense land trade route

▨ area of Myrrh cultivation

▨ area of Frankincense cultivation

● major town

● main cities of the four main "peoples" according to Greek geographer Eratosthenes

RED SEA

GULF OF ADEN

Socotra

Najran
Sa'da
Ma'in
Sana'a · *dam*
Thamud
Axum
Zafar
Muza
Al-Muktha
Ta'izz
Al-Bayda
Miswar
Shabwa
Shibam
dam
Qana
Aden

noting that the moon-centered paganism of pre-Christian, pre-Islamic Syria survived at Harran well into the 11th century AD.

Safe behind the bulwark of northern and central Arabia, the civilizations of ancient Yemen were rarely threatened with interference by the superpowers of Rome and Persia. The Romans made an entirely unsuccessful attempt at invasion, but after that the south Arabians were largely left to play the role of merchants and middlemen in international trade between the Mediterranean, India, East Africa, and the Far East.

INTO DECLINE

For thousands of years southern Arabia and the Horn of Africa had earned considerable revenues by cultivating frankincense and myrrh. These two aromatic resins were essential for religious observances in the ancient and classical civilizations of the Mediterranean and Middle East.

With the triumph of Christianity, however, the market for myrrh and frankincense slumped. This had a major impact on the economies of the southern Arabian kingdoms. Trade routes shifted elsewhere, along with the wealth they brought, while the collapse of the western

Roman empire, and the difficulties experienced by the rival Sassanis, all contributed to political and social change in southern Arabia.

As a result the southern Arabia that existed in the sixth and early seventh centuries, immediately prior to the coming of Islam, was a pale shadow of its former glory. Many parts were now inhabited by tribes who spoke the Arabic of central and northern Arabia rather than the Sabaean and other ancient languages of the south. Nevertheless some communities continued to use non-Arab and even non-Semitic language.

A few continue to do so today—for example the Qara of Dhufar, between the Hadhramawt and Oman. These people still speak Shahari, which is believed to be related to the dialects of northeast Africa. Cattle remain central to Qara life, along with some pre-Islamic superstitions that seem to recall ancient southern Arabian paganism in which bulls represented the moon god Sin. Other beliefs hint at a forgotten cultural connection with Hindu India.

A pre-Islamic relief of warriors with spears; southern Arabia.

The ancient southern Arabian city of Marib was famous for its dam, which harnessed the waters of several seasonal inland rivers for irrigation.

Neighboring Empires

The states north of Arabia had almost always been more powerful. Only with the coming of Islam would this balance of power change, and even then the center of Islamic power soon moved northward, out of Arabia.

Medieval Islamic buildings cluster by the Greco-Roman ruins of the Temple of Bacchus at Baalbek in the Lebanon.

Following the collapse of the Hellenistic Greek Seleucid kingdom in Iran and Iraq during the third century BC, the territory east, north, and west of Arabia was divided between two rival powers. To the northwest was the seemingly eternal Roman empire which, from the sixth century AD onward, western historians usually call the late Roman or Byzantine empire. This dominated most of Anatolia (present day Turkey), Syria, and Egypt, while Nubia, the Sudan, and Ethiopia lay within its sphere of influence.

To the northeast lay the Persian empire, initially represented by that of the Parthians, and then, from the third century AD onward, by that of the Sassanians. It dominated Iran, Iraq, most of the Caucasus region, and sometimes the eastern provinces of what is now Turkey. Despite frequent and occasionally epic wars between these superpowers, the frontier between them rarely moved very far. On the other hand smaller states, such as Armenia and Georgia, occasionally managed to maintain a precarious independence between the two giant states.

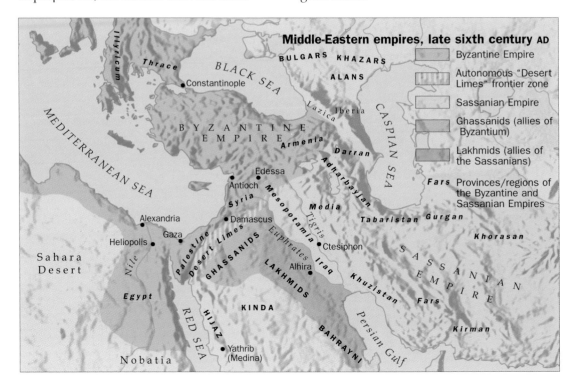

Middle-Eastern empires, late sixth century AD

- Byzantine Empire
- Autonomous "Desert Limes" frontier zone
- Sassanian Empire
- Ghassanids (allies of Byzantium)
- Lakhmids (allies of the Sassanians)
- *Fars* Provinces/regions of the Byzantine and Sassanian Empires

BETWEEN TWO WORLDS

The steppe and desert that lay south of the frontier between the Roman and Persian empires was generally controlled by Aramaic or Arab tribal states. Those that usually controlled the western side of the steppe and desert were federated allies or dependencies of the Roman empire, while those that dominated the eastern side were linked to the Parthian or Sassanian empires. The degree of autonomy which such desert surrogates enjoyed depended on the power and goodwill of their patrons.

Sometimes these kingdoms played an almost independent role in the power-politics of their day. Nabataean Petra dealt with the Roman imperial authorities in Syria almost on terms of equality, while Zenobia, the ruler of Palmyra, even attempted to replace Roman power in the east during the mid-third century AD. Such an ambition could only have been considered when Roman power was at a low ebb, and the strong emperor Aurelian ended her pretensions.

The Persians' Arab surrogates on the desert fringes of Iraq never attempted anything quite so ambitious. Here the Lakhmid tribal kingdom was usually a loyal auxiliary of the Sassanian empire, and its capital at al-Hira was effectively inside Sassanid territory. Nevertheless the Lakhmid state played a major role in Arabian affairs during the pre-Islamic period and had grown very powerful by the sixth century AD, profiting from a decline in Sassanian prestige.

But before the Lakhmids could challenge the Sassanian empire within Iraq, the Sassanids abolished the Lakhmid dynasty and took over direct control of the desert frontier. This strategic error made the subsequent Arab-Islamic invasion of Iraq much easier.

The rival Ghassanids played a comparable role along the opposing late Roman or early Byzantine frontier, competing with the Lakhmids for influence deep within Arabia. Their supposed capital, like that of the Lakhmids, actually lay within the territory of their sponsors, being on what is now the Syrian Golan plateau.

One of the most effective weapons available to the Byzantines and Ghassanids was religion, for in those days conversion to Christianity usually indicated political as well as cultural allegiance. This would be a very significant factor in Arabian affairs during the immediate pre-Islamic period.

Ruins of the Sassanian palace at Ctesiphon, downstream from Baghdad, Iraq.

c.450 AD	c.500–583	505	522	534	539–562	570	570
Christian kingdom of Axum in Ethiopia at the height of its power	Ghassanids (allies of Byzantium) and Lakhmids (allies of Sassanians) engaged in war	Hun invasion through Caucasus allies Byzantium and Sassanians to fight common threat	Axumite occupation of Yemen	Byzantines control North Africa after their defeat of Vandal kingdom	Second Byzantine-Sassanian War under Emperor Justinian I	Axumites invade Hijaz but fail to take Mecca	Birth of Prophet Mohammed in Mecca, on August 20

Links to the East

Most merchants who plied the ocean between the Middle East and India during the pre-Islamic period seem to have been Persians, Greeks living in Egypt, or Indians. Arabs only played a secondary role, but their influence spread in tandem with the rise of the Sassanids.

Below right:
Terracotta plaque of an Indian warrior with sword and shield. Indian swords were much-prized in Arabia.

Below: Carving of a warrior in Iranian or Middle Eastern garb; subsidiary figure of a Hindu god.

Most Persian merchants seem to have come from the Gulf and southern Iraq, so many of them may have been Arabic-speaking subjects of the Persian empire. Arabian countries like Oman and Yemen, which were later to dominate long-distance trade across the Indian Ocean, only traded in small numbers. Nevertheless, it is clear that Arab merchant communities settled in East Africa in pre-Islamic times.

The coastal regions of Oman were incorporated into the Sassanian Persian empire in the mid-third century AD, and the Sassanians would also occupy Yemen just over 300 years later. Trade with India, southeast Asia, and East Africa was already very important to these parts of Arabia, whether or not Arab merchants and sailors played a significant part.

Some of the ships involved were large, three-masted vessels capable of carrying bulk cargoes. They crossed the oceans using predictable and seasonal monsoon winds. One such ship appears on a little-known wall-painting in the rock-cut temple complex at Ajanta, northeast of Bombay in India. It dates from about AD 600.

A more detailed picture of a similar vessel was scratched on a plaster wall at Siraf on the Gulf coast of Iran several centuries later. This was, of course, at a time when the sailors of Rome and Greece rarely ventured out of sight of land. Knowledge of deep-sea sailing was clearly more advanced in the east where the navigational skills of sea captains was, to some extent, built upon the remarkably sophisticated astronomical observations which had characterized Mesopotamian and Indian civilizations.

RISE OF OMAN

The decline of southern Arabia and the Red Sea trading route was associated with a notable increase in the importance of Oman and the Persian Gulf as a major artery of trade. The Sassanian empire was also keener on promoting international commerce than its Parthian predecessors had been. This was one reason why the Sassanians put such effort into dominating both coasts of the Persian Gulf. They imposed direct rule on what are now Bahrain and Qatar, and along the coasts of Oman, which they called Mazun.

with Kalah in what is now Malaya. Occasionally some courageous merchants and seamen ventured as far as Vietnam and even southern China. Meanwhile Chinese ships sailed west as far as Sri Lanka but do not seem to have reached Arabia, at least not on a regular basis.

Given this well-established pattern of long distance trade, it is hardly surprising to find that Indian swords were highly prized in Arabia and featured prominently in pre-Islamic Arabic poetry. The best were made of Indian steel, which was then considered the finest available in the Middle East. But whether they were usually imported as completed blades or were forged within Arabia from imported ingots of Indian steel called *wootz* remains unclear.

Trade between Arabia, India, and the Indies did not only involve small volumes of high value goods such as bales of silk or sword blades. There was also a bulk trade in iron ore, iron, and steel ingots, and even of horses. These animals were shipped from Arabia and the Gulf to India across the open ocean—a feat of maritime transportation that would have astonished the mariners of the Greco-Roman world. Paradoxically, the resulting legends of "horses from the sea" that developed in India were later sent back to the Arab world, where they can be found in the *Tales of One Thousand and One Nights*.

Left: Wall-painting of an ocean-going ship, part of the extensive decorations within the Ajanta caves, near Bombay, India; c.AD 600.

The Omani port of Sohar rose to prominence and its seafarers, both Arab and Persian, competed with the more famous Silk Road across central Asia to import silk and other exotic goods from the east. Most of their voyages went no further than southwest India and the island of Sri Lanka, but some ships traded

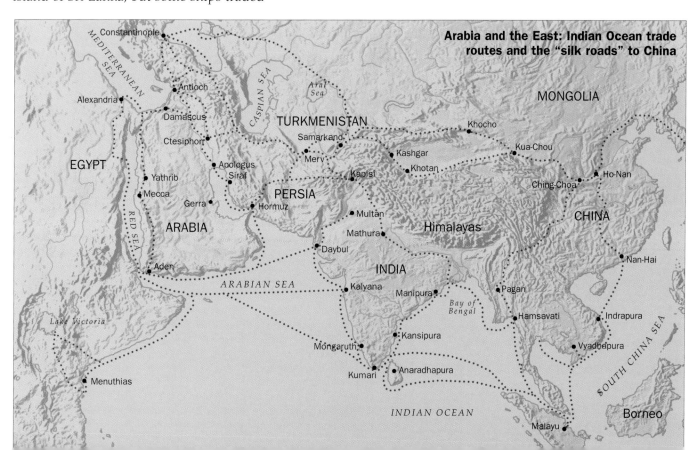

Arabia and the East: Indian Ocean trade routes and the "silk roads" to China

Judaism in Pre-Islamic Arabia

Many historians believe that the Jewish population of southern Mesopotamia was one of the most numerically and culturally significant since the Babylonian captivity of the Jewish people in the sixth century BC. The Jews in what is now Iraq steered worship toward synagogue attendance, and were influential upon the Persian empire.

Facing below: The supposed tombs of Esther and Mordecai in their mausoleum at Hamadan, Iran.

Below: "Battle between Israelites and Philistines for possession of the Ark of the Covenant;" wall painting from the ruined 3rd-century AD synagogue in the Roman Euphrates frontier fortress of Dura Europus.

By the fifth and sixth centuries AD, the main center of Jewish population and culture was not in Palestine but in Iraq. These people would be instrumental in developing Judaism into the form that exists today. There were also significant Jewish populations in Egypt, Syria, Anatolia (present day Turkey), and Persia (western Iran), as well as elsewhere within the Roman empire. Other smaller Jewish communities flourished much further afield, beyond the frontiers of both the Roman and Persian empires. Meanwhile there was, of course, still a Jewish minority within the Roman and early Byzantine provinces of Palestine, but its importance was religious and perhaps symbolic rather than numerical or economic.

Another rarely recognized aspect of Judaism during the early Christian era was the fact that it had become a proselatizing religion, welcoming and indeed seeking converts among other peoples whether they be fellow Semites in the Middle East, or non-Semitic peoples in Europe, Asia, and Africa. The remarkable spread of Judaism was not simply a result of the dispersal of a nation that had been exiled from its Palestinian homeland, first by the Babylonians and subsequently by the Romans following the Jewish revolts in the first and second centuries AD. The Romans had not driven the Jews from rural Palestine following these uprisings, but only from its cities.

DEVELOPMENT OF THE TALMUD

Iraq was also where Jewish religious practice as it is now known—based on attendance at synagogue rather than focusing on sacrifice in the Temple of Jerusalem—had evolved since the sixth century BC. Here too the religious and scholarly elite of rabbis emerged as an alternative to the ancient

Jewish priestly caste. They and other scholars in Palestine had codified Jewish law as the basis of the corpus of learning now known as the Talmud.

More surprisingly, perhaps, the large Jewish communities in what are now Iraq and western Iran wielded considerable political influence with the Persian empires. Those of Iraq had even provided troops for the armies of the Herodian kings in Palestine during the first century BC and the first century AD.

In contrast the Jewish or Judaized tribes of western Arabia were not known for their scholars. Instead they played a major though localized political, economic, and military role. The Herodian dynasty itself stemmed from the Idumaeans, an early Arab tribe in southern Palestine. They had been assimilated into Syrian Aramaic and then Jewish culture, absorbing many aspects of non-Semitic Greco-Roman civilization before returning to their cultural roots following the collapse of the Herodian dynasty. They are then believed to have re-emerged as the Judham Arab tribe of southern Palestine in the immediate pre-Islamic period.

Further south other Arabic-speaking Jewish tribes in the Hijaz region of what is now western Saudi Arabia were similarly descended from local converts, plus a few Jewish settlers. They were powerful and wealthy enough to pose a serious challenge to the initial rise of Islam in this area.

Whereas the Jewish tribes of western Arabia were eventually absorbed within Arab-Islamic society, the large Jewish population of Yemen continued to flourish down to modern times, when it was persuaded to migrate to the new state of Israel. The Jews of pre-Islamic Yemen briefly became the dominant local power, having been drawn into the rivalries between the Roman and Persian empires as Sassanian allies.

It was then that the epic figure of Dhu-Nuwas converted to Judaism, seized the throne of Yemen, and made war on the Byzantine empire's local Christian surrogates. He is remembered as a heroic figure in Arab legend, finally being defeated by a Christian Ethiopian army that invaded Yemen as allies of the Byzantine empire.

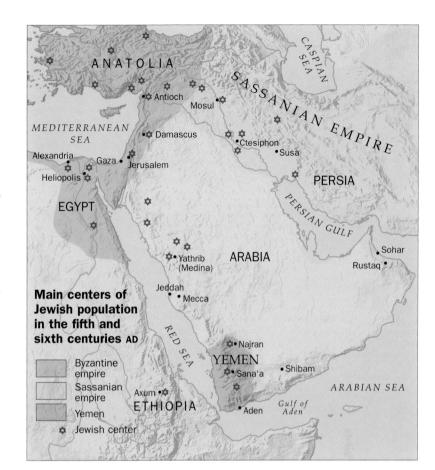

Main centers of Jewish population in the fifth and sixth centuries AD

- Byzantine empire
- Sassanian empire
- Yemen
- ✡ Jewish center

Christianity in Pre-Islamic Arabia

Christians from the east and south of the Arabian peninsula spread their religion in different directions with Monophysite and Nestorian sects. Monophysites worked in Africa, the Yemen, and the Syrian frontier, while Nestorians met with success in Iran and central Asia.

The distribution of Christian and Jewish peoples within pre-Islamic Arabia shows an apparent paradox. The Jews, whose political and cultural links were with the Persian empires in Iraq, were mostly in the west of the Arabian peninsula. The Christians, whose links might be assumed to have been with the Romano-Byzantine empire, were concentrated in the east and south of the peninsula as well as the Syrian frontier zone. This situation was a result of the way in which Christianity spread during its early years.

The conversion of neighboring Arab, Iranian, and African peoples was not carried out by missionaries from the Orthodox

Right: 6th–7th century Coptic carved relief of a man leading a loaded camel, "Labors of the Month."

Below: Ruins of the Cathedral of Saints Sergius and Bacchus in Bosra, Syria.

Christian Church, as might be presumed. The separation of the Orthodox Greek Church from the Latin or Catholic Church had not occurred at this period.

The Church had, however, been split by several earlier disagreements. The Monophysites, for example, maintained that Christ had one nature and that it was wrong to see him as having both human and divine aspects. This was regarded as an extreme position by the Orthodox or Catholics. In contrast the Nestorians represented the other end of this debate. They maintained that Christ was a man who had been inspired by God and as such had two quite distinct natures. This Nestorian view of Jesus Christ is remarkably close to the Islamic view, since Muslims regard Jesus as a divinely inspired prophet like those of the Old Testament, and like Mohammed himself.

Detailed matters of religious faith were so important in the Romano-Byzantine world that these differing opinions caused major social and political problems. Whereas the Monophysites were generally tolerated by the imperial authorities, being strongest in Armenia, southern Palestine, and Egypt, the Nestorians were unacceptable and so their main centers lay outside the Romano-Byzantine frontier, but inside those of the rival Persian empires.

LARGE-SCALE CONVERSION

Monophysite missionaries converted the Arab tribes of the Syrian frontier as well as the African peoples of Nubia, Sudan, and Ethiopia. From there Monophysite Christianity reached Yemen. Meanwhile Nestorian missionaries spread their faith across much of Iran, deep into central Asia, and probably to southern India. Closer to home Nestorian Christians may actually have become the majority faith in pre-

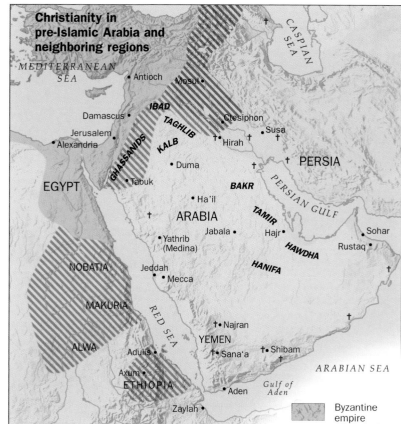

Islamic Iraq, and won numerous converts among the Arab tribes of eastern Arabia.

The Christianity practiced by uneducated tribesmen in pre-Islamic Arabia was of an unsophisticated and even heretical form. This probably accounts for the fact that the Christian religious figures mentioned in early Islamic sources differ from those seen within most Christian churches. Nevertheless Christian stories and beliefs, along with their Jewish counterparts, were widely known in Arabia at the time of Mohammed and had a significant impact on his own Revelation.

Christianity in Yemen was more mainstream, although still Monophysite, presumably because an established church hierarchy and system of organization developed here. It was this structured Christian community that became involved in Romano-Byzantine political ambitions at the southern end of the Red Sea.

Unlike the significant Jewish population in Yemen, the Yemeni church did not survive and little evidence of its existence remains. Aspects of its history are, however, embedded in garbled accounts of some of its martyrs, including those killed at Najran by Dhu-Nuwas in the early sixth century AD.

The map legend reads:

- Byzantine empire (Christian)
- Sassanian empire (officially Zoroastrian)
- Regions of Sassanian empire with probable Christian majority by late sixth century AD
- Christianized by late sixth century AD
- † Other significant Christian communities
- **IBAD** Substantially Christianized Arab tribes

Right: Stele with architectural carving at Axum in Ethiopia.

Pre-Islamic Arabian Paganism

Pagan gods and goddesses had much in common with the pagan religions of earlier Semitic civilizations to the north. It had elements of past and future beliefs, with deities related to the Greek pantheon, and Mecca as a center of pilgrimage.

Most of what is known about pre-Islamic paganism comes from the writings of those who were hostile to its beliefs and practices. A few inscriptions and carvings have been found by archaeologists, but artifacts are few. However, the general nature of Arabian religion, and the pantheon of gods that were worshipped, is known.

Right: A 3rd-century inscribed stele, dedicated to the Lihyanite deity Thu Hgebbat now stands upside down at al-Ula.

Like the pagan peoples of pre-Christian Syria, the pagan Arabs, including those of Yemen, sometimes associated their deities with those of the ancient Greek and Roman pantheon when the god or goddess in question had similar characteristics. This may be why some stone carvings and

bronze statuettes found in Arabia look so similar to Hellenistic Greek art. Some of them may even have been imported from the Mediterranean world.

Nothing remains of the pagan statues which once stood in the Ka'aba, in the center of Mecca. Nevertheless descriptions of these idols, based on lost earlier writings,

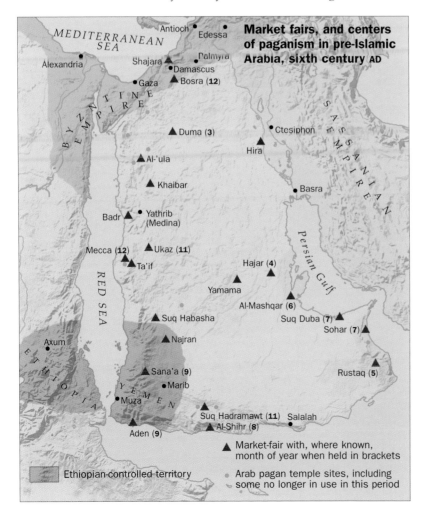

Market fairs, and centers of paganism in pre-Islamic Arabia, sixth century AD

Antioch
Edessa
MEDITERRANEAN SEA
Alexandria
Shajara
Palmyra
Damascus
Gaza
Bosra (12)
BYZANTINE EMPIRE
SASSANIAN EMPIRE
Duma (3)
Ctesiphon
Hira
Al-'ula
Khaibar
Basra
Badr
Yathrib (Medina)
Mecca (12)
Ukaz (11)
Ta'if
Hajar (4)
Persian Gulf
Yamama
RED SEA
Al-Mashqar (6)
Suq Habasha
Suq Duba (7)
Sohar (7)
Axum
Najran
Rustaq (5)
ETHIOPIA
Sana'a (9)
Marib
Muza
YEMEN
Suq Hadramawt (11)
Salalah
Al-Shihr (8)
Aden (9)

▲ Market-fair with, where known, month of year when held in brackets

Ethiopian-controlled territory

● Arab pagan temple sites, including some no longer in use in this period suggest that some of them had characteristics in common with statues from pagan Arab temples in Petra, Palmyra, and Dura Europus. One war god was, for example, dressed in armor and some carried two swords, or one sword and a large dagger, as was typical of comparable carvings in Iraq and Iran.

The most important of these deities were al-Lat, al-Uzza, Manat, and Hubal. The first three were regarded as the daughters of Allah, the supreme God. Since they could intercede with Him on behalf of humanity, they were at the center of many popular cults. Al-Lat was also worshipped in pagan Syria but was represented by many different symbols: in Arabia as a pure white stone; in Petra as the sun; and as a lion in Palmyra.

Al-Uzza was worshipped in the form of three palm trees and was the patron deity of the Quraysh, Mohammed's own tribe. Manat was the goddess of fate and death while Hubal was the male god of fertility, spring, and agriculture. His cult had probably been introduced from Syria where he was also known as Baal, Adonis, or Tammuz.

Al-Zuhara was the goddess of physical love like the Greek Aphrodite or Roman Venus, but she ranked lower than the three daughters of Allah. Other deities protected caravans in the desert, or were personifications of the moon and sun. Lesser deities came to be associated with sacred trees, rocks, and wells in the often threatening landscape in which the pagan Arabs lived.

TRIBAL MEETING PLACES

There were several centers of pagan pilgrimage in pre-Islamic Arabia, Mecca being one of them. Here the rites associated with one or more deities took place at the same time as markets, when the surrounding tribes gathered to exchange their produce and to trade with merchants. Such fairs were usually a time of truce between the often warring tribes; it being agreed that feuds must stop during the sacred period and within the sacred zone.

Each fair was held at the same time each year, and since most were in different months, the merchants moved from one to the other. Furthermore these fairs became major cultural festivals where poets gathered to compete and seek patronage.

Like the pagan pantheon of the ancient Greeks, the deities of ancient Arabia were ranked according to seniority, with Allah as the supreme god. With the coming of Islam all the others were swept away, and it became a central tenet of the Islamic faith that there is only one god—Allah. Nevertheless, the ancient gods and goddesses were not entirely forgotten. They survived in legends, folk tales, and children's stories. Some shrank to being one of the host of devils, angels, jinnis, and other immortal beings which most Muslims believed to exist.

Above: Bronze statuette of a kneeling man, possibly praying, found at Qaryat al-Faw; 3rd century BC.

Left: Modern-day pilgrims surround the Ka'aba in Mecca during the Hajj. The city was a center of worship in pre-Islamic times, when the Ka'aba housed images of pagan deities.

CHAPTER ONE

Rumors of War

The long struggle between the Romano-Byzantine and Persian empires came to a head in the late sixth and early seventh centuries. Their eras were drawing to a close—soon Muslim armies would pour out of Arabia, destroying the Persian empire and threatening the Byzantine realm.

Bronze statuette of the Sassanian Shahinshah; late 6th–early 7th century AD

About AD 574 a Sassanian expedition drove the Byzantine empire's Ethiopian allies out of Yemen, and in 597 the Persians imposed direct rule on southern Arabia. It is, however, unclear whether the Sassanian garrisons already based in Oman also linked up with the expeditionary force in Yemen to establish Sassanian authority along the entire Indian Ocean coast of Arabia.

In 602 the Sassanids abolished the autonomous Lakhmid Arab kingdom on the desert frontier of Iraq, and ten years later made a dramatic breakthrough against its Romano-Byzantine rival. Sassanian armies launched a heavy assault, overrunning much of Anatolia and occupying Syria, Palestine, and Egypt. Jerusalem fell, to the horror of the Christian world but to the delight of many Jewish Sassanid supporters.

Some Sassanian troops may even have penetrated North Africa and the Sudan, and clearly overrun Egypt. As a result the whole Arabian peninsula must have fallen within the Sassanian empire's sphere of influence. This was, of course, precisely the period when the future Prophet Mohammed was a young man in Mecca. The only surviving Christian powers in this part of the world were in Ethiopia and the newly converted kingdoms of Nubia in the Sudan.

In the early seventh century there was a dramatic reversal in the fortunes of the rival empires. A new Romano-Byzantine emperor named Heraclius imposed his authority throughout what remained of his empire, than launched a devastatingly effective counter-offensive against the Sassanians and their allies.

By 627 the war was over. Heraclius's troops had not only retaken Egypt, Syria, and eastern Anatolia, but had driven deep into enemy territory to occupy the Sassanian empire's economic and political heartland in Iraq. Realizing that it would be impossible to conquer the entire Sassanian empire, Heraclius opened negotiations. These seem to have gone on for some time, and several Romano-Byzantine garrisons had still not withdrawn from nominally Sassanian territory when a new threat to both empires suddenly emerged from an unexpected

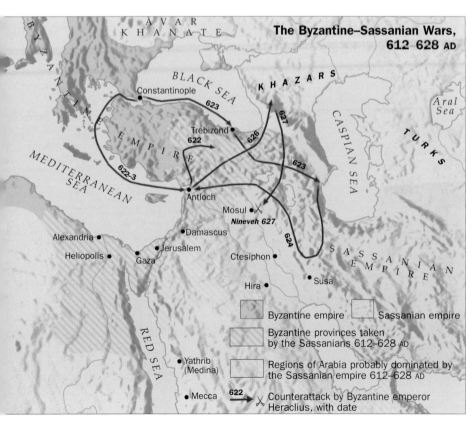

The Byzantine–Sassanian Wars, 612–628 AD

Byzantine empire Sassanian empire

Byzantine provinces taken by the Sassanians 612–628 AD

Regions of Arabia probably dominated by the Sassanian empire 612–628 AD

622 ⟶ Counterattack by Byzantine emperor Heraclius, with date

existing political relationships, and there seems to have been a significant increase in the availability of advanced modern weaponry. This not only included arms and armor but also siege weaponry, and a new development in equine technology—the stirrup, which the Huns had brought to Europe. Many Arabs, including some early Muslim leaders, despised this new invention and believed that it weakened a horseman rather than giving him any military advantage.

Meanwhile many Arab soldiers had taken part in the war between the Romano-Byzantine and Sassanian empires, being present on both sides and often serving far from Arabia itself. Perhaps this resulted in a significant strengthening in the Arabs' military self-confidence, as experienced soldiers returned home with well-honed military skills.

Top left: Silver-gilt plate of a mounted Sassanian-style horse-archer.

Below left: A gold coin portrays the Romano-Byzantine emperor Heraclius.

Below: One of the silver Byzantine so-called "David Plates" from the early 7th century includes a depiction of two Hebrew soldiers dressed like those who served Heraclius against the Sassanians.

direction. The Arabs had erupted from the Arabian peninsula under the banner of a new religion—Islam.

IN THE NAME OF ALLAH

The precise sequence of events within Arabia during the epic struggle between the empires of Rome and Iran remains unclear. There had been fighting between different tribes and groups, some sponsored by one of the neighboring empires, others acting independently.

Trade was disrupted, as were many of the

Enemies in the South

The struggle for southern Arabia involved not only the people of Yemen and neighboring regions of the peninsula, but also invading armies from Ethiopia and the Sassanian empire. The region became embroiled in part of a larger war for the whole of Arabia.

Right: A Coptic textile fragment shows a seated Persian-style prince and a battle between Arabs and Ethiopians.

Below: Ruins of the Dengur palace at Axum in Ethiopia.

Anew battle for control of Arabia began when Ethiopia was converted to Christianity in the middle of the fourth century. This was more than merely a religious event, since it meant that the kingdom of Ethiopia had now become a client and ally of the Romano-Byzantine empire. There was also a growing Christian minority in Yemen, and so to counter a possible extension of Romano-Byzantine power there on the other side of the Red Sea, the rival Sassanian empire cultivated good relations with the pagan and Jewish populations of Yemen.

Matters came to a head when Dhu-Nuwas became king of the country in 523–4. He is believed to have been the son of a previous ruler of Yemen, while his mother was Jewish and came from the Sassanian province of Iraq. Dhu-Nuwas decided to adopt the religion of his mother, and his campaigns to win control of Yemen resulted in the persecution of local Christians. This gave the Byzantine empire justification to act, to save the threatened minority. Rather than invading Yemen themselves, the Byzantines encouraged the Ethiopian Christians to do so, even though they were Monophysites. They also supplied ships from the Byzantine province of Egypt, to ferry Ethiopian armies across the Red Sea.

Dhu-Nuwas defeated the first Ethiopian assault but was killed during the second, while the kingdom of Ethiopia installed its own governors and garrisons in part of southern Arabia. Nevertheless Ethiopian control never seems to have extended across all of southern Arabia, and was instead concentrated on the Red Sea coast and mountains around the Yemeni capital of Sana'a.

One of the Ethiopian governors in Yemen was named Abraha, and although he rebelled against direct control by Ethiopia, he remained loyal to the Ethiopian and Christian cause. It has been suggested that he wanted to build a great new church which would become the religious center of Arabia and the focus of Arab pilgrimage. Since religious pilgrimages were so closely associated with market fairs, such a move would also have brought considerable economic and political benefits. But to succeed in this attempt Abraha would have to destroy the main pagan pilgrimage centers.

A CHRISTIAN MECCA

In the year 570 and in alliance with the Kinda Arab tribal confederation, Abraha marched against the town of Mecca with its still pagan sanctuary of the Ka'aba. According to Islamic legend Abraha's army, which included at least one war elephant, was forced to turn back as a result of divine intervention. This, the well-remembered

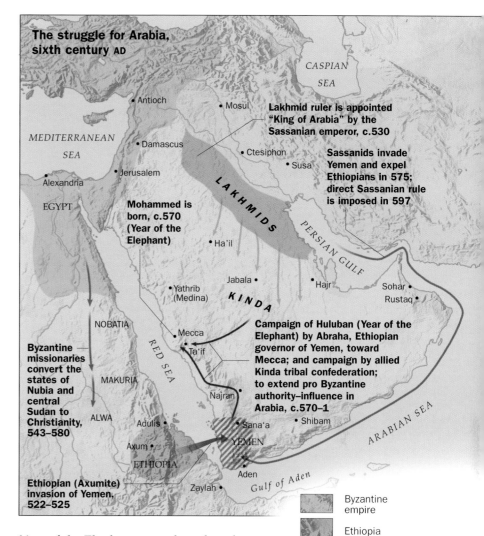

The struggle for Arabia, sixth century AD

Lakhmid ruler is appointed "King of Arabia" by the Sassanian emperor, c.530

Sassanids invade Yemen and expel Ethiopians in 575; direct Sassanian rule is imposed in 597

Mohammed is born, c.570 (Year of the Elephant)

Byzantine missionaries convert the states of Nubia and central Sudan to Christianity, 543–580

Campaign of Huluban (Year of the Elephant) by Abraha, Ethiopian governor of Yemen, toward Mecca; and campaign by allied Kinda tribal confederation; to extend pro Byzantine authority–influence in Arabia, c.570–1

Ethiopian (Axumite) invasion of Yemen, 522–525

CASPIAN SEA

Antioch • Mosul

MEDITERRANEAN SEA

• Damascus • Ctesiphon • Susa

• Jerusalem

• Alexandria

EGYPT

LAKHMIDS

PERSIAN GULF

• Ha'il

Jabala • • Hajr Sohar • Rustaq •

• Yathrib (Medina) KINDA

NOBATIA • Mecca

• Ta'if

MAKURIA RED SEA

Najran •

ALWA Adulis • Sana'a • Shibam

Axum • YEMEN

ETHIOPIA Aden

Zaylah • Gulf of Aden

ARABIAN SEA

- Byzantine empire
- Ethiopia
- Probable extent of Ethiopian occupation of Yemen, 525–575 AD
- Sassanian empire
- Lakhmids

Year of the Elephant, was also when the Prophet Mohammed was born.

During the Ethiopian occupation of Yemen it was Jews and pagans who were persecuted by Christians, but the Sassanian empire's decision to send an expeditionary force to conquer southern Arabia was probably a result of strategic rather than religious considerations. The Ethiopians were expelled in 575 and thereafter Yemen remained under somewhat tenuous Sassanian rule until the coming of Islam.

The decline of southern Arabia during the troubled fifth and sixth centuries can, however, be overstated. The area was capable of providing much of the military manpower and sophisticated military know-how seen in several of the earliest Arab-Islamic conquests. Furthermore, Yemen's own culture clearly survived, not least in its architecture, and it remained culturally distinct from the rest of Arabia even after converting to Islam.

Right: A mounted warrior saint, equipped with primitive stirrups, charges forth on a Coptic textile of the 7th century AD.

Mohammed the Merchant

Mohammed was born into the Quraysh tribe, who dominated Mecca and its surroundings but were divided into sometimes quarrelsome clans. In his youth, legend says it was predicted that he would become a great man.

Below right: Mosaic with Greek inscriptions showing an Arab warrior with his bow and arrow, on Mount Nebo, Jordan.

Mohammed, the merchant

The main caravan and maritime trade routes between the Arabian Red Sea coast and Syria

Mohammed is believed to have been born on August 20, 570, at a time of great political, religious, and social change in Arabia. His father, Abdullah Ibn Abd al-Muttalib, had died a few months before, so the baby and his mother were cared for by Mohammed's paternal grandfather, Abd al-Muttalib, who was recognized as the leading figure of his tribe.

As an infant Mohammed Ibn Abdullah was handed over to a woman of the neighboring Banu Sa'ad tribe, it being customary for children of elite families to be brought up in what was regarded as the free and healthy air of the desert rather than in a hot, dusty, and perhaps unhealthy town like Mecca.

When he reached six years of age, Mohammed returned to his immediate family, but within a year his mother died, leaving him an orphan to be looked after by a devoted slave woman known as Umm Ayman. When Mohammed was only eight, his highly respected grandfather Abd al-Muttalib also died, leaving the boy with few to

protect him in a dangerous and competitive world. His uncle, Abu Talib, accepted this responsibility but he was a relatively poor man with many children of his own.

Mohammed is said to have visited the Syrian frontier town of Bosra twice. Here camel caravans from Mecca and elsewhere in Arabia assembled after their long journeys across the desert. Many of their merchants would go on to trade in Damascus or the coastal cities of Syria, yet Bosra was also a thriving market in its own right.

GIFTED YOUTH

According to some accounts of his life, Mohammed was only 12 years old when he first went to Bosra, while on one of his uncle Abu Talib's trading missions to Syria. According to a legend, which not all Muslims accept, a local Christian monk named Bahira saw the youthful Mohammed as the merchants were passing through Bosra on their way home.

This story goes on to say that the monk, who is more likely to have been an abbot or other senior figure in a monastery or church at Bosra, invited everyone in the caravan to a meal before they set out into the desert. During this meal Bahira questioned

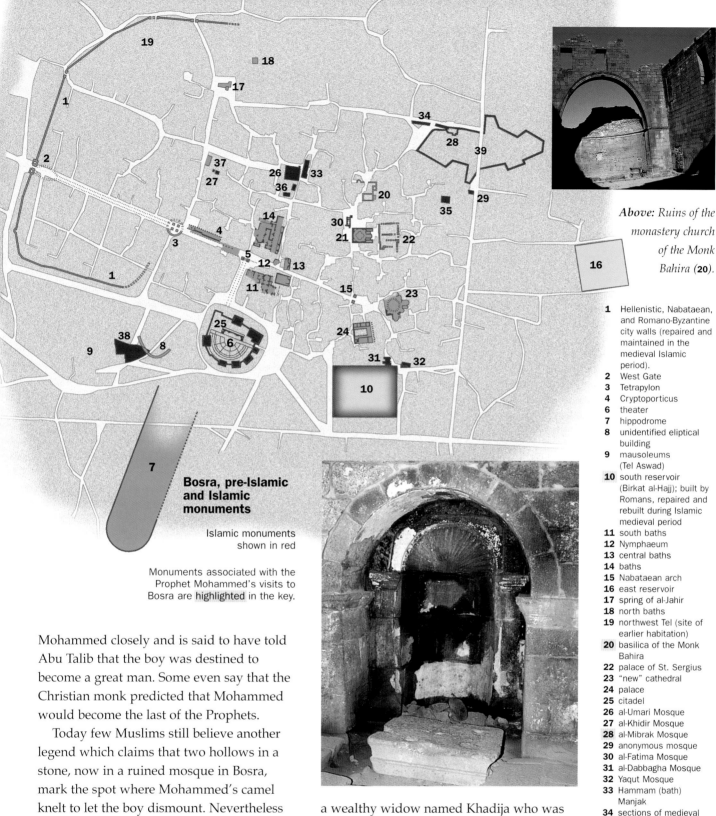

Bosra, pre-Islamic and Islamic monuments

Islamic monuments shown in red

Monuments associated with the Prophet Mohammed's visits to Bosra are highlighted in the key.

Above: Ruins of the monastery church of the Monk Bahira (20).

1 Hellenistic, Nabataean, and Romano-Byzantine city walls (repaired and maintained in the medieval Islamic period).
2 West Gate
3 Tetrapylon
4 Cryptoporticus
6 theater
7 hippodrome
8 unidentified eliptical building
9 mausoleums (Tel Aswad)
10 south reservoir (Birkat al-Hajj); built by Romans, repaired and rebuilt during Islamic medieval period
11 south baths
12 Nymphaeum
13 central baths
14 baths
15 Nabataean arch
16 east reservoir
17 spring of al-Jahir
18 north baths
19 northwest Tel (site of earlier habitation)
20 basilica of the Monk Bahira
22 palace of St. Sergius
23 "new" cathedral
24 palace
25 citadel
26 al-Umari Mosque
27 al-Khidir Mosque
28 al-Mibrak Mosque
29 anonymous mosque
30 al-Fatima Mosque
31 al-Dabbagha Mosque
32 Yaqut Mosque
33 Hammam (bath) Manjak
34 sections of medieval fortified city walls
35–37 unnamed Islamic buildings
38–39 Islamic cemeteries

Mohammed closely and is said to have told Abu Talib that the boy was destined to become a great man. Some even say that the Christian monk predicted that Mohammed would become the last of the Prophets.

Today few Muslims still believe another legend which claims that two hollows in a stone, now in a ruined mosque in Bosra, mark the spot where Mohammed's camel knelt to let the boy dismount. Nevertheless this was a popular legend during the medieval period.

Life remained uncertain and far from easy for the young Mohammed. He earned what he could where he could, sometimes as a shepherd, sometimes as a small-scale merchant. Nevertheless he earned a reputation for being totally reliable and trustworthy.

When Mohammed was 25, his uncle Abu Talib suggested that he accompany a large trading caravan to Syria, acting as agent for a wealthy widow named Khadija who was also one of Mecca's wealthiest merchants. Khadija was so pleased with the young man's honesty and success on this trip that she married Mohammed.

She subsequently bore him two sons who, however, died in infancy. Supported by Khadija's wealth, Mohammed and his wife went on to become a successful merchant partnership. Meanwhile, however, Mohammed continued his growing habit of seeking solitude in the desert where he could think in peace.

Above left: The legendary stone on which Mohammed's camel knelt, in the al-Mibrak Mosque (28).

Mohammed the Prophet

Mohammed's discontented life was turned upside-down after he received a series of visions that formed the tenets of Islam. His faith was not accepted, its followers forced to flee Mecca and fight for their beliefs.

Right: An 18th-century Islamic depiction of "Verses of the Koran revealed to Mohammed during a Battle" follows the rules of not depicting the Prophet's face.

As he grew older, Mohammed struggled to make sense of humans' relationship with God and with each other. He found the paganism in which he had been brought up inadequate and he was disturbed by the selfishness and immorality he saw in his own town of Mecca. Mohammed had also learned much about Judaism and Christianity during his various trading expeditions. He would now begin to have a series of divine revelations.

There was a cave on the slopes of Mount Hira outside Mecca, and here Mohammed found a quiet place to think. After several years wrestling with religious and moral problems, Mohammed had his first vision. The Angel Gabriel appeared before him and ordered Mohammed to read, or proclaim, an inscription on a brocade the angel was carrying. Mohammed was, however, illiterate. But after Gabriel repeated the order four times Mohammed began to understand. This was the beginning of his mission to preach Islam to the people of Mecca.

Other revelations followed, becoming the text of the Koran, Islam's holy book. Mohammed preached the Five Pillars, or what became the basic tenets of Islam: the Unity of God; the duty of prayer; fasting during the month of Ramadan; paying the Zakat tax to support the needy; and making the Hajj or pilgrimage to the Ka'aba in Mecca. This ancient structure would have been purified by the removal of its idols after Mecca fell to the Muslims. During the course of his mission Mohammed also revealed the rules of an entire way of life which would became the foundation of Islamic civilization.

In many ways Mohammed's religious mission was more like those of some Old Testament Jewish prophets than of Jesus. His preaching was practical and, when necessary, ruthless.

FIRST MUSLIM CITY

Rejected by all but a few in Mecca itself, he and the first persecuted converts to Islam fled to a smaller town further north. It was called Yathrib but came to be known simply as Medina or "The City." There Mohammed was invited to take control and end the inter-clan quarrelling which had been tearing Yathrib apart. As a result Yathrib-Medina became the first Islamic state, and remained the model for all subsequent Islamic governments.

Now the pagans of Mecca decided that Mohammed and his followers were a threat and so attacked them. Mohammed's preaching did not embrace pacifism and so the Muslims fought back. The struggle that ensued was both economic and military, and resulted in Mecca's submission to the Prophet Mohammed in 630.

During the course of this bitter struggle, other Arab tribes were drawn in. In 629 a

574	610	616	622	625	628	630	632
Sassanian Persian occupation of Yemen	Mohammed has first vision of the Archangel Gabriel	Sassanian Persian conquest of Romano-Byzantine Syria and Egypt	Mohammed's Hejira from Mecca to Medina, start of the Islamic Hejira calendar	Mohammed begins his Prophetic Mission	Conclusion of peace between Romano-Byzantine and Sassanian empires	Muslims take control of Mecca	Death of the Prophet Mohammed

small Islamic raiding force under Zayd Ibn Harithah, the Prophet's adopted son, set off northward to avenge the murder of some Muslim emissaries by a northern Arab tribe. This tribe lived in the nominally Byzantine frontier zone in what is now southern Jordan. The Muslims, however, were defeated at Muta and Zayd Ibn Harithah was killed.

Since the war between the Byzantine and Sassanian empires had only ended the previous year, it is not clear that the targets of this raid were really subjects of the Byzantine empire. Yet in Islamic historical tradition the defeat at Muta is seen as the first armed clash between the Islamic and the Christian-Byzantine worlds.

Two years after taking control of Mecca,

in June 632, Mohammed died, but in the intervening period tribes from distant regions recognized him as the senior ruler of the Arabian peninsula. This did not mean the imposition of Islamic rule along the Gulf coast or in Yemen, but it did mean that some degree of unity was achieved among the traditionally fractious peoples of Arabia.

Above: Ruins of the Mosque of the Martyrs of the battle of Muta; Muta, Jordan. Islamic tradition holds this battle to be the first between the Muslim and Christian-Byzantine worlds.

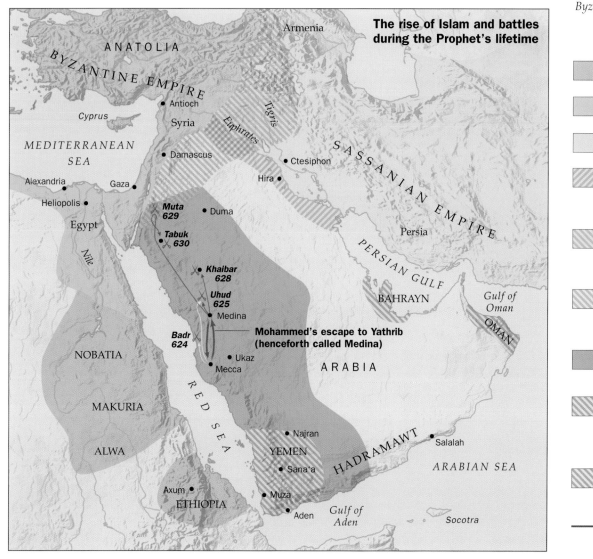

The rise of Islam and battles during the Prophet's lifetime

Christian states in Africa

Byzantine empire

Sassanian empire

Sassanian direct rule over Lakhmid kingdom, 602

Byzantine occupation under Heraclius, 627

Ghassanid territory as Byzantine allies, 627

Territory accepting Islam, 630

Sassanian territory accepting Islamic authority, 631

Other regions accepting Islam, 631

Hijra route, 622, attack on Mecca, 630

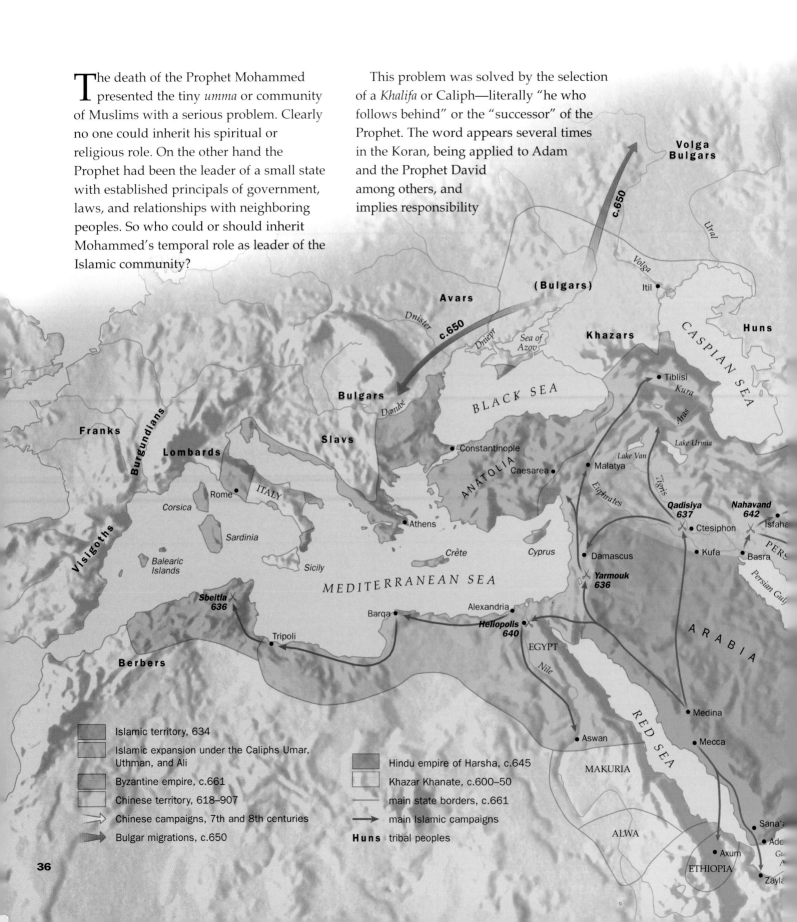

CHAPTER TWO

The Rightly Guided Caliphs

Ideal rulers and the development of Islam

The death of the Prophet Mohammed presented the tiny *umma* or community of Muslims with a serious problem. Clearly no one could inherit his spiritual or religious role. On the other hand the Prophet had been the leader of a small state with established principals of government, laws, and relationships with neighboring peoples. So who could or should inherit Mohammed's temporal role as leader of the Islamic community?

This problem was solved by the selection of a *Khalifa* or Caliph—literally "he who follows behind" or the "successor" of the Prophet. The word appears several times in the Koran, being applied to Adam and the Prophet David among others, and implies responsibility

Volga Bulgars

Ural

Volga

c.650

(Bulgars)

Itil

Avars

Dniester

c.650

Dniepr

Sea of Azov

Khazars

CASPIAN SEA

Huns

Bulgars

Danube

BLACK SEA

Tiblisi

Kura

Araxes

Lake Urmia

Slavs

Constantinople

ANATOLIA

Caesarea

Malatya

Lake Van

Euphrates

Tigris

Qadisiya 637

Nahavand 642

Isfaha

Franks

Burgundians

Lombards

Rome

ITALY

Corsica

Athens

Sardinia

Crète

Cyprus

Damascus

Ctesiphon

Kufa

PERS

Basra

Balearic Islands

Sicily

Visigoths

MEDITERRANEAN SEA

Yarmouk 636

Persian Gulf

Sbeitla 636

Barqa

Alexandria

Heliopolis 640

ARABIA

Tripoli

EGYPT

Berbers

Nile

RED SEA

Medina

Aswan

Mecca

Islamic territory, 634

Islamic expansion under the Caliphs Umar, Uthman, and Ali

Byzantine empire, c.661

Chinese territory, 618–907

Chinese campaigns, 7th and 8th centuries

Bulgar migrations, c.650

Hindu empire of Harsha, c.645

Khazar Khanate, c.600–50

main state borders, c.661

main Islamic campaigns

Huns tribal peoples

MAKURIA

ALWA

Sana'a

Ade

Gi

A

Axum

ETHIOPIA

Zayla

over the world or some aspect of it. Whether or not the first Caliph, Abu Bakr, actually used the title is a matter of debate, but from the time of the second Caliph onward it was generally given to the leader of the expanding Islamic community. His role was to uphold and spread the new faith as well as promoting the well-being of Muslims. Caliphs were also expected to interpret the faith or at least supervise the deliberations of experts when difficult religious questions arose.

Although there was heated discussion about the nature and extent of the Caliph's

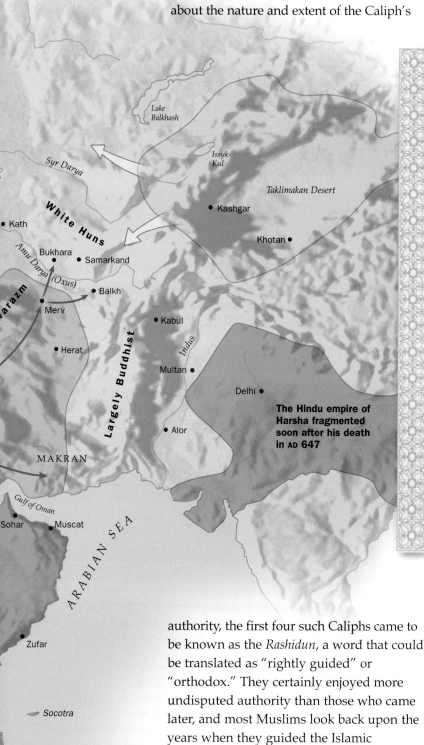

Lake Balkhash

Issyk Kul

Syr Darya

Taklimakan Desert

Kashgar

White Huns

Kath

Khotan

Amu Darya (Oxus)

Bukhara

Samarkand

warazm

Balkh

Merv

Kabul

Herat

Indus

Largely Buddhist

Multan

Delhi

The Hindu empire of Harsha fragmented soon after his death in AD 647

Alor

MAKRAN

Gulf of Oman

Sohar

Muscat

ARABIAN SEA

Zufar

Socotra

authority, the first four such Caliphs came to be known as the *Rashidun*, a word that could be translated as "rightly guided" or "orthodox." They certainly enjoyed more undisputed authority than those who came later, and most Muslims look back upon the years when they guided the Islamic

community (from 632 to 661) as a model of correct government, second only to that of the Prophet Mohammed's own government in Medina and Mecca.

CUSTODIANS OF THE FAITH

These four Rashidun Caliphs did not, however, form a dynasty. All had been close "Companions" of the Prophet, a status of great prestige during the first decades of Islamic history. All were also related to Mohammed either by family or through marriage.

The first, Abu Bakr, was the father of Mohammed's most beloved wife Aisha and had been one of his earliest supporters. It was under his firm leadership that the Muslims re-established their authority across the Arabian peninsula.

The second Caliph, Umar, was the father of another of the Prophet's wives and is credited with introducing the first rudimentary civil administration required by the fast expanding Islamic state. He also established a *diwan* or register of troops that began to change the tribal Arab-Islamic army into a modern fighting force capable of defending the fast expanding Islamic state.

The third Caliph, Uthman, was the Prophet's son-in-law and was elected to his position by a council of the leading Companions of the Prophet following the assassination of Umar. Unfortunately the discontent that had led to the murder of Umar continued to foment, and Uthman's Caliphate ended with rebellion and his assassination.

The strife that followed Uthman's death was known as the *fitna*, literally meaning the "temptation" or "trial of faith." Ali, the fourth and last of the Rashidun Caliphs, was the Prophet Mohammed's cousin, son-in-law, and childhood companion. During his rule strife and discord rumbled on and would end in outright civil war.

Nevertheless some Muslims regarded Ali as the most suited of all to have been Caliph, and those who held to this view eventually emerged as the *Shi'at Ali* or "Party of Ali." Known simply as the Shi'a, they now form the largest minority within Islam, whereas the majority is known as the Sunni because they base their religious practices on the *sunnah*, or "customs" of the Prophet.

The Unification of Arabia

Almost as soon as the Prophet Mohammed died, many parts of Arabia that had acknowledged his overlordship withdrew their allegiance from his successor. The resultant rise and fall of false prophets in the Ridda wars strengthened Arabia and its army.

Facing top: The Mihrab Sulayman in the Well of Souls cave beneath the Dome of the Rock, Jerusalem.

Arabians' rejection of the Caliphate was fully within the volatile traditions of pre-Islamic politics, but those who threw off the suzerainty of Medina—the first capital of the Islamic Caliphate—were now dealing with an entirely new and more determined power. The result was a bitter and bloody conflict in which a remarkable number of the original Companions of the Prophet were slain. These were the Ridda wars, or wars of Apostasy.

Under the leadership of the first Caliph, Abu Bakr, the Muslims reimposed their authority over Najd in central Arabia, Bahrayn, which then included not only the present island state of Bahrain but also the Qatar peninsula and neighboring coasts of the Persian Gulf, as well as Oman and Yemen in the far south. Furthermore, these bloody campaigns extended Islamic rule over parts of Arabia that had not previously accepted the suzerainty of Medina, and they

Facing below: Interior of the main hall, Qasr al-Haranna, Jordan, late 7th–early 8th centuries.

resulted in the Arabian peninsula being united under one highly effective government, probably for the first time in its history. This unity would survive for centuries, which had certainly never happened before.

FALSE PROPHETS

The struggle to reassert Islamic hegemony over Arabia was made urgent because men claiming to be prophets had emerged elsewhere among the Arabian tribes. The most dangerous of these were Tulaiha and Musailama. What we know of these "false prophets" is seen through the eyes of their Islamic foes and so is very unfavorable.

Tulaiha Ibn Khuwailid was one of the tribal commanders of the Banu Asad, who had already submitted to Mohammed and is said to have converted to Islam. But even before Mohammed's death Tulaiha rebelled and assumed the title of a prophet. During

Right: A section of floor mosaic depicts a stylized town, from Khirbat al-Samra c.650, Mount Nebo, Jordan.

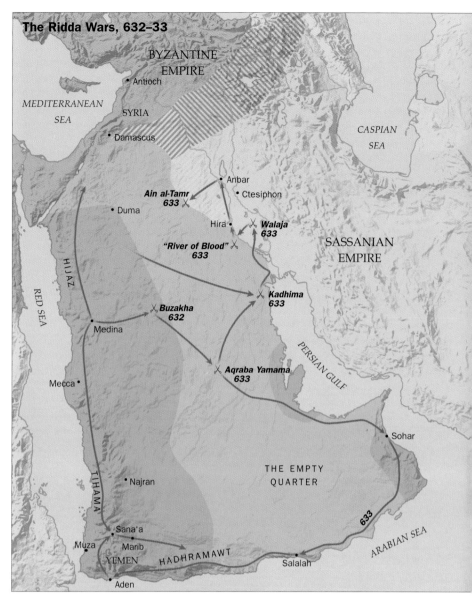

The Ridda Wars, 632–33

BYZANTINE EMPIRE

MEDITERRANEAN SEA

• Antioch

SYRIA

CASPIAN SEA

• Damascus

• Anbar

Ain al-Tamr 633 ✗

• Ctesiphon

• Duma

Hira •

✗ Walaja 633

SASSANIAN EMPIRE

"River of Blood" ✗ 633

✗ Kadhima 633

HIJAZ

RED SEA

✗ Buzakha 632

• Medina

PERSIAN GULF

Mecca •

✗ Aqraba Yamama 633

• Sohar

THE EMPTY QUARTER

TIHAMA

• Najran

633

• Sana'a

Muza

• Marib

HADHRAMAWT

ARABIAN SEA

YEMEN

Salalah

• Aden

the Ridda wars he joined in a widespread revolt but was defeated by an Islamic column commanded by Khalid Ibn al-Walid, the Islamic community's finest general, at the battle of Buzakha in 632. Tulaiha himself escaped and fled, perhaps to Syria, but subsequently rejoined the Islamic faith. He then fought valiantly during the conquest of Iraq and western Iran.

Musailama's proper name was Maslama Abu Thumama, and he came from the Banu Hanifa tribe. He proclaimed himself a prophet during or perhaps even before Mohammed's own mission and he seems to have been strongly influenced by the Christianity which was already widespread in the Yamama region. According to some sources Musailama offered to divide Arabia between himself and Mohammed.

The Banu Hanifa followed him into battle against the Muslims during the Ridda wars but, like Tulaiha, he was defeated by Khalid Ibn al-Walid. Musailama and many of his followers were killed at the battle of Aqraba Yamama in 633, but several sayings attributed to this strange man apparently survived and were still quoted in central Arabia in the 19th century.

By the time the Ridda wars were over, the Islamic state had proved its cohesion and had acquired a highly experienced, battle-proven army capable of overcoming enemies that appeared far stronger than itself.

 Byzantine empire

 nominally Byzantine (control by local Arab tribes)

 Sassanian empire

 nominally Sassanian (control by local Arab tribes)

 Sassanian territory garrisoned by Byzantine troops

 nominally Islamic territory at the death of Mohammed

 Arabian territory gained by Islam during the Ridda Wars

 Islamic campaigns of the Ridda Wars

The Focus of Prayer

The Ka'aba in Mecca had been the object of pilgrimage in what Muslims call the *Jahiliya* or Age of Ignorance. Its pagan idols were destroyed when Mohammed returned to Mecca as its spiritual leader and ruler. The Ka'aba then became the focus of Islamic prayer and pilgrimage.

According to some traditions, one statue in the pre-Islamic Ka'aba temple was a Christian representation of the Virgin Mary. This story states that, unlike the pagan statues, that of Mary was treated with respect though it was, of course, still removed. Since then the Ka'aba has been empty of idols, serving solely as a focus of Islamic prayer.

Right: Pilgrims on the Hajj to Mecca, illustration in a copy of the Maqamat of al-Hariri, Iraq, AD 1237.

It is a symbolic structure to be venerated and kept scrupulously clean, but not itself being the object of prayer like a pagan idol. The Ka'aba is, of course, also the focus of Islamic pilgrimage; not only of the annual Hajj in which hundreds of thousands of Muslims converge on Mecca, but also of individual pilgrimages at other times of year.

According to Islamic tradition, the original Ka'aba was erected by the Prophets Ibrahim (Abraham) and Isma'il (Ishmael) in ancient times, though the earliest historical references date from the second century AD. When Mohammed himself was a young man, an accidental fire destroyed this first low, roofless Ka'aba. Wood from a wrecked Byzantine ship was used to make a new Ka'aba which consisted of alternating rows of timber and stone, an architectural style recalling those of ancient Ethiopia and perhaps southern Arabia. This new structure was taller than the first and had a roof.

It was also the young Mohammed who solved the problem of who should have the honor of placing the sacred meteoric black stone which now lies in the corner of this building. He had been carrying stones during the building operations and suggested placing the sacred stone on a cloth; then the heads of the rival clans of families should hold the edges of the cloth as the black stone was moved into place.

Damaged by stone-throwing siege machines and yet another fire in 683, the Ka'aba was again rebuilt, this time entirely of stone. Smaller alterations would follow, but the Ka'aba was now essentially in the form it is today.

HOLY PLACE OF PEACE

Surrounding the Ka'aba was a *haram* or sacred area, as was typical of sacred places

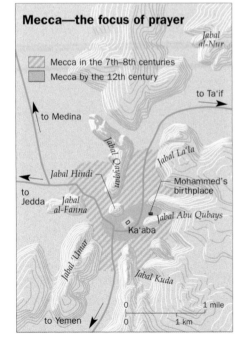

Mecca—the focus of prayer

Mecca in the 7th–8th centuries
Mecca by the 12th century

Jabal al-Nur
to Ta'if
to Medina
Jabal Omar
Jabal La'la
Jabal Hindi
Mohammed's birthplace
to Jedda
Jabal al-Fanna
Jabal Abu Qubays
Ka'aba
Jabal Umar
Jabal Kuda
to Yemen

0   1 mile
0   1 km

633	**634**	**c.634**	**635**	**636**	**644**	**c.650**	**656**
"False prophet" Musailama and several followers are killed at Aqraba Yamama	On Abu Bakr's death, Umar ibn al-Khattab is the second Rashidun caliph	The Byzantine empire loses most of its Middle Eastern territory to Muslim armies	Muslim Arabs seize Damascus (September)	Islamic army defeats Byzantines at Yarmouk; victory is repeated in 637 at Qadisiyah	Uthman ibn Affan succeeds Umar ibn al-Khattab as Rashidun caliph on the latter's death	Islamic settlements are established on the African coast by traders	Caliph Uthman is murdered (June); Ali is nominal successor but divides Islam

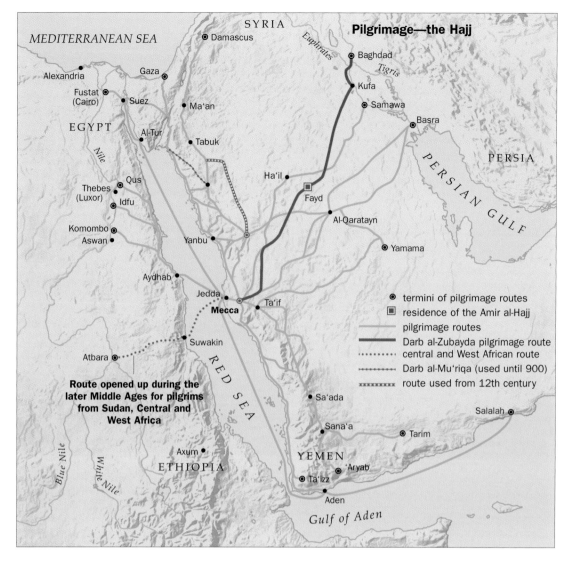

Pilgrimage—the Hajj

MEDITERRANEAN SEA

SYRIA
● Damascus

● Baghdad

Gaza ●
Alexandria ●

Fustat ◉ ● Suez
(Cairo)

● Ma'an

Kufa

Tigris

● Samawa

Basra

EGYPT

Al-Tur

● Tabuk

PERSIA

Nile

Thebes ◉ Qus
(Luxor) ◉ Idfu

Ha'il ●

Fayd

PERSIAN GULF

Komombo ◉
Aswan ●

Yanbu ●

Al-Qaratayn

Aydhab ●

Jedda ●
Mecca

Ta'if ●

◉ Yamama

◉ termini of pilgrimage routes
■ residence of the Amir al-Hajj
—— pilgrimage routes
—— Darb al-Zubayda pilgrimage route
········· central and West African route
---------- Darb al-Mu'riqa (used until 900)
▭▭▭▭ route used from 12th century

Suwakin ●

Atbara ◉

**Route opened up during the
later Middle Ages for pilgrims
from Sudan, Central and
West Africa**

RED SEA

● Sa'ada

Salalah ◉

Sana'a ●

● Tarim

Blue Nile

White Nile

Axum ●

ETHIOPIA

YEMEN ● 'Aryab

◉ Ta'izz

Aden ●

Gulf of Aden

---

in Semitic religious tradition. Within this *haram* there was no bloodshed. Instead there would be a truce between quarrelling groups, it was forbidden to carry arms, and the *haram* served as a place of refuge for fugitives. Animals, except those considered dangerous to man, were not chased from the *haram*, while trees and shrubs which took root would not be cut down, except for one species which was used for building houses.

The Ka'aba was not, however, the focus of prayer for the first Muslims. Perhaps because of its pagan associations, Mohammed and his earliest converts at Medina prayed toward Jerusalem, which was their first *qibla* or orientation of prayer. This practice they shared with the Jews, but 16 or 17 months after his *hijra* or migration to Medina, Mohammed received a revelation which told him to change the *qibla* to Mecca

and the Ka'aba. This significant development reinforced the autonomy of Islam as a local religion rather than being seen by non-Muslims as an offshoot of Judaism or Christianity.

Despite being by far the most important location in the Islamic world, Mecca was not its political capital. This role first fell to Medina, and subsequently to other cities further north like Damascus and Baghdad. Mecca was a spiritual center.

It expanded over the centuries but never became a major metropolis. Its permanent inhabitants took part in trade and the other ordinary activities of life but, after the coming of Islam, the primary function of the city was to maintain and preserve the Ka'aba, and to look after the vast numbers of Muslim pilgrims who arrived each year. This remains Mecca's primary function to this day.

656	**656**	**657**	**661**	**661**	**673-8**	**680**	**685**
Zubayr and Talha form an army with Mohammed's wife Aisha against his cousin, Caliph Ali	Zubayr and Talha are killed at the Battle of the Camel (December)	Battle of Sifin ends in a truce led by troops of Mu'awiya Ibn Abi Sufyan, governor of Syria	Ali is assassinated; Mu'awiya becomes caliph at request of Mohammed's son Hasan	End of the Rashidun caliphate, start of the Umayyad caliphate	First Islamic siege of Constantinople	Husayn is killed in a conflict between Umayyads and the "descendants of Mohammed"	Conflict between Palestine, Syria, and Iraq divides the Islamic state

Medina and the Hijaz

With the sudden expansion of Islam, Mohammed's home region lost its isolated position and became the spiritual center of the new empire. The elite of the Muslim empire made the Hijaz their spiritual home, and developed the area almost beyond recognition.

Right: Fragments of carved architectural decoration in south Arabian style, Hamam al Sarakh, Jordan, early 8th century AD.

Yathrib, or Medina as it was now called, was the first capital of the expanding Islamic state. It was also where the Prophet Mohammed was buried in his own house, which had become the first and most important mosque.

As the caliphate grew, increasing wealth flowed into this small oasis town while the surrounding region became the political heartland of a great empire. Even after the political center of the Islamic world shifted

northward to Syria in 661, the Hijaz remained popular among the Arab social, cultural, and religious elites, who built small palaces in its lush oases and seasonally watered *wadis* or valleys.

Nevertheless the Hijaz remained prone to droughts, which could in turn lead to famine. In 639 Arabia was struck by one such drought, but this time the efficient and more powerful caliphal government arranged for camel caravans to bring supplies of grain and other foodstuffs from the newly conquered provinces of Syria, Palestine, and Iraq. The problem of ensuring food supplies for the Hijaz was eventually solved by sending grain from newly conquered Egypt, long the granary of the Roman and Byzantine empires.

This shift in trade caused severe problems in Constantinople and also led to the clearing of the ancient Amnis Trajanus canal linking the River Nile to the Red Sea. Renamed the Canal of the Commander of the Faithful, it enabled ships to travel between the Mediterranean and the Indian Ocean.

Most of what we know of the structures built by the new Arab-Islamic aristocracy in western Arabia comes from written sources.

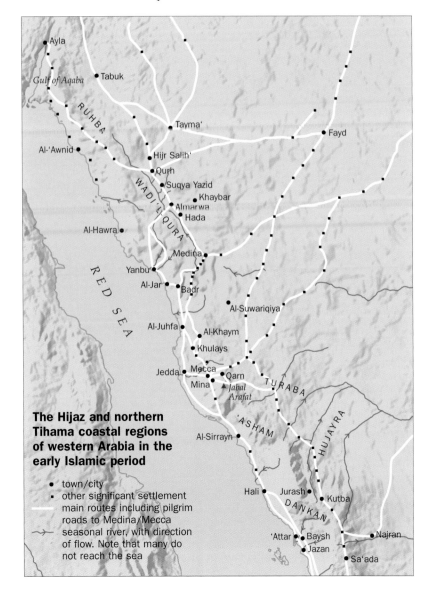

The Hijaz and northern Tihama coastal regions of western Arabia in the early Islamic period

- town/city
- other significant settlement
- main routes including pilgrim roads to Medina/Mecca
- seasonal river, with direction of flow. Note that many do not reach the sea

Palaces and fortified castles were built, which had audience halls where the nobility received guests or listened to poets.

WATER FOR THE MASSES

Considerable efforts were also made to maintain and extend the water-storage system which had for centuries controlled what little rainfall the Hijaz received. One ancient pre-Islamic dam which was kept in working order is at Samalaqi, south of Taif. Designed to store water from flash-floods, it was made of stone, with a plastered summit, and is 600 feet long.

Large pools to store water were also constructed along the pilgrimage routes to Mecca and Medina. One of the best preserved is called the Birkat al-Khurabah and is about 60 miles north of Taif. Built in the mid-eighth century of basalt stone, it is circular and has a depth of 18 feet, with 26 steps to reach the bottom. A small settling basin was located nearby, to filter water before it entered the main pool. The water itself was brought along a sluice or channel from the Wadi Aqiq, 15 miles away.

Further north the ancient settlements

around Khaybir similarly continued to flourish. Another pre-Islamic dam was carefully maintained at al-Khasid, while at al-Ula, on top of a rocky outcrop, there are still the remains of the Qalaat Musa Ibn Nusair, which is said to have been built for the general who conquered much of North Africa and the Iberian peninsula.

Other fortified palaces stand in and around the strategic northern oasis of al-Jawf. Here the foundations of the Qasr Maris castle are believed to date from about 300 BC, though most of the surviving ruins are early Islamic.

Above: The Birkat al-Khurabah northeast of Taif on the Darb Zubaida, recently restored.

Below: Abandonded remains of al-Ula, which sat below the fort of Qalaat Musa Ibn Nusair.

A Place of Prayer

The first mosque was part of Mohammed's house in Medina, rebuilt and extended many times to enclose the Prophet's tomb and an ever-increasing numbers of pilgrims. Subsequent mosques developed features now recognized in mosques all over the world.

Right: Plan of the House of the Prophet in Medina (the "first mosque"), reconstructed from several written descriptions.

Below right: Church of Shemun al-Safar, 5th–7th centuries, Mosum, Iraq.

Below: Plan of the congregational mosque at Kufa, AD 637, rebuilt in 670.

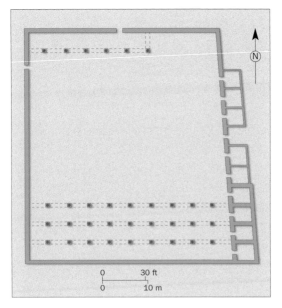

A mosque is not usually a sacred building in the way that a Christian church is sacred. It is simply a place set aside for prayer. As such a mosque should be kept scrupulously clean and treated with respect, but apart from a few vital conventions, it does not have to be of any particular architectural style.

From the start of Islamic history, the representation of living animals and human beings was banned from the interior and exterior of mosques. Yet exceptions can be found, either in the form of animal-like decorative elements on some medieval Turkish mosques or in the representation of sacred figures in some Shi'a mosques.

Mosques also come in many shapes, usually reflecting the architectural traditions of those who built them or the climatic conditions which worshippers had to face. The smallest mosques are often known simply as *musallas* or "places where the *salat* [prayer] is performed." At the other extreme a large open place can be marked out and have no more than a *mihrab* or indication of the direction of prayer on one side. Here crowds can pray together in the open air during major congregational events.

The first mosque was installed in Mohammed's house, a typical early Arabian domestic structure consisting of an enclosed courtyard with covered rooms and storage chambers on two or more sides. This form remained characteristic of other early mosques, including the huge but now ruined example at Kufa in Iraq dating from 637. The basic design would be elaborated in later centuries.

The entire structure of a mosque was orientated so that one wall, the *qibla* wall, faced Mecca. Concern with correct orientation led to considerable interest in geography, astronomy, and mathematics in medieval Islamic civilization, but even today a handful of the most ancient mosques, or their remains, are still incorrectly aligned.

REGIONAL STYLES

Other features now began to make an appearance. The first, mentioned above, was the *mihrab* on the *qibla* wall, showing worshippers the correct direction of prayer. The second was the *minaret* or tower from which the *muezzin* summons the faithful to prayer. A third feature is found in mosques that are used for congregational worship, although it also exists in smaller mosques. This is the *minbar*, which serves the same function as the pulpit in a Christian church.

Throughout Islamic history pre-Islamic religious buildings have been modified so that they could serve as mosques, this being one of the factors which influenced the development of different architectural styles. As a result the Ottoman mosques of Turkey and the Balkans share similarities with Orthodox Christian churches, those in India show the influence of Hindu and Buddhist temples, while some mosques in central Asia have a Chinese architectural style.

The Great Mosque in Damascus had originally been a pagan temple but then had a small church erected within its huge

courtyard. During the Islamic conquest of Syria the Muslims' seizure of Damascus is said to have involved one Arab force entering after peaceful negotiations while another Arab force broke into the far side of the great city, sword in hand.

Legendary or otherwise, this story was used to explain the fact that instead of either taking the entire temple-church as their new mosque, or leaving it in the hands of the Christians as was normally done when a city surrendered peacefully, the huge temple complex was shared between Muslims and Christians for several decades. Both communities entered by the south door, and while the Christians turned left toward their church the handful of resident Muslims turned right. This is supposedly why the *mihrab* in the eastern section of the *qibla* wall is called the Mihrab of the Companions of

the Prophet—namely those who knew Mohammed personally and then went on to serve in the army which conquered Syria.

Left: South wall of the Great Mosque of Damascus, showing the door (now blocked) originally shared by Christians and Muslims.

Center: The golden dome of the Shrine of Ibn Akri rises above the ruins of Kufa, Iraq.

Below: Shrine of the Head of John the Baptist in the Great Mosque, Damascus, and below that a plan of the ancient temenos *(temple) in Damascus, shared between Christians and Muslims, 635–705.*

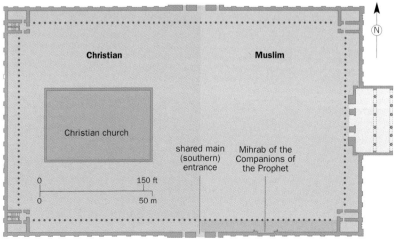

Christian   Muslim

Christian church

shared main (southern) entrance   Mihrab of the Companions of the Prophet

0   150 ft

0   50 m

The Word

For Muslims the Koran is the uncorrupted and unchangeable Word of God. Early variations and omissions were a potential source of conflict, so Caliph Uthman acted to standardize the sacred text.

Below: Stucco statue, possibly of the Caliph, Umayyad mid-8th century.

Any suggestion that there could be variations to the text of the Koran, even of a minor nature, can cause major problems in the Islamic community. The discovery, during the 20th century, of very early copies of the Koran that contained tiny differences to the accepted text led to tensions almost incomprehensible to non-Muslims. Despite quarrels then and very early on in Islamic history, the fact that the text was standardized soon after Mohammed's death diffused conflicts over the issue.

limited. On the other hand Muslims enjoyed one major advantage over some other religious groups. Islam became an established faith with political power and a recognizable community of believers within the lifetime of Mohammed. Many of those who had heard and memorized his revelations were still alive when the caliph accepted the need to write down such texts. Further, traditional Arab society was one in which the memorization of texts, be they religious or poetic, had been central to culture.

Mohammed's revelations had been inspired piecemeal, some at Mecca and some at Medina. It was only after the Prophet died that his Companions collected the *Suras* or chapters together and began to assemble them into one text. The most widely accepted

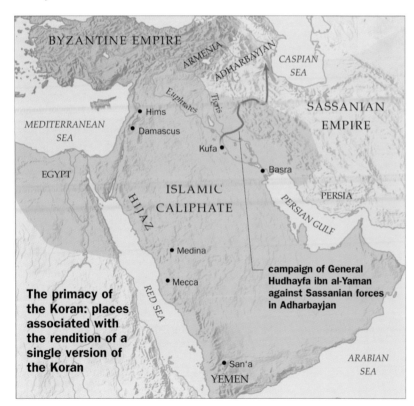

The primacy of the Koran: places associated with the rendition of a single version of the Koran

campaign of General Hudhayfa ibn al-Yaman against Sassanian forces in Adharbayjan

The first Muslims very quickly recognized the need for agreement on the Sacred Text, for they only had to look at their Christian and Jewish neighbors to see how divisions could easily arise from disputes about important religious texts.

The art of writing was known in pre-Islamic Arabia but its use was extremely

leadership of the young Islamic state in 644 the potential for minor disagreements becoming significant problems was already apparent.

Ubay Ibn Ka'b's version of the Koran was accepted in Damascus, Miqdad Ibn Amr's in Hims, Abd Allah Ibn Ma'sud's in Kufa, and Abu Musa Abd Allah al-Ash'ari's in Basra. Each city was also the military base of a significant army. Things had already almost boiled over in the expeditionary force that the Arab leader Hudhayfa had commanded in Adharbayjan, far to the north. Here various units had quarreled over whose version of the Koran was correct.

Caliph Uthman accepted the need to avoid division, so he asked Umar's daughter Hafsa if he could borrow her father's copy of the sacred book. He then had copies made and distributed among the Islamic communities. Whether Uthman ordered other versions to be destroyed remains doubtful, and some medieval scholars claim to have seen copies of those Korans which had eventually been rejected.

The Islamic world would suffer from plenty of other differences of opinion and interpretation, but Uthman's efforts were successful and quarrels about the text of Islam's Holy Book did not become a serious problem.

account of how the final text of the Koran was brought together indicates that many of those who could recite the *Suras* had been killed in the Ridda wars. Consequently there was a danger that some sacred verses might be forgotten. So the Caliph Abu Bakr had the oral and written texts collected together. This first text was inherited by the second caliph, Umar, who bequeathed it to his daughter Hafsa, one of the Prophet's widows.

UTHMAN'S FORESIGHT

Four other men were credited with bringing together texts of the Koran but their collections seem to have differed. When the third Caliph, Uthman, took over political

Below: The word written down—pages of an early medieval copy of the Koran.

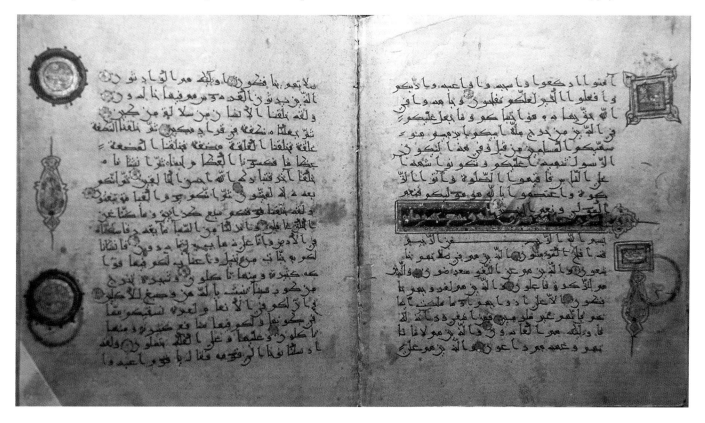

Islam for the Arabs or the World?

The expansion of Islamic-ruled territory under the four Rashidun Caliphs was remarkable by any standards, yet it remains one of the least known series of campaigns in world history.

Unlike most comparable waves of conquest, Islamic expansion in the seventh century had a permanent impact upon the culture, religion, and languages of all those regions involved. The exploits of Alexander the Great and the Greeks, Genghis Khan and the Mongols, and even the Roman empire, pale in comparison.

This expansion was primarily a cultural phenomenon but it was also a significant chapter in military history. Nevertheless the skilled military commanders who led small and often poorly equipped Arab armies to victory over the Byzantine and Sassanian empires, as well as many lesser foes, remain virtually unknown outside the Arab and Islamic worlds. Their exploits and those of their men seem consciously neglected by Western historians, perhaps because they do not fit into an interpretation of history in which the West led the supposed "march of civilization."

In the early years there was doubt within the early Islamic community about whether Islam should be exported to non-Arab peoples. Some aspects of the Prophet Mohammed's religious mission seemed to suggest that he was "The Prophet of the Arabs," whose role was to overcome paganism among the Arab peoples.

Even if this interpretation was correct, however, the fact remained that many Arab peoples already lived within the territory or spheres of influence of the neighboring empires. To unify the Arabs—even those

Below: Wall paintings of soldier-guards in the throne room of the Umayyad castle of Qusayr Amra, early 8th century, Jordan.

who still clung to paganism rather than having already converted to Christianity—meant clashing with the great powers of the Middle East. This was how the first serious clashes with Byzantine and Sassanian troops started.

DYNAMIC EXPANSION

Once the confrontation was underway there seemed no way of turning back, especially since both empires had been so weakened by their recent mutual wars that resistance to Arab-Islamic incursions proved ineffective. Some subsequent Islamic scholars would interpret the relative ease of those first campaigns in Syria and Iraq as "a way prepared." In other words, the fatal weakening of the Byzantine and Sassanian empires was a result of Divine Will, permitting small Arab-Islamic armies to take control of richer territories where Islamic power could take root and grow stronger.

The first Arab-Islamic armies have often been dismissed as tribal hordes motivated by religious enthusiasm and desire for booty. In reality they were well organized, supported by an effective supply system, and the influence of Byzantine, Sassanian, and South Arabian or Yemeni military traditions.

The volatile and often unreliable nomadic Bedouin played only a secondary role; the bulk of these first armies consisted of disciplined infantry from the towns and oases of Arabia, with only small numbers of cavalry from the tribal elites. Their tactics reflected these military limitations, yet they still managed to defeat the armies of the neighboring empires.

The Byzantines lost their richest provinces of Palestine, Syria, and Egypt along with what are now eastern Turkey and Libya. Even the island of Cyprus was shared with the Byzantine empire, despite the Caliph's supposed reluctance to commit his troops across water. To the east the battered Sassanian empire crumbled after a series of hard-fought battles in Iraq and Western Iran.

Fighting would continue for many years but the Caliphate eventually found itself ruling the main provinces of the ancient Persian empires. In so doing, however, the Muslims inherited the Sassanians' troublesome eastern frontier. Here the Arabs would face much more determined foes, especially among the warlike Buddhist peoples of what is now Afghanistan.

The largely Buddhist peoples of what are today the Turkish republics of central Asia resisted the Arab-Islamic invasion but then accepted the new regime because it, like themselves, was dedicated to expanding trade. Here in central Asia the Muslim Arabs would also come up against a rival expanding power, the Chinese empire, which was trying to extend its domination westward along the wealthy trade route known as the Silk Road.

Above: A medieval Islamic bridge at Bisaton, Iran, stands on pre-Islamic Sassanian foundations.

CHAPTER THREE

The Umayyad Century

Stabilizing the new Islamic culture

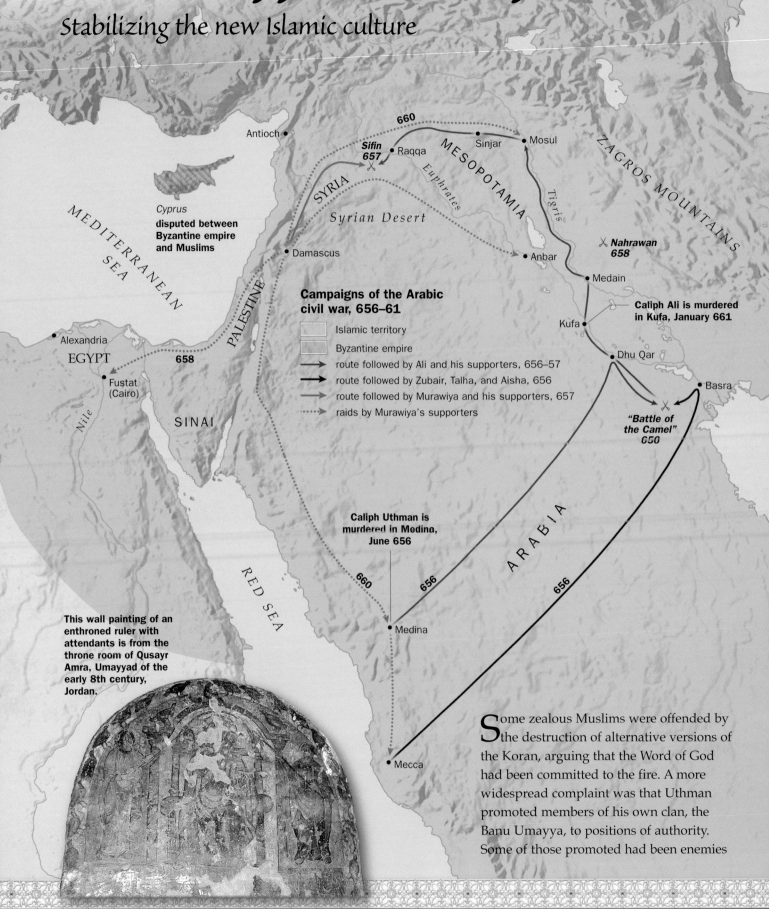

Antioch

660

Sifin 657 · Raqqa

Sinjar · Mosul

MESOPOTAMIA

ZAGROS MOUNTAINS

Euphrates

SYRIA

Syrian Desert

Tigris

Cyprus
disputed between Byzantine empire and Muslims

MEDITERRANEAN SEA

· Damascus

Anbar

✄ **Nahrawan 658**

Medain

PALESTINE

· Alexandria

EGYPT

658

· Fustat (Cairo)

Nile

SINAI

Campaigns of the Arabic civil war, 656–61

Islamic territory

Byzantine empire

→ route followed by Ali and his supporters, 656–57

→ route followed by Zubair, Talha, and Aisha, 656

→ route followed by Murawiya and his supporters, 657

···· raids by Murawiya's supporters

Caliph Ali is murdered in Kufa, January 661

Kufa ·

Dhu Qar ·

· Basra

✄ **"Battle of the Camel" 656**

ARABIA

Caliph Uthman is murdered in Medina, June 656

RED SEA

660   656   656

This wall painting of an enthroned ruler with attendants is from the throne room of Qusayr Amra, Umayyad of the early 8th century, Jordan.

· Medina

· Mecca

$\mathbf{S}$ome zealous Muslims were offended by the destruction of alternative versions of the Koran, arguing that the Word of God had been committed to the fire. A more widespread complaint was that Uthman promoted members of his own clan, the Banu Umayya, to positions of authority. Some of those promoted had been enemies of Mohammed earlier in their lives. Furthermore, many members of the new elite lived luxurious lives, contrary to the example of the Prophet. Outright rebellion seemed inevitable.

Discontent was particularly rife in the newly founded barrack-city of Kufa in Iraq, the main base for Islamic armies on the eastern front. There was then a mutiny in

Ruins of the central hall of the Umayyad Palace on the Citadel, late 7th century, Amman, Jordan.

Persian Gulf

Medina, during which Caliph Uthman was murdered, in June 656. The Koran that he was reading at the time, stained with the caliph's blood, would later become a sacred relic for those who demanded vengeance for Uthman.

This assassination ended the dream of a united Islamic people ruled by a religious theocracy. Further remarkable conquests would follow, and Islamic civilization was yet to achieve its Golden Age of art and science, but the unity of the early decades was over. The Islamic Caliphate gradually become much like any other state or empire, although religion always remained at the heart of its ideology.

Ali, the Prophet's cousin, was now proclaimed caliph by the mutineers in Medina and by those supporters of Uthman who believed that he could heal the rifts that were threatening the Islamic community. Nevertheless anarchy was spreading among the Bedouin of Arabia.

The armies in Iraq and Egypt had been involved in the previous uprising while the one in Syria was commanded by Mu'awiya,

a senior member of the Umayyad clan, and long the rival of the Hashimite clan to which Ali belonged. Rivalry between the Banu Umayya and Banu Hashim had existed long before the coming of Islam, despite the fact that both formed part of the Prophet Mohammed's own tribe of the Quraysh.

OVERCOMING TRIBAL RIVALRY

These tensions left Ali with few options. Many provincial governors had been promoted by Uthman and were themselves members of the Banu Umayya. Ali demanded that several step down, including Mu'awiya in Syria. In the meantime, Ali's reluctance to avenge the murder of Uthman lost him the support of several elder statesmen in Medina.

Matters came to a head in September 656 when two of these men, Zubayr and Talha, left Medina for Mecca. There they joined Aisha, who had been the Prophet's most beloved wife and had a personal grievance against Ali. Together with a small army of supporters they raised the standard of revolt and crossed the desert toward Basra in Iraq.

The events that followed involved several military engagements. In December 656, Zubayr and Talha were killed at the Battle of the Camel. Then Mu'awiya, the highly efficient governor of Syria, led his forces in rebellion, demanding vengeance for Uthman.

Between May and July 657, a prolonged stand-off near the Euphrates resulted in a major battle at Sifin. This, however, ended after some of Mu'awiya's troops tied pages from the Koran to their spears and demanded a truce, shouting "The Word of God, let the Word of God decide!"

Ali ruled as caliph until January 661, when he too was assassinated by a puritanical zealot in Kufa. This crime united the majority of Muslims for the first time in years. Mu'awiya was proclaimed as the new caliph after Ali's son Hasan asked him to accept.

He pardoned those who had previously fought against him and tried where possible to rule by consensus. In fact Mu'awiya become one of the most effective rulers in the early medieval period, and the dynasty which he founded not only endured for over century but consolidated Islamic power from the Atlantic Ocean to India.

Damascus: Capital of a New Empire

When Mu'awiya Ibn Abi Sufyan, the governor of Syria, became caliph in 661, the administrative center of the Islamic state moved from Medina in Arabia to Damascus in Syria. Although the city retained its Roman character, Islamic elements were introduced.

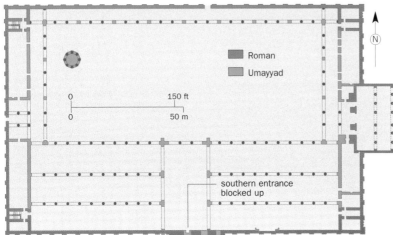

southern entrance blocked up

Roman
Umayyad

0   150 ft
0   50 m

The shifting of the Islamic capital to one of the most ancient, prosperous, and sophisticated cities in the Middle East would have a profound impact upon the secular aspects of the Islamic state. The Arab army based in Syria was already an elite before Mu'awiya became caliph, having campaigned with great success against the Byzantine empire. Under the new Umayyad Caliphate the status of Syrian regiments increased still further.

The overwhelming majority of the Syrian population was, however, still Christian with significant Jewish and other minorities. These communities were more literate and more experienced in administration, trade, the arts, and science than were the newly arrived Arabs, who remained a military and ruling class. On the other hand the Arabs themselves now included tribes that had lived within Byzantine Syria and were themselves more cultured than the newly arrived tribes from Arabia.

In turn, the presence of the Umayyad court inevitably had a major impact on Damascus. Under Roman rule this city had become a typical Syro-Roman metropolis. Its plan was rectangular, surrounded by walls and gates that symbolized Roman power rather than being primarily defensive. The main colonnaded street, known in Christian history as The Street called Straight, ran through the city from east to west. Near the center were two triumphal arches that the Romans erected to demonstrate their authority.

Other typical Greco-Roman structures included a theater, an agora or public open square, and various imposing administrative buildings. Damascus also included a vast walled enclosure that surrounded its huge temple, linked to the agora by another colonnaded street.

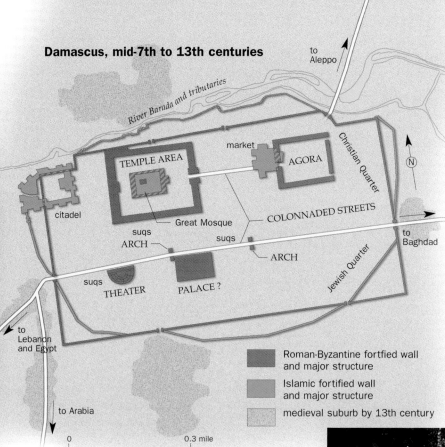

Damascus, mid-7th to 13th centuries

to Aleppo

River Barada and tributaries

TEMPLE AREA

market

AGORA

Christian Quarter

N

citadel

Great Mosque

COLONNADED STREETS

to Baghdad

suqs

ARCH

suqs

ARCH

Jewish Quarter

suqs

THEATER

PALACE ?

to Lebanon and Egypt

to Arabia

Roman-Byzantine fortfied wall and major structure

Islamic fortified wall and major structure

medieval suburb by 13th century

0   0.3 mile

0   500 m

the craftsmen who made these remarkable mosaics were probably local Syrian Christians, rather than from an empire with which the Umayyads were still at war.

Left: Damascus, capital of a new world empire.

Facing top: Mid-7th-century Umayyad mosaics on the front of the main prayer hall of the Great Mosque of Damascus, and, *below*, plan of the Great Mosque as rebuilt by Caliph al-Walid in 706.

Below: Detail of the so-called Barada Panel mosaic in the Great Mosque of Damascus, dating from the mid-7th century

ARCHITECTURAL HERITAGE

During the early Byzantine period a small church had been built inside the courtyard of the pagan temple. This was the city that the Muslim Arabs seized in September 635. Its huge ancient edifices would influence subsequent urban developments to a remarkable degree, resulting in the fascinating city seen today.

The individualism and mercantile character of Semitic culture returned to the ancient city, which molded itself around the authoritarian relics of Rome. Some of the latter disappeared, including the ancient city wall. Others, like much of the colonnaded main street, were absorbed within later structures. Only recently have some of the cheerful but cluttered *suqs* or markets of central Damascus been cleared to expose the forbidding edifices erected by the Romans.

The first Islamic monument to appear in Damascus was the Great Mosque, rebuilt by Caliph al-Walid in 706. It remains one of the most splendid Islamic buildings ever erected, yet it dates from a period when Islamic art and architecture were in their infancy. As a result some historians still refer to the mosaics that decorated al-Walid's mosque as Byzantine rather than Islamic art. In reality

The Dome of the Rock

The Dome of the Rock was the first great aesthetic achievement in Islamic civilization, yet it was built at a time of uncertainty for the new religion. It symbolizes not only Islam's differences to Judaism and Christianity, but also traditions shared with the older religions.

Right: Umayyad mosaics dating from the mid-7th century inside the Dome of the Rock.

Below: Gold dinar coin of the Umayyad Caliph Abd al-Malik, pre-reform style, late 7th century.

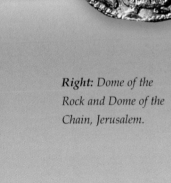

Right: Dome of the Rock and Dome of the Chain, Jerusalem.

Some chroniclers stated that Umayyad Caliph Abd al-Malik built the Dome of the Rock on the Haram al-Sharif or Noble Sanctuary in Jerusalem to divert Muslim pilgrims away from Mecca during a civil war. Many Muslims believe that the Dome commemorates Mohammed's miraculous night-time journey from Mecca to Jerusalem, where he prayed before a similarly miraculous journey to Heaven on a celestial animal named Buraq. Many early Islamic scholars simply did not accept that the place where the Prophet prayed that night was Jerusalem.

In reality it seems more likely that the Dome was a statement of Islamic superiority over Christianity and Judaism. Certainly the position of Islam in Jerusalem and the Middle East was by no means assured when it was built in 690–92, and the Dome of the Rock may actually have been more defensive than triumphalist. The Dome's first function was apparently to claim the Patriarch Abraham for Islam, where he was known by the Arabic form of his name, Ibrahim. At that time many Jews believed that the Rock was the site of Adam's grave, was the place where Abraham had been willing to sacrifice his son, and was the Omphalos or center of the world. The Christians had, however, transferred this Navel of the World, plus some of the other associations, to nearby Golgotha—the site of Christ's crucifixion.

The second function, symbolizing the defeat of the Byzantine and Sassanian empires, is clear in the design and content of the surviving mosaics. They include imperial Byzantine and Sassanian symbols of rank and power, perhaps represented as trophies for a victorious Islam.

SITE OF THREE FAITHS

The third function—informing Christians and Jews that Islam had superceded their revelations—may also be seen in mosaic verses from the Koran. These summon non-believers to accept the truth of Islam, and their content is critical of certain Christian beliefs. Yet these inscriptions are very hard to see and are in Arabic, which few non-Muslims could then have read. Perhaps they were intended to stiffen the morale of a small, though politically dominant, Muslim community surrounded as it was by splendid Christian churches. Only a few years later Christian sources do indeed mention a Muslim-Arab soldier who was converted to Christianity and suffered martyrdom.

The political and military circumstances of the caliphate were not very secure at the time the Dome of the Rock was built. Despite staggering Islamic military victories and some equally spectacular conquests still to come, a three-way civil war had been tearing the Islamic state apart since 685.

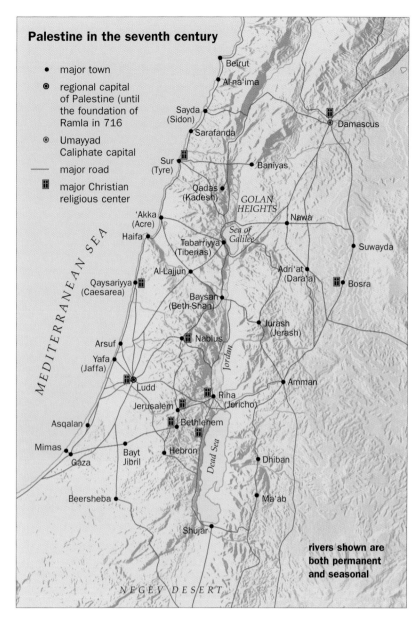

Palestine in the seventh century

- major town
- ⊙ regional capital of Palestine (until the foundation of Ramla in 716)
- ◉ Umayyad Caliphate capital
- — major road
- ⊞ major Christian religious center

Beirut
Al-na'ima
Damascus
Sayda (Sidon)
Sarafanda
Sur (Tyre)
Baniyas
Qadas (Kadesh)
GOLAN HEIGHTS
'Akka (Acre)
Nawa
Haifa
Sea of Galilee
Tabarriyya (Tiberias)
Suwayda
Al-Lajjun
Adri'at (Dara'a)
Qaysariyya (Caesarea)
Bosra
Baysan (Beth-Shan)
Jurash (Jerash)
Arsuf
Nablus
Yafa (Jaffa)
Jordan
Amman
Ludd
Riha (Jericho)
Jerusalem
Bethlehem
Asqalan
Mimas
Dead Sea
Dhiban
Gaza
Bayt Jibril
Hebron
Beersheba
Ma'ab
Shujar
MEDITERRANEAN SEA
rivers shown are both permanent and seasonal
NEGEV DESERT

Only in 691 did Caliph Abd al-Malik reunite Palestine, Syria, and Iraq. The following year he completed the restoration of caliphal authority by re-taking Mecca.

Nor was the Byzantine empire a spent force. In 678 Islam had suffered a serious reverse outside the walls of the Byzantine capital, Constantinople, and Caliph Mu'awiya had accepted a humiliating peace. Subsequently the Byzantines harassed the Islamic frontier, obliging the new caliph Abd al-Malik to pay a heavy tribute.

One aspect of this Byzantine counterattack was a guerrilla army which took advantage of the Islamic civil war to raise a revolt in the Christian coastal mountains of Syria and Lebanon. Although this Byzantine military revival was short-lived, it might have played a part in Abd al-Malik's decision to erect the Dome of the Rock, and in his choice of symbolic decorations for this magnificent structure.

Left: The Dome of the Rock seen from the Muslim Quarter in the Old City of Jerusalem.

55

The Emergence of Islamic Art

Quite when Islamic art or architecture emerged as a specific style remains a matter of controversy. Its most striking early characteristic was its eclecticism, readily accepting influences from surrounding cultures.

Right: Gateway of the Umayyad palace at Qasr al-Hayr al-Gharbi, mid-8th century, re-erected in the National Museum, Damascus.

Islamic art could not have emerged fully developed, but must have been the result of traditional Arab styles that were combined with the forms found in conquered territories during the early years of Islamic conquest. Traditional Western art historians have maintained that the Muslim Arabs who first carried the Faith beyond Arabia had no art or architecture of their own. Others claim that for many decades the non-religious and non-literary creations of early Islamic society were not really Islamic but were mere continuations of existing cultural traditions borrowed from peoples whom the Muslim Arabs had conquered. All that such scholars usually admit is that these

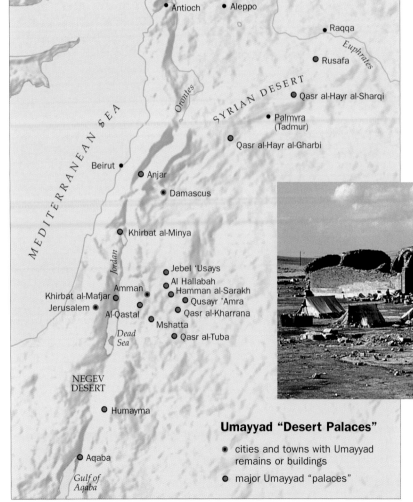

Umayyad "Desert Palaces"

- cities and towns with Umayyad remains or buildings
- major Umayyad "palaces"

artforms had been slightly modified to accommodate Islamic religious sensibilities. More recently some have maintained that Islam is essentially anti-art and that there

690-2	691	692	697	705	711	712-3	c.715
Muslims take Byzantine territory then share Cyprus in the Arab War	Umayyad Caliph Abd al-Malik reunites Palestine, Syria, and Iraq	Caliphal authority is completed when Abd al-Malik takes Mecca	Byzantine Carthage is destroyed by an Arab army	Islam reaches Turkistan, central Asia	Start of the Islamic conquest of the Iberian peninsula	Umayyads cross the deserts of Mukran and invade Sind (south Pakistan)	Muslim armies take Spanish territory from the Visigoths

can therefore be no such thing as Islamic art!

Archaeological research within the Arabian peninsula has shown that the pre-Islamic Arabs had their own artistic and architectural traditions. Like those of almost all the peoples who lived near the cultural powerhouses of Greece and Rome, the pre-Islamic Arabs were deeply influenced by these great Mediterranean cultures. At the same time they were clearly also under strong artistic influence from Iran. Nevertheless their existing artistic traditions retained their own character and cannot have simply disappeared during the few years that the Prophet Mohammed preached Islam in the western part of the Arabian peninsula.

Yet it is undeniably true that the first surviving Islamic buildings, especially non-religious structures, were powerfully influenced by the architecture of those regions where they were built. Surviving decoration, whether it is of stucco in Iran or mosaic and carved stone in Syria, is similarly deeply rooted in existing pre-Islamic cultures. In each case, however, there are already identifiable differences.

MANY INFLUENCES

In the ex-Byzantine provinces this is most noticeable in the lack of human or animal representations in any Islamic religious buildings. Such iconoclasm became a typical although by no means universal characteristic of Islamic art. Highly naturalistic wall paintings would continue to be made within a non-religious context, especially in palaces. Here heroic, domestic, and even erotic scenes were found in the private or family quarters known as the *harim*, and in public spaces such as reception or banqueting halls and *hamams* or communal baths.

Paradoxically, a greater amount of such wall-painting survives from the Umayyad Caliphate, which lasted just over a century, than from the subsequent and more enduring Abbasid Caliphate. Other later examples have been found in provincial palaces in Afghanistan, Iran, Iraq, Egypt,

Above: Wall painting of a turbanned man in the Throne Room at Qasr Amra, from the mid-8th century.

and the Iberian peninsula.

Several of the famous but misnamed Umayyad "desert palaces" of Syria, Lebanon, Jordan, and Palestine were decorated with wall-paintings and in some cases with high relief carving and free-standing statues. In most cases their style could be described as provincial Byzantine, although closer study shows that it was actually a continuation of a Syrian form of Romano-Byzantine art. The surprisingly explicit and erotic character of some paintings in the little desert reception hall and *hamam* at Qusayr Amra in Jordan clearly fall within an ancient Semitic tradition.

During this first period of Islamic art the most striking characteristic was an eclecticism in artistic styles. In addition to Romano-Byzantine and Semitic strands, Iranian and even Turkish central Asian influences can be found, particularly by the final years of the Umayyad Caliphate in the mid-eighth century. Openness to outside influences in everything except religion was and would remain the single most important characteristic of early Islamic civilization. It was also, perhaps, its greatest strength.

Facing: Ruins of the Umayyad "Desert Palace" at Mshatta, mid-8th century.

Literature and Reborn Sciences

The Arabic language remains one of the richest and most expressive in the world. Post-Islam, its lyrical strengths were applied to the translation of existing texts, from which sciences were revealed and developed.

Despite apparently humble tribal origins, history has demonstrated that when the newly Muslim Arabs pushed out from Arabia they brought with them an adaptable language and an openness to new ideas that was simply not present in Christian and Jewish societies of the time. This fresh approach meant that during the early medieval era Islamic society became the world's most advanced across a range of disciplines.

The Arab people's most developed form of cultural expression during the pre-Islamic era was language. Before the Koran was revealed, the highest artistic form within Arabic was poetry. Other aspects of the language were less developed and in many cases may not have existed at all.

Below: Plan and cross section of the Umayyad palace at Al-Qastal, part of an Arab settlement in Jordan.

After the coming of Islam and the creation of the Caliphate or Islamic state, Arabic rapidly showed itself to be very well suited to many other forms of expression. These ranged from a broader array of poetic forms, through prose literature to philosophy, geography, the sciences, and practical technology.

Arabic came to equal the great languages of ancient civilization such as Greek and Latin in the west and Chinese in the east. Like Greek and Latin, Arabic also became an international tongue, being used by scholars, merchants, travelers, and ordinary citizens as a means of communicating across linguistic barriers.

The process of translating the existing body of knowledge from Greek, Latin, Syrian, Aramaean, Persian, Sanskrit, and various other languages began at a very early date, long before the Muslim Arabs could themselves add much that was new.

In medicine, during the reign of Umayyad Caliph Marwan I, a Jewish physician named Masarjawayh who came from Basra in Iraq translated the *Pandects of Ahron* into Arabic. This was soon followed by the translation of equally important Greek medical texts. Meanwhile, law and history became the first fields in which Arab-Islamic scholars made a distinctive contribution.

BUILDING ON DISCOVERIES

The suitability of Arabic as a means of cultural and scientific communication was, however, only one reason why civilization witnessed one of its most dramatic leaps

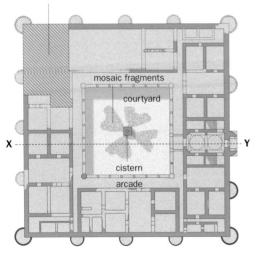

unexcavated area

mosaic fragments

courtyard

X — — — Y

cistern

arcade

Restored section
A main entrance
B domed chamber above entrance
C central courtyard with two-tiered arcade surrounding it
D cistern beneath the courtyard
E tower

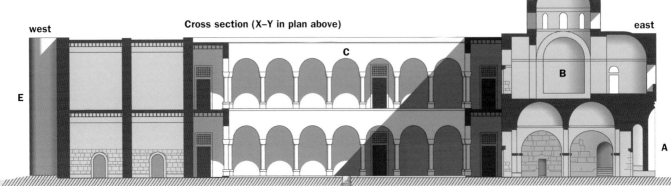

Cross section (X–Y in plan above)

west

east

E

C

B

A

D

Left: Remains of Umayyad-period houses in front of Roman columns at Jerash, Jordan.

forward within the medieval Islamic world. The other was the nature of Islamic civilization and society itself.

For example, the contrast between the attitudes and achievements of Christian Byzantine and medieval Islamic scholarship are striking. Both civilizations were dominated by religion, but whereas Byzantine science largely remained stuck in the past, the only area where Islamic beliefs inhibited new thinking was in secular philosophy. Here several medieval Islamic scholars did find themselves in trouble for putting forward unorthodox ideas.

In terms of pure science, the Muslims have been called "the pupils of the Greeks." Yet this ignores the fact that medieval Arab, Persian, and Turkish scientists also learned from their pre-Islamic Iranian, Indian, Chinese, and other predecessors. Furthermore, as a result of their own researches, Islamic scholars added a huge amount of new information and several daring new concepts to what the ancient Greeks had produced.

The progress in technology achieved by Islamic engineers, craftsmen, and farmers has received far less acknowledgment than that of Islam's leading scientists, doctors, and geographers. Yet there were spectacular advances in many aspects of practical and applied science.

Irrigation is perhaps the most obvious,

but technological developments similarly underpinned other industries. These included the distillation techniques used in manufacturing scent from the essential oils of flowers, as well as in the preparation of terrifyingly effective incendiary weapons.

While medieval Islamic civilization inherited the pure sciences of several earlier civilizations, it was the Muslims' own concern with the precise time and direction of prayer that stimulated notable advances in lunar calendars, astronomical tables, and map-making. Despite their lack of accurate chronometers, Islamic geographers tackled the problem of measuring longitude so effectively that their results are amazingly accurate even by modern standards.

Islam's greatest achievements in pure science and technology date, of course, from the Abbasid period or later. Nevertheless, the foundations were already being laid during the century of Umayyad rule.

Above: A floor mosaic in the Umayyad palace of Khirbat al-Mafjar, Palestine, early 8th century.

The Great Arab Conquests

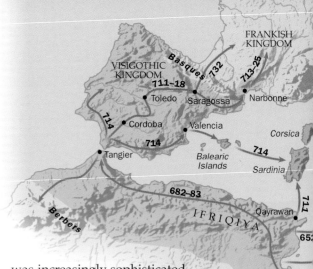

By the time Mu'awiya, governor of Syria, took over as the first Umayyad caliph in 661, Islamic armies were professional forces of largely Arab troops. Most had settled within the conquered territories. Now, a new generation of Muslim warriors pushed the frontiers of Islam still further.

Below: Stucco statuette of a guardsman, from Khirbat al-Mafjar, Palestine, mid-8th century.

The elite of what became the Umayyad army were the *ahl al-Sham* or "people of Syria," who included descendants of Arab tribesmen who had previously fought for the Romano-Byzantine empire. In addition to this urbanized force there were tribesmen from the Syrian desert and from a loosely defined frontier zone facing Byzantium.

Separate from the Islamic military elite were troops from Christian tribes in northern Syria, some of whom were known as *musta'a'riba* or "those who became Arabs." These were not, however, individually listed by the *Diwan al-Jaysh* or army ministry. In other parts of the caliphate, Arab provincial troops declined into a local militia.

By the mid-eighth century non-Arab soldiers had become an important element within the eastern armies. They sometimes came as volunteers, and sometimes as levies from conquered Iranian and Turkish peoples. Persians had been stationed in Palestine and Syria since the mid-seventh century. Other troops were recruited or captured in the mountains of Afghanistan and Transoxania, some then being formed into guard units for the Arab commanders who had conquered them.

Non-Arab soldiers also included Armenian mercenaries, Christian auxiliaries from the coastal mountains of Syria, and Coptic Egyptians. Of greater military significance, however, were large numbers of Berber tribesmen who were enlisted by the Umayyad governors of North Africa.

The organization of these varied armies was increasingly sophisticated. The *jund* or regional structure of Islamic armies is traditionally attributed to Umar, the second Rashidun caliph, but in reality it was probably due to the first two Umayyad caliphs, Mu'awiya and Yazid. These *junds* were based on fortified provincial cities, their soldiers being registered with the Army Ministry and receiving regular pay. Mu'awiya also turned the old communal treasury and weapons store into a government department dealing with military salaries and pensions.

EFFICIENT SYSTEM

The earliest Syrian *junds* of Damascus and Hims were those most closely associated with the caliph himself, but others soon followed, the most important consisting of loyal *ahl al-Sham* Syrian Arabs. There was also a clear distinction between internal security forces, whose role was essentially static, and the field or frontier armies. Meanwhile *ahl al-sham* based in the east were rotated back to the Arab heartlands with each change of governor.

Provincial governors usually relied on *jund* troops from the same tribe as themselves. However, the entire tribal system was restructured during the Umayyad period because the original tribes were too small to provide effective army units. So smaller tribes were assembled into larger tribal divisions while several artificial tribes were created to accommodate those who fell outside the existing system. These may also have camouflaged the presence of a large number of non-Arab troops.

Regimental units were commanded by *quwwad* officers, while senior command positions went to members of the Umayyad

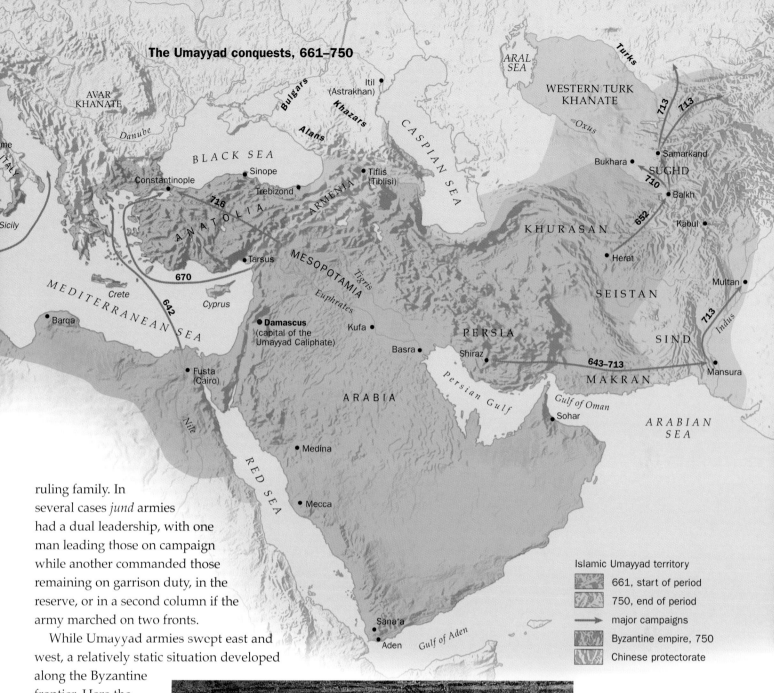

The Umayyad conquests, 661–750

AVAR KHANATE

Danube

Rome

ITALY

Sicily

BLACK SEA

Constantinople

Sinope

Trebizond

ANATOLIA

716

670

642

Tarsus

Crete

Cyprus

MEDITERRANEAN SEA

Barqa

Fusta (Cairo)

Nile

RED SEA

Medina

Mecca

Sana'a

Aden

Gulf of Aden

ARABIA

Bulgars

Khazars

Alans

Itil (Astrakhan)

Tiflis (Tiblisi)

ARMENIA

ARAL SEA

CASPIAN SEA

WESTERN TURK KHANATE

Turks

Oxus

713 713

Samarkand

Bukhara

SUGHD

710

Balkh

652

Kabul

KHURASAN

Herat

SEISTAN

Multan

713

Indus

SIND

Mansura

MESOPOTAMIA

Euphrates

Tigris

Damascus (capital of the Umayyad Caliphate)

Kufa

Basra

PERSIA

Shiraz

Persian Gulf

643–713

MAKRAN

Gulf of Oman

Sohar

ARABIAN SEA

Islamic Umayyad territory

661, start of period

750, end of period

→ major campaigns

Byzantine empire, 750

Chinese protectorate

ruling family. In several cases *jund* armies had a dual leadership, with one man leading those on campaign while another commanded those remaining on garrison duty, in the reserve, or in a second column if the army marched on two fronts.

While Umayyad armies swept east and west, a relatively static situation developed along the Byzantine frontier. Here the second Umayyad caliph strengthened the previously improvized defenses to protect Damascus, and as a launch pad for further invasion of Byzantine territory.

By the late Umayyad period proper military frontier provinces called *thughur* faced the Byzantine empire. They were positioned around two or three major strategic passes through the mountains and they would be greatly strengthened by the subsequent Abbasid caliphal dynasty.

Left: Wall painting from Qasr al-Hayr, Syria depicting a mid-8th-century horse archer.

People of the Book

Islam is one of the few major religions that recognizes that other faiths also result from divine revelation. In Islamic doctrine these valid and therefore tolerated religions are those of the People of the Book.

Right: A wall painting showing Arab camel riders from Afrasiab, late 7th–early 8th century, now in the Afrasiab Archaeological Musuem, Samarkand, Uzbekistan.

The term "People of the Book" reflects the importance of a revealed sacred text in Islamic religious thinking. Chief among the People of the Book are the Jews and Christians, and their freedom to practice their religion was guaranteed by the Prophet Mohammed himself.

Islamic scholars would, however, claim that the religious texts of the Jews and Christians have survived in a corrupted or falsified form. Also, followers of religions which do not possess a divinely revealed book are generally regarded as heathens. Unlike heathens, the People of the Book were allowed to worship in public, to

Below: Ruins of a Zoroastrian fire temple near Nantaz, Iran.

maintain their own religious buildings, and to have their own religious organization.

In return for being excused military service, which was expected of all Muslims, they had to pay an additional tax, the *jizya*, as their contribution toward the defense of the state. In return such communities became *ahl al-dhimma* or "protected people," who were offered unconditional legal and military protection by the Islamic authorities.

Facing: The tomb of St. Jacob, dating from the 4th–6th centuries, is situated in the Monastery of Mar Yacub, Nusaybin, Turkey.

For any Islamic government to violate the protected status of the *dhimmis* was a serious crime. As the Prophet Mohammed was himself recorded as saying: "He who wrongs a Jew or a Christian will have myself as his accuser on the Day of Judgment."

An exception to this principle of toleration was, however, based on another supposed saying of the Prophet: "Two religions may not dwell together in Arabia." This soon resulted in the disappearance of non-Islamic communities in what is now Saudi Arabia, although they survived for much longer around the periphery. For example the Jewish population in Yemen flourished until it relocated en masse to the newly created state of Israel in the 20th century.

Many non-Islamic scholars regard the famous Treaty of Umar between the second caliph and the Christians of Jerusalem as a later invention. Nevertheless it became a model for subsequent agreements, especially as Umar reportedly refused to pray inside the Church of the Holy Sepulcher because he feared his followers would use this as a pretext to convert the building into a mosque. Instead Umar prayed not far from

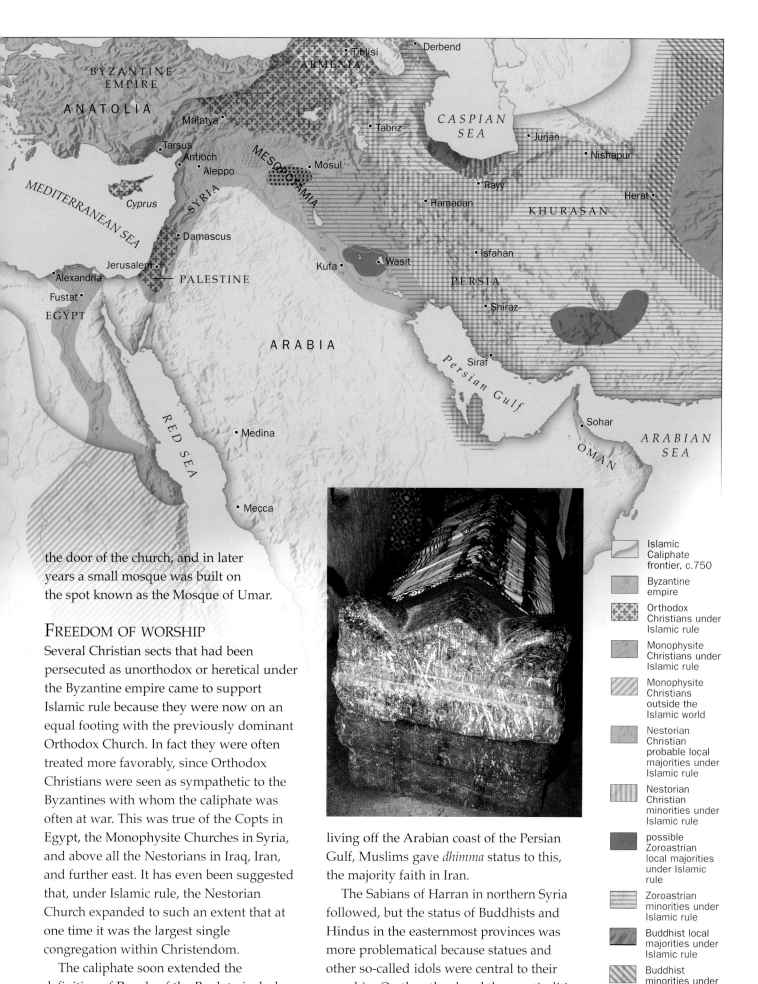

the door of the church, and in later years a small mosque was built on the spot known as the Mosque of Umar.

FREEDOM OF WORSHIP

Several Christian sects that had been persecuted as unorthodox or heretical under the Byzantine empire came to support Islamic rule because they were now on an equal footing with the previously dominant Orthodox Church. In fact they were often treated more favorably, since Orthodox Christians were seen as sympathetic to the Byzantines with whom the caliphate was often at war. This was true of the Copts in Egypt, the Monophysite Churches in Syria, and above all the Nestorians in Iraq, Iran, and further east. It has even been suggested that, under Islamic rule, the Nestorian Church expanded to such an extent that at one time it was the largest single congregation within Christendom.

The caliphate soon extended the definition of People of the Book to include other religious communities. Basing this decision on the fact that Mohammed had accepted the *jizya* tax from Zoroastrians

living off the Arabian coast of the Persian Gulf, Muslims gave *dhimma* status to this, the majority faith in Iran.

The Sabians of Harran in northern Syria followed, but the status of Buddhists and Hindus in the easternmost provinces was more problematical because statues and other so-called idols were central to their worship. On the other hand the practicalities of ruling over a large Buddhist population in Afghanistan and central Asia meant that toleration was necessary.

Legend:

- Islamic Caliphate frontier, c.750
- Byzantine empire
- Orthodox Christians under Islamic rule
- Monophysite Christians under Islamic rule
- Monophysite Christians outside the Islamic world
- Nestorian Christian probable local majorities under Islamic rule
- Nestorian Christian minorities under Islamic rule
- possible Zoroastrian local majorities under Islamic rule
- Zoroastrian minorities under Islamic rule
- Buddhist local majorities under Islamic rule
- Buddhist minorities under Islamic rule
- Yayidis under Islamic rule
- Sabians under Islamic rule

CHAPTER FOUR

The Golden Age

Abbasid expansion of trade, knowledge, and empire

The last years of the Umayyad Caliphate were wracked with problems. These included tensions on the frontiers and uprisings in various provinces, some close to the center of Umayyad power. Despite the loyalty and effectiveness of the elite *ahl al-sham* Syrian regiments, the last Umayyad caliphs did not have enough troops to control the situation, and in 750 the dynasty was overthrown by the rival Abbasid clan. The Abbasids established their own dynasty, with its administrative center in Iraq rather than Syria, because it was closer to the real center of early Abbasid power, which was Khurasan in eastern Iran.

The reasons for the Umayyad collapse are complex, and unfortunately the truth is sometimes difficult to uncover because sources sympathetic to the Umayyad dynasty were systematically destroyed by the victorious Abbasids. The Umayyad's reputation has resultingly been tarnished by exaggerated stories of drunkenness, lack of religious commitment, and administrative

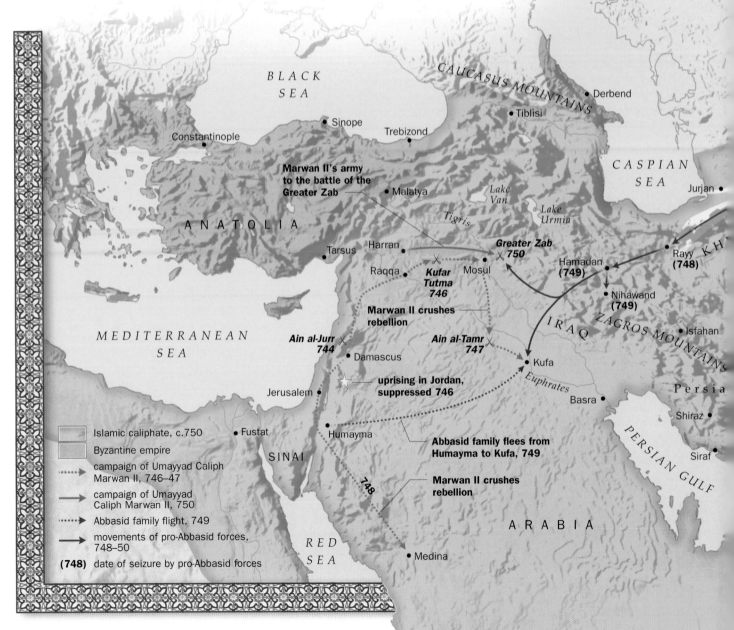

Islamic caliphate, c.750

Byzantine empire

········▶ campaign of Umayyad Caliph Marwan II, 746–47

──────▶ campaign of Umayyad Caliph Marwan II, 750

·······▶ Abbasid family flight, 749

──────▶ movements of pro-Abbasid forces, 748–50

(748) date of seizure by pro-Abbasid forces

corruption. Nevertheless simple and barely alcoholic forms of wine were widely consumed in early Islamic society, and animal and human representations were used in wall-paintings, textiles, ceramics, and metalwork. There was even a flourishing tradition of mildly erotic poetry.

The Umayyads faced particularly strong opposition from a puritanical sect known as the Kharijis who believed that authority stemmed from God alone. These zealots attempted to establish theocratic republics and tried to assassinate leaders of whom they disapproved. Driving off Kharijite raids absorbed much effort, and even led to the writing of the earliest known book of military advice in Arabic.

Supporters of the descendants of Ali as claimants to the title of Caliph gradually evolved into another religious sect subsequently known as the Shi'a. Meanwhile new converts to Islam, who included the *mawali* or clients, played an increasingly important military and administrative role. Unfortunately many felt that they did not enjoy the equality that conversion to Islam was supposed to give, and complained that Arabs were still given preferential treatment.

CENTER OF POWER MOVES EAST

These sources of discontent were exploited by a skilful political agitator named Abu Muslim who was operating in the eastern province of Khurasan. Paradoxically this was a part of the Iranian world that had been heavily colonized by Arab tribes following the Islamic conquest. The descendants of these settlers, some of whom had married locally, were strongly influenced by Iranian culture and Iranian military traditions, yet they still considered themselves Arabs. It was here that Abu Muslim succeeded in creating a revolutionary movement which won a series of victories that culminated in a major battle in the valley of the Greater Zab river in northern Iraq, in the year 750.

The last Umayyad caliph, Marwan II, fled westward, perhaps attempting to reach North Africa or al-Andalus in Spain, where there were still significant Umayyad armies. He was, however, killed in Egypt; this being followed by a massacre of the Umayyad clan by the victorious Abbasids. One survivor did, however, reach the Iberian peninsula where in time he re-established Umayyad power.

One significant advantage that the Abbasids enjoyed over their Umayyad rivals was that they stemmed from Mohammed's uncle, al-Abbas, who was himself from the Hashimite clan. This gave them greater legitimacy in the eyes of orthodox Sunni Muslims. On the other hand it did not stand them in good stead with the supporters of Ali's descendants, who also had a strong claim to the role of caliph.

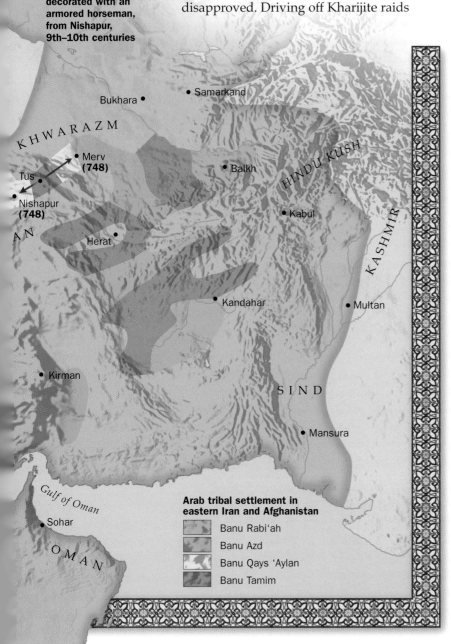

Ceramic bowl decorated with an armored horseman, from Nishapur, 9th–10th centuries

Bukhara

Samarkand

KHWARAZM

Merv
(748)

Tus

Nishapur
(748)

AN

Herat

Balkh

HINDU KUSH

Kabul

KASHMIR

Kandahar

Multan

SIND

Kirman

Mansura

Gulf of Oman

Sohar

OMAN

Arab tribal settlement in eastern Iran and Afghanistan

Banu Rabi'ah

Banu Azd

Banu Qays 'Aylan

Banu Tamim

Baghdad: Round City or Round Palace?

Baghdad became synonymous with the caliphate in the eyes of medieval western Europeans, and even today children's stories often assume that caliphs lived in Baghdad. In fact the city was not the first Abbasid capital, although it was the most successful.

Right: Wall painting of dancers from the throne room of Jawsaq al-Khaqani palace, 9th century, Samarra, Iraq.

Below: The Baghdad Gate in Raqqa, built during the late 8th–early 9th century.

When Abu'l-Abbas al-Saffah assumed the title of caliph in 749, he did so in Kufa, which remained his seat of government until he moved to Anbar, further up the Euphrates. Here he built two palaces, the second of which was really a new town.

Al-Saffah's heir Abu Ja'far al-Mansur similarly accepted the title of caliph in Kufa, but within a few years he decided that Kufa was politically and religiously unreliable, having been involved in several uprisings. Nor did Anbar appeal to al-Mansur and, like Kufa, it was cut off from the Abbasids' power-base in Khurasan by the Tigris.

What the caliph needed was a new capital that would be entirely loyal to the new Abbasid dynasty while at the same time being situated at the center of the vast Islamic state. Al-Mansur's choice of what is now the Iraqi capital was an inspired one.

The site stands on the west bank of the Tigris, close to a point where the great rivers Tigris and Euphrates almost meet. Furthermore, an ancient irrigation and communications canal from the Euphrates joined the Tigris at this point. Consequently the produce of Syria could reach the new city down the Euphrates, the trade of India could arrive via the Persian Gulf and Tigris, and ships could bring the produce of northern Iraq down the Tigris. Also the Imperial Road of the ancient Persian empires emerged from the Zagros Mountains, not far away. The whole region was densely populated, the bulk of the local inhabitants being Christians or Zoroastrians.

The name Baghdad came from a local village. Its official name of Madina al-Salam (City of Peace) was only used in official documents, while its nickname of Mansuriya reflected that of its founder.

DISTINCTIVE DESIGN

The plan to make the city round was novel and daring, although Baghdad was not the first round city. Furthermore the famous

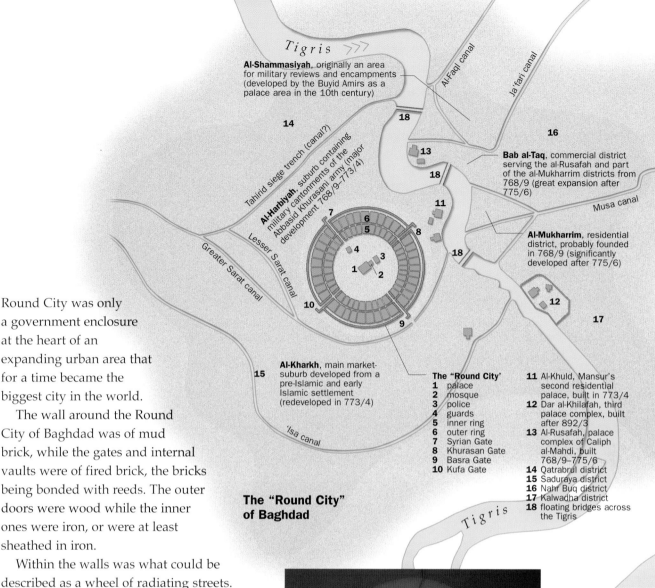

Tigris

Al-Shammasiyah, originally an area for military reviews and encampments (developed by the Buyid Amirs as a palace area in the 10th century)

Al Faql canal

Ja'fari canal

14

18

16

13

Tahirid siege trench (canal?)

Al-Harbiyah, suburb containing military cantonments of the Abbasid Khurasani army (major development 768/9–773/4)

18

Bab al-Taq, commercial district serving the al-Rusafah and part of the al-Mukharrim districts from 768/9 (great expansion after 775/6)

Greater Sarat canal

Lesser Sarat canal

11

Musa canal

7

6
5

8

Al-Mukharrim, residential district, probably founded in 768/9 (significantly developed after 775/6)

4

3
1   2

18

10

9

'Isa canal

15

Al-Kharkh, main market-suburb developed from a pre-Islamic and early Islamic settlement (redeveloped in 773/4)

12

17

The "Round City'
1 palace
2 mosque
3 police
4 guards
5 inner ring
6 outer ring
7 Syrian Gate
8 Khurasan Gate
9 Basra Gate
10 Kufa Gate

11 Al-Khuld, Mansur's second residential palace, built in 773/4
12 Dar al-Khilafah, third palace complex, built after 892/3
13 Al-Rusafah, palace complex of Caliph al-Mahdi, built 768/9–775/6
14 Qatrabrul district
15 Saduraya district
16 Nahr Buq district
17 Kalwadha district
18 floating bridges across the Tigris

**The "Round City"
of Baghdad**

Tigris

Round City was only a government enclosure at the heart of an expanding urban area that for a time became the biggest city in the world.

The wall around the Round City of Baghdad was of mud brick, while the gates and internal vaults were of fired brick, the bricks being bonded with reeds. The outer doors were wood while the inner ones were iron, or were at least sheathed in iron.

Within the walls was what could be described as a wheel of radiating streets. The inner part of the city consisted of an open area or park containing al-Mansur's palace, with a dome surmounted by a bronze statue of a horseman, plus a mosque and barracks for the caliphal guards and police.

The caliphal mosque was again constructed of mud brick, and supported by wooden columns, but this simple building was rebuilt in a more magnificent form by al-Mansur's grandson, Caliph Harun al-Rashid. Other enlargements followed but nothing of this mosque survives except, perhaps, for a marble *mihrab* found in a later mosque. It is believed to have been the *mihrab* of al-Mansur's mosque inside the original Round City of Baghdad.

Subsequent Abbasid caliphs felt constricted inside the Round City and so had palaces built outside. Then in the ninth century Caliph al-Mu'tasim moved the capital away from Baghdad to another new city, Samarra, but this project did not prove a lasting success and eventually the Abbasid court returned to Baghdad.

Left: A side passage in the sunken throne room of the Jawsaq al-Khaqani palace, Samarra.

From New Emperor to King of Kings

Whereas most of the Umayyad caliphs had intended their dynasty to become Islamic successors to the Romano-Byzantine empire, the Abbasids either saw themselves as heirs to the ancient Iranian King-of-Kings, or as a totally new and dominant world power.

The failure of two major assaults on the Byzantine capital of Constantinople in 670–7 and 716–17, and the stiffening of resistance along the Anatolian frontier, meant that the Byzantine empire did not collapse as the Sassanian empire had done. Yet this was only one reason why the caliphate began to see itself as successor to the Persian rather than Roman empire. A consequent shift in political and cultural emphasis started during the later Umayyad period, even before the Abbasid dynasty moved the capital of the caliphate from ex-Roman Syria to ex-Sassanian Iraq.

The ideology of the caliphate was, of course, primarily religious. Nevertheless some members of the ruling Umayyad elite saw themselves as part of what could be called the "Family of the Rulers of the World." This Iranian concept is believed to be behind an otherwise enigmatic painting on a side-wall in Qusayr Amra. Here six pre-Islamic rulers salute the figure of an Umayyad prince painted on the end wall. At one time this was thought to represent the rulers defeated by the Arab-Islamic conquerors, but it now seems that these three emperors and three kings are welcoming a new member into their "family"—namely the Umayyad Caliph.

REGIONAL INTERESTS

A change in the center of gravity of the Islamic world would prove significant, yet the Abbasids did not lose interest in the Mediterranean world or North Africa. The Islamic part of the Iberian peninsula would soon be lost to a revived Umayyad dynasty and Morocco would be taken over by a dynasty which refused to acknowledge Abbasid authority. Nevertheless the

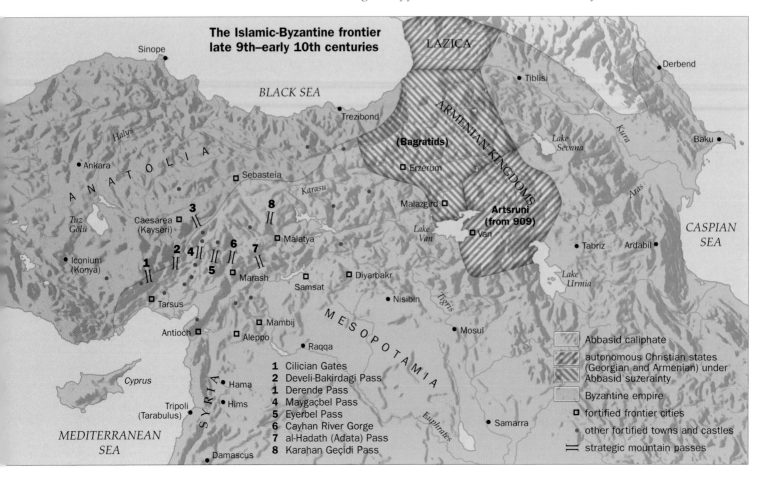

The Islamic-Byzantine frontier late 9th–early 10th centuries

1 Cilician Gates
2 Develi-Bakirdagi Pass
1 Derende Pass
4 Maygaçbel Pass
5 Eyerbel Pass
6 Cayhan River Gorge
7 al-Hadath (Adata) Pass
8 Karahan Geçidi Pass

Abbasid caliphate
autonomous Christian states (Georgian and Armenian) under Abbasid suzerainty
Byzantine empire
fortified frontier cities
other fortified towns and castles
strategic mountain passes

Abbasids continued to support loyal though often autonomous governors in Tunisia, Egypt, and Syria. Here, the Abbasids also sometimes imposed direct rule.

At the same time the frontier with the Byzantine empire could not be neglected. Instead several Abbasid caliphs launched major invasions deep into Anatolia while strengthening and reorganizing the frontier zones. *Thughur* military provinces along the vulnerable central and southwestern sections of the frontier were defended by fortified towns and castles with permanent garrisons. The northeastern part of the frontier was eventually left to autonomous Christian vassal states, most notably Armenia.

The shift of cultural, political, and economic emphasis which led the caliphate from being a post-Roman to a post-Sassanian empire was not, of course, merely a matter of abandoning western ambitions. It also involved the Abbasid caliphate adopting new priorities and, on a more superficial level, new court ceremony and even costume. The fact that the early Abbasids depended upon an army rooted in the eastern province of Khurasan meant that eastern Iranian influences now rivaled those from western Iran and Iraq.

Still further east the central Asian provinces of Khwarazm and Ma wara al-Nahr, "That which is beyond the river" or Transoxania, became more than mere recruiting grounds for soldiers. They now provided the Abbasid caliphate with dedicated administrators, cultural figures, and some of its most enterprising merchants.

Baghdad and the other cities which Abbasid caliphs used as temporary or permanent capitals, like Samarra and Raqqa, may not have been much further east than Damascus. The real change was in attitudes and ambition.

Reviving World Trade

From the late eighth to early tenth centuries, the Abbasid caliphate became the economic powerhouse of the Old World and the hub of international trade. Long-distance trade expanded to an extent never seen before.

Right: Sacks of spices outside a spice-seller's store in Cairo.

Below: Pack donkeys on a track in mountainous Syria.

Bottom: A carved wooden panel from the Fatimid Caliphal Palace, Cairo, depicts a camel with howdah and guards.

Thanks to vastly increased trading links, the Islamic Middle East became even more economically powerful than the massive and highly productive Chinese empire. There was a huge expansion of agricultural land, especially the irrigated land used for intensive agriculture. This in turn led to a rapid increase in population within the Islamic heartlands and of outlying regions such as central Asia and the Iberian peninsula. A remarkably high proportion of this growing population was now urban, having been drawn to the booming towns and cities by the prospect of work and prosperity.

For a while Baghdad became the most populous city in the world and would remain a thriving metropolis, despite civil wars, riots, and social upheavals, until it was brought to its knees by the invading Mongols in the early 13th century. Other cities like Damascus, Cairo, Cordoba, Bukhara, Samarkand, and Nishapur may have been smaller but were still huge in comparison to anything seen elsewhere outside China. They dwarfed the unsanitary so-called cities of western Europe, and within the Byzantine empire only the capital of Constantinople was in the same league.

These Islamic cities flourished as centers

of manufacture, often specializing in goods intended for export to distant lands both inside and outside the Islamic world. The increasing significance of such trade also meant that entire provinces became famous for the production of specific goods for export. These, of course, reflected the major local primary products, be they leather or wool, fish or horses, or whatever.

This astonishing network of international trade had a profound impact upon many of the Islamic world's immediate neighbors, as well as several that lay much further afield. For example, large parts of sub-Saharan Africa were linked to Egypt and North Africa by busy camel-caravan routes across the desert long before the peoples of sub-Saharan Africa converted to Islam.

To the edges of the World

Similarly, East Africa was tied into international trade by sea, where Arab merchants and mariners now dominated the western half of the Indian Ocean. East Africa became, in fact, an essential participant in a triangular trade involving the export of iron ore or ingots to India. There the metal was forged into swords and other more peaceful items, some of steel rather than mere iron, to be exported to the Islamic Middle East and elsewhere. The products of the Middle East, including luxury items and textiles, were then exported to East Africa to complete the triangle.

More dramatic, though on a smaller scale, was maritime trade between the Islamic Middle East and southeast Asia, again involving iron ingots as well as spices and more exotic goods. The extension of this trade northward to the Chinese coast was, perhaps, the most remarkable of all. At the same time the ancient Silk Road, from the Middle East across central Asia to China, enjoyed a boom in traffic. This brought great prosperity to the Islamic frontier provinces of Transoxania and eastern Iran.

In turn these regions opened up a series of important trade routes into what is now Russia. There they linked up with other trade routes to Scandinavia and northern Europe. As a result places as apparently isolated as the British Isles, Ireland, and Iceland were drawn into a virtually worldwide network of trade without even really being aware of it.

dates	
fish	
fruit and foodstuffs	
olives	
spices	
cotton	
hides	
silk	
textiles and embroidery	
paper	
porcelain	
glassware	
perfume	
soap	
amber	
gold	
precious stones	
other minerals	
ivory	
pearls	
ebony	
horse raising	
shipbuilding	
weapons	

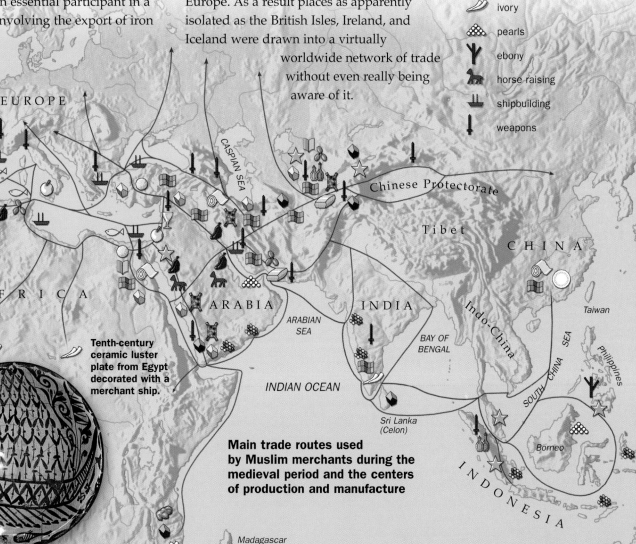

Tenth-century ceramic luster plate from Egypt decorated with a merchant ship.

Main trade routes used by Muslim merchants during the medieval period and the centers of production and manufacture

ATLANTIC OCEAN

EUROPE

CASPIAN SEA

Chinese Protectorate

Tibet

CHINA

Taiwan

AFRICA

ARABIA

ARABIAN SEA

INDIA

BAY OF BENGAL

Indo-China

SOUTH CHINA SEA

Philippines

INDIAN OCEAN

Sri Lanka (Celon)

Borneo

INDONESIA

Madagascar

The Fervent Translators

The revival of learning started during the century of Umayyad rule, but it was under the Abbasid caliphate and its successors that Islamic civilization achieved its golden age in the fields of science, medicine, and philosophy.

Right: Carved stone inkpot from Nishapur, 9th–10th centuries.

Below: This carved stone lamp from Nishapur, which also dates from between the 9th and 10th centuries, was designed to hold 25 flames.

Academies that had many of the characteristics of modern universities were established at Baghdad, Mosul, and Basra in Iraq, and also at Nishapur in Khurasan. Other less official centers developed elsewhere, and the major cities of the Islamic world from the Iberian peninsula to northwestern India became thriving centers of learning.

Much intellectual effort naturally focused upon essentially religious matters such as Islamic law and interpretation of the Koran. Nevertheless other deeply religious scholars put their efforts into non-religious studies. Several are credited with clarifying and commenting on the works of the ancient Greek philosophers, especially Aristotle, whose ideas dominated non-religious thought in both medieval Islamic and medieval Christian civilizations. It was such men who transmitted Aristotelian concepts back to Europe and, as a result, became recognized authorities themselves. Hence Ibn Sina became Avicenna to European scholars, while Ibn Rushd became Averroes.

Most Greek knowledge was translated into Arabic via Syrian or Aramean, the previously dominant Semitic languages of the Middle East. Because of its huge and extremely flexible vocabulary Arabic was well equipped to absorb ideas from as far afield as China and India, as well as being able to cope with new scientific theories. Many scientific and mathematical words still used in European languages are of Arabic origin.

The greatest period of Islamic scientific advance was during the tenth and eleventh centuries, yet the vital translation work was carried out, and the intellectual foundations were laid, by previous generations. This was done under the supportive rule of the Abbasid caliphs during their period of greatest power and wealth. Significant strides were similarly made in mathematics, medicine, geography, and history.

Right: Bab al-Amma, the monumental gate of Jawsaq al-Khani Palace, Samarra, was built in the 9th century.

750	751	751	756	760	762	789	798
Marwan II, last Umayyad caliph, is overthrown by the Abbasid caliph, Abu al-Abbas	Islamic army defeats T'ang Chinese at Talas in Central Asia	Muslims gain paper-making and wood-block printing from captured Chinese clerks	Revival of Umayyad rule in al-Andalus (Islamic Iberia)	Abbasids take control of Tabaristan	Foundation of the Round City of Baghdad by the Abbasids	Beginning of Shi'a Idrisid rule in Morocco, first fragmentation of the Abbasids	Muslims under Caliph Harun ar-Rashid defeat Byzantines at Heraclea, Anatolia

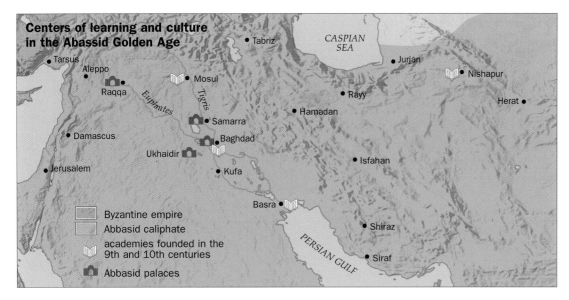

TECHNOLOGICAL REVOLUTION

Another apparently small development was to have a huge impact on the spread of knowledge within the caliphate. This was the arrival of paper-making technology, traditionally attributed to Chinese clerks captured by the Muslims at the battle of Talas in central Asia in 751. It was soon accompanied by woodblock printing.

The cursive character of the Arabic script, and the modified versions of this adopted by the Persians and Turks, did not lend itself to moveable type printing, which was invented much later in Germany. Instead woodblock printing had limited use, mostly in the production of decorated fabrics, though also in the printing of magical charms which used only a few well-established written phrases. Meanwhile, sophisticated chemical knowledge led to the invention of new textile dyes, ceramic glazes, and decorative alloys used in metalwork.

In mathematics the Muslims translated Indian treatises and adopted the Indian concept of the numeral zero. As a result the numbering system still used today is known in most countries as "Arabic numerals" to distinguish it from the cumbersome Roman numerals. The invention of algebra, from the Arabic *al-Jabr* meaning "restoration," as well as analytical geometry, trigonometry, and even spherical trigonometry, were similarly new.

Deep interest in light and optics led to an understanding of refraction, which in turn enabled Islamic scientists to calculate the thickness of the earth's atmosphere with remarkable accuracy. A sun-centered rather than earth-centered interpretation of the solar system would later be suggested by a few Muslim scholars, long before it was "discovered" in Europe.

There were fewer advances in subjects like zoology, which was seen as having little practical application. It was very different with botany, where Muslims could draw on Greek and Indian sources. These, when added to their own traditions of painstaking observation, produced startling results that had a direct impact upon medicine and agriculture, the latter becoming a science in its own right.

Below: An apothecary weighs out medicinal ingredients in this illustration from the Kitab al-Diryaq, a late 12th-century manuscript from either Syria or northern Iraq.

The Professionals

The first Abbasid army was largely recruited from Arab troops resident in eastern Iran, and therefore strongly influenced by Iranian traditions. Later forces were drawn from various nations and made use of military bases and tactical manuals.

Unlike the Umayyad army, the Khurasani-Arab army of the Abbasids was recruited on a regional rather than tribal basis. This reflected the Islamic army's transition from a largely Arab force to a much more cosmopolitan entity.

Meanwhile, the Syrian-Arab *Ahl al-Sham* remained in existence with lowered prestige, and the early Abbasid army included a remarkable variety of other units from

Above: The east side and entrance to the incomplete victory monument built by Caliph Harun al-Rashid at Herakla, Syria in the early 9th century.

different linguistic and geographical areas. The first 50 years of the Abbasid caliphate also saw indigenous Iranian Khurasanis absorbed into the Arab military elite, but it was not until a civil war following the death of the great Caliph Harun al-Rashid that Iranian Khurasanis marched west to become the dominant military force in Baghdad. Existing Arab units remained on the military lists until 833–4 and Arab soldiers from settled land-owning rather than nomadic communities continued to play a very important role in southeastern Anatolia.

Slave-recruited soldiers known as *ghulams* or mamluks, who would later become characteristic of medieval Islamic armies, first made a significant impact on military recruitment during the Abbasid period. Such military slaves formed an elite from the start, Turks from central Asia being considered the best.

Nevertheless the loyalty of such men was not taken for granted and they tended to be well treated and highly paid, having already been freed on completion of their training. There had been some free Turks in the later Umayyad army, but such troops were first recruited in large numbers in the early ninth century, following the Abbasid caliph al-Ma'mun's decision to offer equal military and religious status to Transoxanians who converted to Islam.

The relative importance of these varied sources of recruitment may be reflected in the number of known senior generals from each region during the reign of Caliph al-Mutasim (833–42). These included 24 Khurasanis, 19 Transoxanians, 17 Arabs, 12 Turks, and two descendants of the first Khurasani-Arab army that brought the Abbasids to power.

MILITARY STATE

The huge Abbasid military machine was provided with a completely new and suitably large military base in and around the Round City of Baghdad. Here they formed a vast garrison in the very center of the caliphate, including palace guard regiments, security forces, local police, and paramilitary militias, each with their own

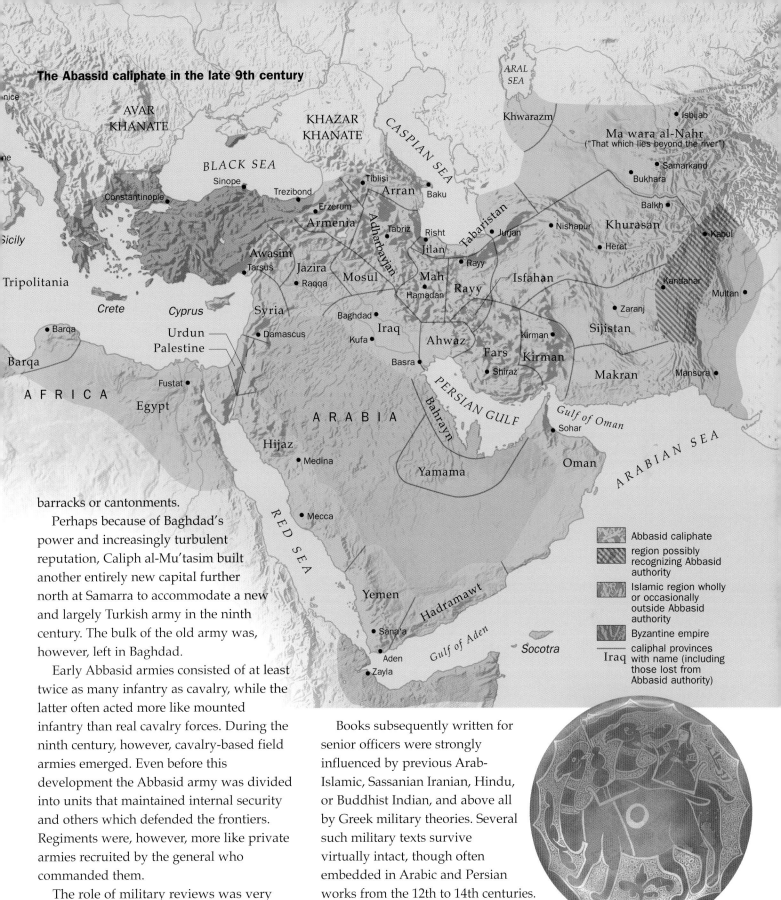

The Abassid caliphate in the late 9th century

AVAR KHANATE

KHAZAR KHANATE

BLACK SEA

CASPIAN SEA

ARAL SEA

Khwarazm

Isbijab

Ma wara al-Nahr ("That which lies beyond the river")

Samarkand

Bukhara

Sinope

Trezibond

Tiblisi

Arran

Baku

Balkh

Constantinople

Erzerum

Armenia

Tabriz

Risht

Jilan

Tabaristan

Nishapur

Khurasan

Kabul

Sicily

Awasim

Adharbayjan

Jurjan

Herat

Tarsus

Jazira

Mosul

Mah

Rayy

Isfahan

Kandahar

Multan

Tripolitania

Crete

Cyprus

Syria

Raqqa

Hamadan

Rayy

Zaranj

Sijistan

Baghdad

Iraq

Ahwaz

Fars

Kirman

Barqa

Urdun

Damascus

Kufa

Basra

Shiraz

Kirman

Makran

Mansura

Palestine

Barqa

Fustat

PERSIAN GULF

AFRICA

Egypt

ARABIA

Bahrayn

Gulf of Oman

Sohar

Hijaz

Medina

Yamama

Oman

ARABIAN SEA

RED SEA

Mecca

Yemen

Hadramawt

Sana'a

Aden

Gulf of Aden

Socotra

Zayla

Abbasid caliphate

region possibly recognizing Abbasid authority

Islamic region wholly or occasionally outside Abbasid authority

Byzantine empire

Iraq — caliphal provinces with name (including those lost from Abbasid authority)

barracks or cantonments.

Perhaps because of Baghdad's power and increasingly turbulent reputation, Caliph al-Mu'tasim built another entirely new capital further north at Samarra to accommodate a new and largely Turkish army in the ninth century. The bulk of the old army was, however, left in Baghdad.

Early Abbasid armies consisted of at least twice as many infantry as cavalry, while the latter often acted more like mounted infantry than real cavalry forces. During the ninth century, however, cavalry-based field armies emerged. Even before this development the Abbasid army was divided into units that maintained internal security and others which defended the frontiers. Regiments were, however, more like private armies recruited by the general who commanded them.

The role of military reviews was very important during the Abbasid period, not least because it was here that a soldier's kit, competence, and pay were assessed. In such a literate and prosperous civilization it is hardly surprising that many books of advice were written for both caliphs and commanders, those for rulers having covered military matters since the mid-eighth century.

Books subsequently written for senior officers were strongly influenced by previous Arab-Islamic, Sassanian Iranian, Hindu, or Buddhist Indian, and above all by Greek military theories. Several such military texts survive virtually intact, though often embedded in Arabic and Persian works from the 12th to 14th centuries.

Such works tended to emphasize caution, fortification, reconnaissance, communications, espionage, and intelligence, as well as the use of deception, ruse, and ambush. Others focused on weaponry and provide remarkably detailed information about swords, maces, helmets, bows, and other items of military equipment.

Above: A lusterware plate showing camels with banner and rider, 10th century, Iraq.

The City, the Land, and the Desert

An agricultural revolution started in the Middle East in the wake of the Arab-Islamic conquests. It spread across the entire Islamic world, leaving prosperity, good health, and social structures in its wake.

The spread of agriculture led to an increase in population and steady improvements in diet, nutrition, and sanitation, especially in cities. The Islamic agricultural revolution led to changes in methods of cooking and in the food crops available. Such new crops then led to the development of new industries.

The expansion of irrigation meant that more effective and newer systems of raising or moving water were required, the most visible being the sometimes enormous vertical waterwheels which spread from Iran to Portugal. Less dramatic was the gradual evolution of a legal system ensuring a fair distribution of irrigation water. These laws grew out of those existing in Syria and Yemen in the pre-Islamic period, and were based upon the principle that the closer a farmer was to the source of water, the greater were his rights of access.

Very fertile areas tended to be dominated by the estates of a new Arab aristocracy. Elsewhere autonomous tribal communities lived under the authority of their own chieftains, who in turn represented the sometimes distant authority of a provincial governor or the caliph.

In almost all regions sharecropping was the most common system. Typically a landlord's tenants had a contract to grow grain on unirrigated land for only one season. Eighty percent of this crop then went to the landlord, but contracts tended to be longer where fruit-growing was concerned.

The distribution of land was even more complex. In some tribal areas freehold farms tended to belong to individual families. Most land ownership was agreed on the basis of established custom, whereas written documentation was only kept by government officials for the high value estates surrounding towns or cities.

In outlying, barren, or war-ravaged regions the condition of the peasantry could be desperately poor. In more favored regions, however, new food crops and agricultural techniques often permitted double cropping where only one had been possible earlier. The extension of existing irrigation systems similarly enabled idle land to be cultivated, and nowhere was this more obvious than in Iraq.

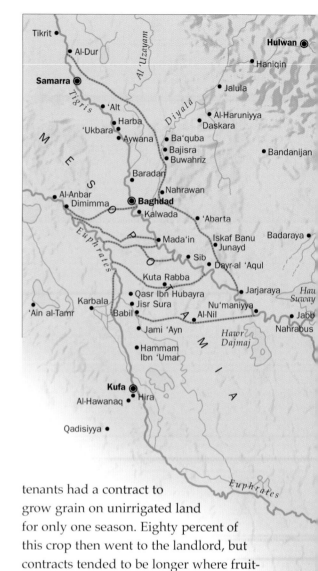

Below: The economy of Egypt was entirely dependent on the annual innundation of the Nile to flood the riverside agricultural land. Through this passage, constructed in 861, the rising waters entered the Nilometer, which helped predict the timing and degree of the essential flood.

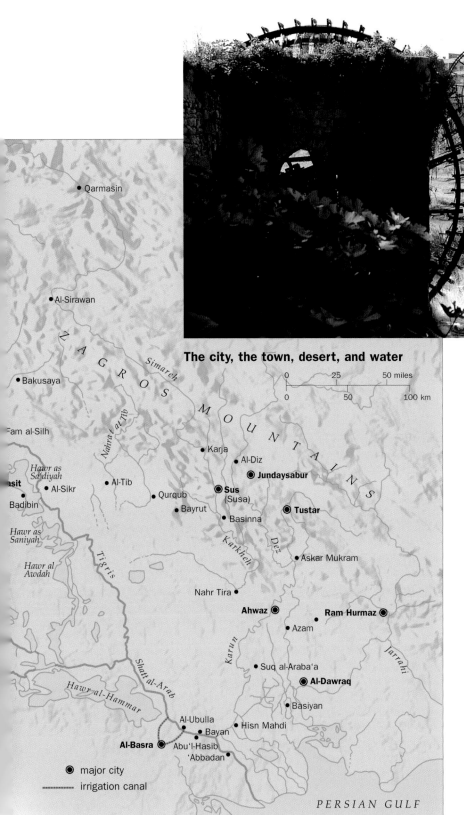

The city, the town, desert, and water

Qarmasin

Al-Sirawan

Z A G R O S

Simareh

Bakusaya

M O U N T A I N S

Fam al-Silh

Nahr at Tib

Hawr as Sa'diyah

asit

Al-Sikr

Al-Tib

Badibin

Hawr as Saniyah

Hawr al Awdah

Tigris

Karja

Al-Diz

Jundaysabur

Sus (Susa)

Qurqub

Bayrut

Basinna

Tustar

Karkheh

Dez

Askar Mukram

Nahr Tira

Ahwaz

Ram Hurmaz

Azam

Karun

Jarrahi

Suq al-Araba'a

Al-Dawraq

Shatt al-Arab

Hawr al-Hammar

Basiyan

Al-Ubulla

Bayan

Hisn Mahdi

Al-Basra

Abu'l-Hasib

'Abbadan

◉ major city

-------- irrigation canal

PERSIAN GULF

0 — 25 — 50 miles
0 — 50 — 100 km

Top: Two of the famous nurias *or water-raising wheels of Hama, on the River Orontes in Syria.*

Above: Women watching the brewing of medicines, illustration from the Kitab al-Diryaq, *late 12th century.*

NEW CROPS IN DISTANT LANDS

During this period oranges and other citrus fruits spread westward from India, along with sugarcane, cotton, rice, and mulberry trees for the new silk industry. The spread of bananas from southeast Asia to Morocco and Iberia was the most remarkable of all, since this plant could not be taken from one place to another in seed form. Instead it had to move as a living plant, one step at a time, generation by generation. Not surprisingly books on agriculture were in great demand, and some

rulers even built botanical gardens staffed by the leading plant experts of their day.

There were fewer changes in animal husbandry but the importance of meat, especially mutton, to Islamic diet and religious practice meant that the economies of many remote peoples became market orientated. Partly as a result, the wool and skins from these animals prompted further developments in the textile and leather industries.

The vital role of long distance trade similarly contributed to the market orientation of agriculture. Large quantities of basic foodstuffs as well as smaller volumes of high-value herbs and spices were carried over great distances by land and sea. Within the Middle East alone, dried fruits, honey, and nuts were transported from country to country, while snow to cool the drinks of the wealthy was packed in lead-lined containers and carried on camel-back from the high mountains before being stored in efficient ice houses throughout the year. During the ninth and tenth centuries ice was similarly used to keep melons fresh while they were carried all the way from central Asia to the caliph's palace in Baghdad.

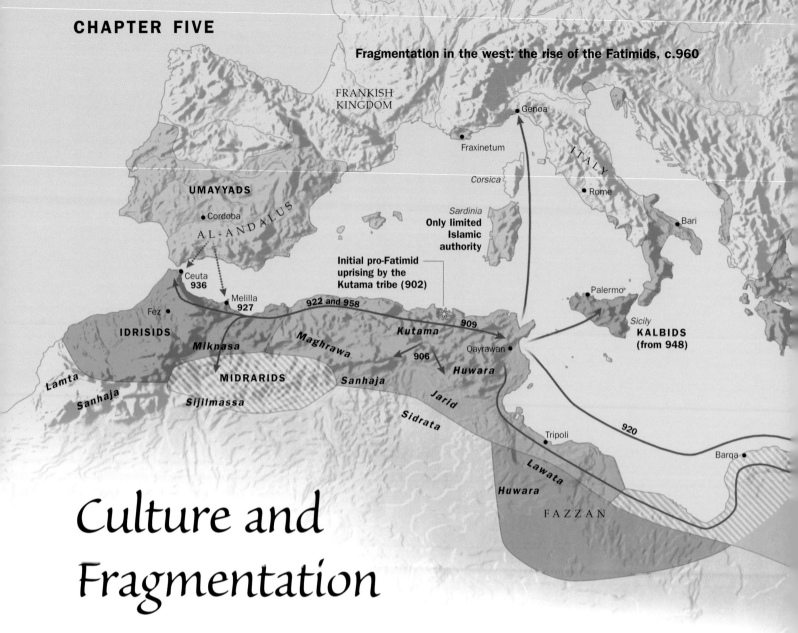

CHAPTER FIVE

Fragmentation in the west: the rise of the Fatimids, c.960

FRANKISH KINGDOM

Genoa

Fraxinetum

Corsica

ITALY

Rome

Sardinia
Only limited Islamic authority

Bari

UMAYYADS

Cordoba

AL-ANDALUS

Initial pro-Fatimid uprising by the Kutama tribe (902)

Palermo

Ceuta
936

Melilla
927

Fez

922 and 958

Sicily
KALBIDS (from 948)

Kutama

909

IDRISIDS

Miknasa

Maghrawa

906

Qayrawan

Huwara

Lamta

MIDRARIDS

Sanhaja

Jarid

Sanhaja

Sijilmassa

Sidrata

920

Tripoli

Barqa

Lawata

Huwara

FAZZAN

Culture and Fragmentation

End and aftermath of the Abbasids

The Umayyads kept their vast state intact for more than a century. Islamic territory continued to expand during the Abbasid caliphate, yet this successor dynasty soon lost control of several outlying provinces. Some regions became entirely independent and refused to recognize the spiritual authority of the Abbasids; an act symbolized by ceasing to mention them in the *khutba* or Friday sermon. Governorship of other provinces fell into the hands of dynasties which continued to recognize the Abbasids but which were too powerful for the caliph to remove even if he wanted to.

The western part of the Islamic world was, of course, difficult to control. This was not merely because of distance and tenuous communications but because North Africa and the Iberian peninsula were poor and economically under-developed when compared with the Middle East, Iran, or Islamic central Asia.

Loyalty to the Umayyads remained strong in al-Andalus or that part of the Iberian peninsula under Islamic rule at the time of the Abbasid revolution. Substantial Umayyad armies had been sent there to restore order, and most of them welcomed a survivor of the Umayyad house who reached al-Andalus as little more than a political refugee. He was able to recreate a Spanish Umayyad state that endured from 756 to 1031.

Morocco was the next to fall away, with the Idrisids taking control in 789 and

Above: A Fatimid sword and shield carved on the Bab al-Nasr Gate, late 11th century, Cairo.

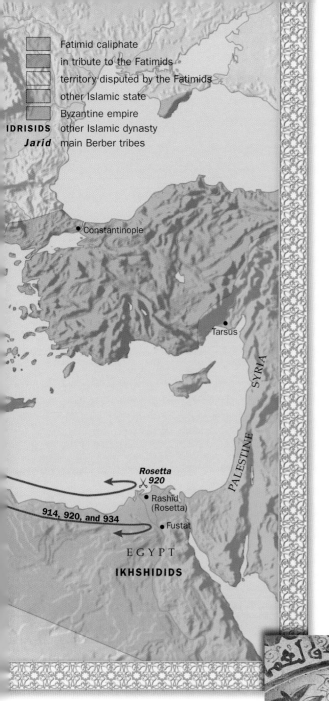

Constantinople

Tarsus

SYRIA

PALESTINE

Rosetta
X 920

Rashīd
(Rosetta)

914, 920, and 934

Fustat

EGYPT

IKHSHIDIDS

*Above: The Bab-
Zuwaila Gate, late
11th century, guards
the late medieval
mosque of al-Muayyad
at Cairo.*

*Below: A Fatimid
mounted man with a
hawk decorates a luster
ceramic plate.*

northern end of one of the most important
trans-Saharan trade routes.

Unlike these dynasties, the Aghlabids
remained loyal servants of the Abbasids.
They controlled Tunisia and much of
Algeria, as well as Malta and Sicily, which
they conquered in the name of the Abbasids.
In return for sending a substantial portion of
their taxes back to the caliphal capital in
Iraq, the Aghlabids were left in peace from
their establishment in 800 to their fall in 909.

In 868 the Abbasid caliph sent a young
Turkish officer named Ahmad Ibn Tulun to
govern Egypt. He went on to take control of
Palestine and Syria. Meanwhile, under
Tulunid rule, Egypt enjoyed a remarkable
economic and cultural renaissance.
In 905 the Abbasid caliph sent another
general to reclaim Egypt but, 30 years
after that, a Turkish governor established
a second autonomous dynasty in Egypt
known as the Ikhshidids.

Next came the Fatimids, whose
dynasty was entirely different. They
rose to power in eastern Algeria and
were dedicated opponents of the
Abbasid caliphate from the start. As
Shi'a Muslims, the Fatimids claimed the
title of caliph for themselves, and from
their powerbase in North Africa the
first Fatimid Shi'a caliphs sent several
armies and fleets to conquer Egypt. In
969 a Fatimid general named Jawhar
finally succeeded. The Fatimid caliph
transferred his court to Egypt and, like
the Abbasids, he decided to build an
entirely new capital. It was called al-
Qahira, "The Victorious"—or Cairo, as it is
known in the Western world.

becoming the first North African
dynasty to introduce Shi'a Islamic
doctrines. At this time
Christianity, Judaism, and
paganism were still strong in
North Africa, as was an
egalitarian Islamic movement
known as Kharijism. Driven
underground elsewhere in North
Africa, some Kharijis created a
small state under the Rustamid
dynasty in the Tahart area of what
is now western Algeria. It
survived until 909.

Another remarkable but small
Berber state was that of the
Midrarids. Based in Sijilmassa on the edge of
the desert in Morocco, it controlled the

Soldiers Become Kings

The fragmentation of Abbasid authority in the east and south was more complex than the decline in the west. The rise and fall of rival dynasties in disparate regions was complicated by Shi'a and Sunni divisions.

Right: Wall-painting of a horseman with a hawk, from Nishapur, 10th–11th centuries.

Facing below: A carved stucco wall-decoration depicts a seated ruler with attendants, from Rayy, 11th century.

A patchwork of ethnic groups and political and sectarian allegiances distinguished the east and south. In the far south of Arabia, an Abbasid governor asserted his autonomy and established the Ziyadid dynasty in 818. Almost 30 years later, another leader who claimed descent from a family of pre-Islamic Yemenite rulers won control of the mountainous interior and established the Yu'firid dynasty. Both dynasties were, however, careful to proclaim their allegiance to the Abbasid caliph in Iraq. He in turn made no effort to reassert direct control.

In 897 a Shi'a Muslim dynasty established itself in the highlands and—as Shi'a—refused to recognize the Sunni Muslim Abbasids. Known as the Zaydi Imams, this remarkable dynasty endured, with one long break in the later medieval period, until it was overthrown by a republican revolution in 1962. Shi'a achieved similar success in another remote region, Tabaristan on the Caspian coast of Iran, which was cut off from the rest of the Islamic world by high mountains and almost subtropical forests. In fact Tabaristan had not been conquered during the first wave of Arab-Islamic expansion. Even after accepting Umayyad suzerainty, Tabaristan remained politically autonomous and Zoroastrian in religion.

The Abbasids overthrew the indigenous rulers in 760 but another local dynasty, the Bawandids, had already seized power in the highlands. By converting to Islam and using great political skill as well as their geographical remoteness, these Bawandids survived for over 600 years into the mid-14th century.

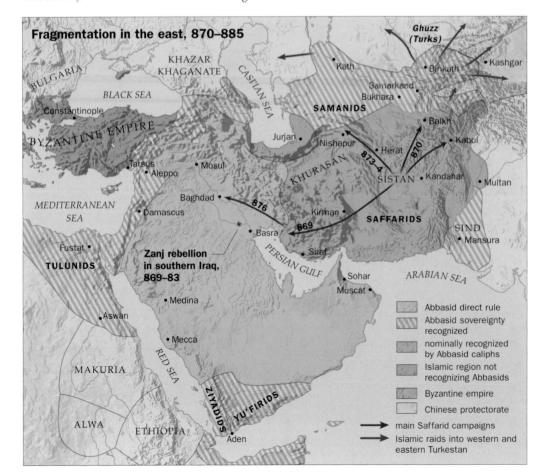

Fragmentation in the east, 870–885

Zanj rebellion in southern Iraq, 869–83

Abbasid direct rule
Abbasid sovereignty recognized
nominally recognized by Abbasid caliphs
Islamic region not recognizing Abbasids
Byzantine empire
Chinese protectorate
main Saffarid campaigns
Islamic raids into western and eastern Turkestan

RENEGADE STATE

Shi'a missionaries continued to be active in these regions, undermining loyalty to the Abbasid caliphate. Things came to a head with the emergence of a fiercely Shi'a Islamic dynasty called the Ziyarids, who at one point seemed likely to take most of northern Iran. The murder of their founder by his own troops removed this threat. Subsequent Ziyarids continued to rule a small, highly cultured yet often warlike state until the last Ziyarid was overthrown in about 1090.

The northernmost province of the central Islamic world was largely left to its own devices under the local Sharwan Shahs from the late eighth to early 17th centuries. One of the most loyal yet still autonomous dynasties of the Abbasid caliphate was that of the Samanids. They ruled much of what are now the independent republics of central Asia during a time of prosperity and remarkable cultural achievements. Though largely peaceful, the Samanids did expand the frontiers of Islam northward and eastward, sometimes by military means but usually by persuasion.

Strictly Sunni in religion, the Samanids also earned the gratitude of the Abbasid caliph by halting a dangerous rebel, Amr Ibn al-Layth, second of the Saffarid rulers of what is now Afghanistan. The Saffarids carved out a large but transient empire that included most of what is now Iran. Unable to destroy the Saffarids completely, the Abbasid caliph reluctantly recognized them as legitimate governors of several regions. For their part the Saffarids accepted these titles but rarely hid their contempt for the caliph's authority.

Beyond Saffarid territory lay the distant provinces of Multan and Mansura in what is now Pakistan. Here descendants of the Arab conquerors and of local converts remained loyal to the Abbasids, except for a brief period when Multan recognized the rival Fatimid caliphate in Egypt. This region dedicated its energies to trade and religious scholarship rather than expansion.

The mausoleum tower of Sultan Kawus, built in 1007, is situated in Gumbad-i Kawus, Iran.

Pupils Become Teachers

Ibn Sina dominated the great age of Islamic science. He was an expert in many fields, but is remembered for his medical discoveries and books such as *Qanun*, made while searching for a safe and stable home.

Right: Two cupping glasses of the 9th–10th centuries used for collecting blood during medicinal bleeding of the patient, from Gurgan (Jurjan), Iran.

Below: Detail from the side of the original tombstone of Ibn Sina in the Ibn Sina Mausoleum, Hamadan, Iran.

Ibn Sina was born in 980 in what medieval Muslims knew as *Ma Wara al-Nahr* ("That which is beyond the river") or Transoxania in what is today Uzbekistan. Transoxania was a cultural and political frontier in the northeastern corner of the Islamic world, yet it was wealthy and powerful with trade links across most of the known world. One of its most important cities was Bukhara, which had been the capital of the ruling Samanid dynasty. While Ibn Sina was a child, however, Bukhara was threatened by invaders and when he was a young man the Samanid state was swept away.

Ibn Sina, whose full name was Abu Ali al-Husayn Ibn Abd Allah Ibn Sina, first studied Islamic law then, from age 10 to 15, philosophy. Next his interests turned to medicine, and he soon earned such a reputation that doctors sought his advice when he was still only 16. When the aged ruler Nuh Ibn Mansur fell ill none of his doctors could understand the problem. Ibn Sina's name was remembered and his diagnosis must have impressed because the next ruler allowed the young doctor to use his famous library. As a result Ibn Sina started to write his first book at the age of 21.

Forced by unknown problems to leave

Facing: Scaffolding supports the interior of the Ibn Sina Madrasah in Isfahan, Iran, while renovation work is carried out.

Bukhara, he first moved to Gurganj (now called Urgench), where his teacher al-Natili had already gone. Within a few years, however, Ibn Sina decided to make a dangerous journey across the desert to the court of Qabus Ibn Wushmgir, the Ziyarid ruler of Jurjan. Yet even now Ibn Sina did not feel safe, since the conquering Sultan of Ghazna apparently wanted to add him to his collection of scholars. Leaving Jurjan and the threat of abduction, Ibn Sina traveled westward to Rayy where he entered the service of the mother of the Buwayhid ruler, who was suffering from what would today be called depression.

A SAFE HAVEN

It is ironic that Ibn Sina found a relatively safe haven under one of the most anarchic dynasties in medieval Islamic history. The Buwayhids were a clan of competing Shi'a rulers who dominated western Iran and Iraq during much of the 10th and 11th centuries. Although Shi'a Muslims, these Buwayhids had also dominated the Sunni Muslim Abbasid caliphate of Baghdad since 945. This time of paradoxes was, however, one of the most brilliant in cultural, scientific, and artistic achievements.

Again Ibn Sina only remained in Rayy for a while before moving first to Qazwin and then to Hamadan, which was controlled by the Buwayhid ruler Shams al-Dawla. There the young doctor become one of the ruler's friends and was soon promoted to the rank of first *wazir* or prime minister.

The following years of political activity did not stop Ibn Sina practicing medicine and writing an astonishing number of books in Arabic and Persian. At other times he was banished or imprisoned, or accompanied armies on campaign. Some of his works

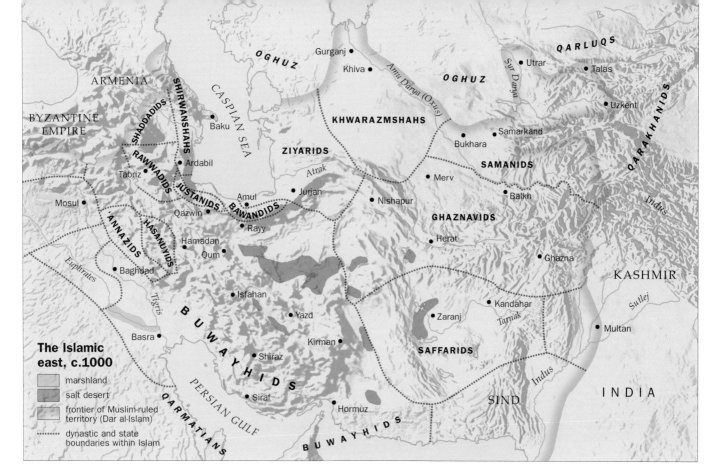

The Islamic east, c.1000

marshland
salt desert
frontier of Muslim-ruled territory (Dar al-Islam)
dynastic and state boundaries within Islam

were even dictated on horseback. At one point Ibn Sina's secretary, pupil, and biographer, al-Juzjani, asked the master to write a commentary on the ancient Greek philosopher Aristotle. Ibn Sina felt too busy but did agree to make a summary, the result being one of his most famous works; the *Shifa* (healing). By now he had also completed the first volume of his massive medical encyclopedia, *Qanun* (rule or principle), the most influential of all Ibn Sina's books, but the death of his patron obliged the doctor to move on again, this time to Isfahan. Here, in the court of Ala al-Dawla, he finally found a stable refuge.

Ibn Sina was a member of the administrative elite called the Men of the Pen, which administered medieval Islamic states while the Men of the Sword served in their armies. During his years in Isfahan, Ibn Sina continued medical research and carried out the experiments recorded in the *Qanun*. He also designed improved types of astronomical instruments and dabbled in philology.

Ibn Sina fell ill while accompanying Ala al-Dawla's army on campaign. Realizing that death was near, he said: "The governor who governed my body is now incapable of governing, and so treatment is no longer of any use." Ibn Sina, scholar, philosopher, and

one of the greatest doctors in the history of medicine, died on the first Friday of Ramadan, June 18, 1037, and was buried at Hamadan.

Sunni and Shi'a

Though the two branches of Islam have much in common, Sunni and Shi'a followers have major differences regarding the interpretation of Mohammed's words and prophecies, and the Prophet's rightful successors, rooted in arguments that occurred over 13 centuries ago.

Right: Stone carving from the mosque of Sarmaj-Kirmanshah, built for Hassnoyeh-Baryekani, 959–79.

In religious terms the Sunni were, and remain, those Muslims who base their practices on the *sunna* or customs of Mohammed. They have always been the majority and are often misleadingly called "orthodox" Muslims by those outside the Islamic faith. The Sunni tend to identify their community in the negative sense of not being Shi'a. Differences in religious doctrine and practice between Sunni and Shi'a are, however, minor compared with the differences between some Christian denominations.

Until the abolition of the Sunni caliphate by the Turkish Republic in 1924, it was recognition of a Sunni caliph as the spiritual and theoretically also the political leader of the Islamic community that most obviously defined a Sunni Muslim. This was the case even when more than one Sunni leader claimed the title of caliph, as happened on several occasions. For example Abd al-

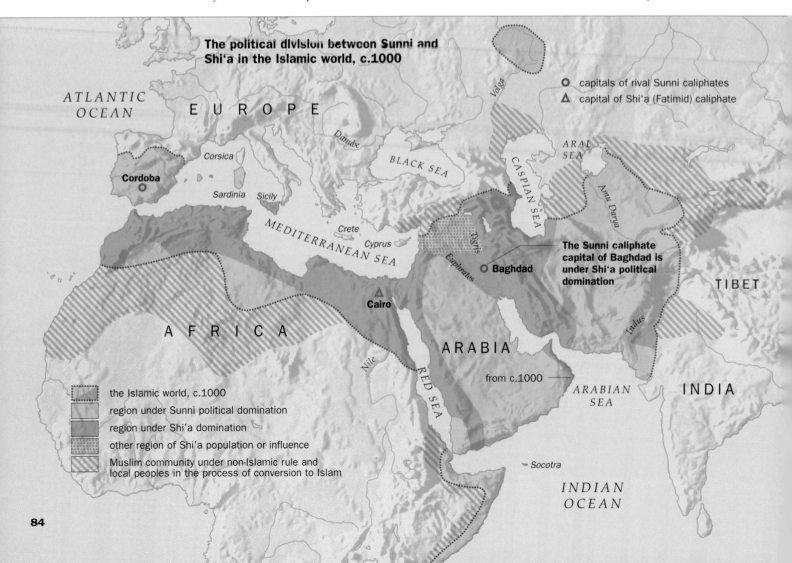

The political division between Sunni and Shi'a in the Islamic world, c.1000

○ capitals of rival Sunni caliphates
△ capital of Shi'a (Fatimid) caliphate

ATLANTIC OCEAN

EUROPE

Volga

Danube

BLACK SEA

ARAL SEA

CASPIAN SEA

Amu Darya

Corsica

Cordoba ○

Sardinia   Sicily

MEDITERRANEAN SEA

Crete

Cyprus

Tigris

Euphrates

○ Baghdad

The Sunni caliphate capital of Baghdad is under Shi'a political domination

TIBET

△ Cairo

AFRICA

Nile

RED SEA

ARABIA

from c.1000 →

ARABIAN SEA

INDIA

Indus

▬ Socotra

the Islamic world, c.1000
region under Sunni political domination
region under Shi'a domination
other region of Shi'a population or influence
Muslim community under non-Islamic rule and local peoples in the process of conversion to Islam

INDIAN OCEAN

Rahman III, the Umayyad ruler of al-Andalus, proclaimed himself caliph in the early tenth century, not primarily in opposition to the Abbasids in faraway Iraq but in the face of the rising Shi'a Fatimid caliphate in North Africa.

It would be misleading to identify the first four Rashidun or "rightly guided" caliphs as Sunni, since they were accepted by the overwhelming majority of all Muslims. It was what happened after the death of the fourth caliph, Ali, that defined the differences between the two main branches of Islam.

The term Shi'a is a shortened form of *Shi'at Ali* or "party of Ali." One of the few features that the many Shi'a sects share is their belief that the role of caliph or Imam should properly have passed from Ali to his descendants, who were themselves also members of the *Ahl al-Bayt*, or descendants of Mohammed. The Shi'a emerged as a political as well as religious movement during Umayyad times. This was when some members of the *Ahl al-Bayt* in the holy cities of Mecca and Medina were urged by various supporters to lay claim to leadership of the Islamic community. This led to conflict with the Umayyad caliphs and their supporters, as a result of which Ali's son, Husayn, grandson of the Prophet, was killed at Karbala in Iraq in 680.

ARGUMENTS OVER SUCCESSION

While Shi'a agree on who the first few successors should have been, they diverge where later members of the family are concerned. The separation of different Shi'a groups largely took place in the ninth century. For example, the Zaydi rulers who won control of central Yemen at the end of the ninth century believed that Ali had been designated by the Prophet Mohammed as Imam, leader of the Muslims or "The Community of the Faithful," because of his personal merits. However, some other Shi'a saw this as a result of Divine Command.

Those who belonged to the same Shi'a sect as the Zaydis also differed from smaller Shi'a groups in maintaining that the Fifth Imam should have been Zayd, grandson of the martyred Husan, who was himself killed when he led another rebellion against

Umayyad authority in 740. Some Shi'a sects maintain that the Fifth Imam should have been Zayd's brother, Mohammed al-Baqir.

These seemingly minor matters of succession still divide the Shi'a movement. Yet such disagreements did not stop the emergence of several Shi'a ruling dynasties in various parts of the Islamic world from the tenth century onward. Until early modern times, the most powerful of these were the Fatimids who, at the height of their power, controlled most of North Africa,

Below: Dating from 1178 and illuminated by eery green light designed to protect its delicate cloth covering from ultra-violet damage, the tomb of Imam Shafi sits in his mausoleum in Cairo.

Egypt, Palestine, much of Syria, parts of Arabia, and even briefly won the allegiance of distant Multan in the later tenth century.

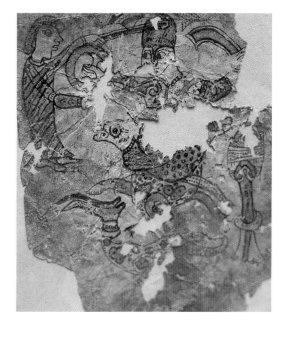

Left: A painted paper "magical charm" from Fustat (Cairo) dates from between the 13th and 14th centuries.

Beyond the River

The river called the Oxus by Greeks and other ancient peoples is now known by its Turkish name of Amu Darya. Transoxania, historically the central Asian lands beyond this river, contained peoples of many ethnicities and faiths.

Right: Interior of the 10th-century tomb of Ismail at Bukhara, Uzbekistan.

Below right: Entrance to the domed Arab Ata mausoleum of the 10th century at Tim, Uzbekistan.

The peoples beyond the Amu Darya (Oxus) were converted to Islam, and the region became one of the Muslim empire's most vital, with trade and science both flourishing. North of the Amu Darya, running a roughly parallel course, is the Syr Darya, which ancients knew as the Jaxartes. Beyond the eastern half of this second river are territories that formed part of the flourishing early Islamic provinces of Ma Wara al-Nahr. In cultural, economic, and political terms, early Islamic Transoxania also included some territory south of the Oxus, including Khwarazm in the west and Badakhshan in the east.

Within this sprawling territory were very different geographical and climatic regions, ranging from huge mountains, through fertile river valleys and oases, to some of the bleakest deserts in the world. Today the great majority of the population speak Turkish and are Muslim. In the early Islamic period, however, the majority spoke Persian-Iranian dialects, while large numbers clung to various pre-Islamic religions.

Above: Decorated 10th–12th-century ceramic fragments from Kuva, Uzbekistan.

Since ancient times merchant caravans had passed through, along a network of routes which linked China and the Mediterranean empires. A 19th-century German scholar named them the Silk Road, and it was a name that stuck. Much more than silk was transported along these roads, of course, and the routes themselves were connected to others leading north and south.

Meanwhile, the impact that such trade had on the peoples of central Asia was immense, stimulating the development of

cities as well as artistic and scientific developments. The introduction of the Islamic caliphate in the eighth century provided greater security, and was serviced by government postal systems where stations were built every half a day's caravan journey. These housed mules and horses, which enabled urgent messages to cover the equivalent of 12 days' journey within one day.

The consolidation of Arab-Islamic authority following the defeat of the Chinese at the battle of Talas halted Turkish encroachment for several centuries and resulted in a remarkable flowering of Sughdian or eastern Iranian civilization. With the rise of the Samanids in the early ninth century, Iranians also took over local government under Abbasid suzerainty. Cities like Bukhara and Samarkand became major cultural centers and several beautiful buildings survive from this period.

TURKISH INFLUX

However, in 1005 the Samanids were succeeded by the Qarakhanids, also known as the Ilig Khans, who were Turks. They had risen to power in the mountains east of the Samanid realm and seem to have been descended from Qarluqs, a Turkish tribal confederacy that had largely converted to Islam in the tenth century.

This was a turning point in the history of central Asia and the long process of Turkification followed, though still within Islamic culture. As a result only one of the new states that achieved independence following the collapse of the Soviet Union in the late 20th century, Tajikstan, still has a non-Turkish majority.

Even some of the ancient differences which distinguished the cultures of various parts of this remarkable corner of the medieval Islamic world are still seen today. For example, Uzbekistan is the most urbanized, being dominated by cities and agricultural communities along its fertile rivers. Turkmenistan is, as its name implies, dominated by the tribal and traditionally

nomadic Turcomans, while most of its territory consists of the forbidding Qara Qum desert. Kyrgyzstan is a land of mountains and high valleys around the upper reaches of the Syr Darya, largely inhabited by nomads and farmers.

Only a small part of what had been early medieval Islamic Transoxania now falls within the territory of the biggest of the new central Asian republics, Kazakhstan. Most of its huge territory consists of steppe, with Chinese central Asia to the east and Russian Siberia to the north. It is also often forgotten that the westernmost corner of Kazakhstan lies beyond the River Ural, and thus is geographically within Europe.

Above: A group of Karakhanid mausoleums dating from the 11th century at Uzgen (Uzkent), Kyrgyzstan.

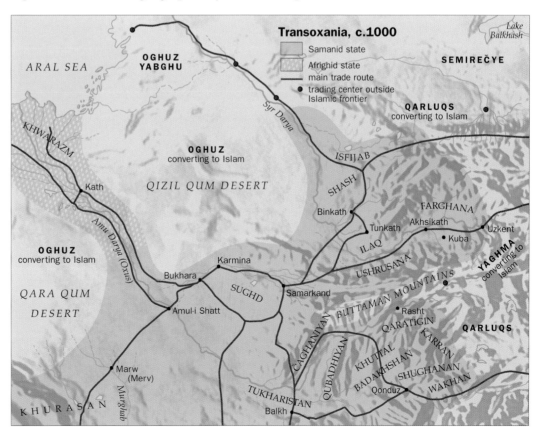

Exploring the World

Islamic culture inherited the ancient cities of the Middle East and the trade routes that linked them to India, China, and East Africa. Medieval Islamic governments and enterprising individuals developed this network much further, across huge land routes and on the high seas.

Facing: A collection of Islamic astrolabes, instruments used by early astronomers to measure the altitude of stars and planets, and which also served as navigational aids. The earliest known Islamic astrolabes date from the 8th century, but greater sophistication was achieved during the 10th and 11th centuries.

While merchants from Syria, Iraq, Iran, and many other parts of the early medieval caliphate traded along the Silk Road and other great land routes of Asia, other merchants took their cargoes by sea to and from ports stretching from southern Africa to what is now Indonesia. Only the tip of southern Africa, the Americas, Australia, and Antarctica remained outside this flourishing trading network and it is possible that some Muslim explorers actually ventured around southern Africa and may have circumnavigated the continent. It is also quite possible—perhaps even likely—that Muslim mariners landed in Australia when blown off course.

Meanwhile, Indian merchants seem to

Right: A mosaic of the late 7th century in the courtyard of the Great Mosque of Damascus illustrates a ship laden with goods.

have abandoned the western half of the Indian Ocean to their Persian and Arab rivals, although they did trade eastward to Burma, Malaya, and Indonesia. Traveling in the opposite direction, settlers and presumably traders from what is now Indonesia were colonizing Madagascar and the east African coast.

The intellectual curiosity that typified the golden age of medieval Islamic civilization encouraged exploration by land and sea. Suleiman the Merchant, Abu Zayd Hassan, and Ibn Wahab of Basra traveled by sea. Others voyaged overland, reaching far into the north of the Asian landmass. Some of these explorers' books still survive, while others are remembered only by their names. But all contributed to an increase in knowledge about the world, its continents, climates, seas, and peoples.

Great navigators

Tales brought back by sailors and merchants also entered popular stories, most notably in the huge collection known as *The Thousand and One Nights*, or *Arabian Nights* as it is better known in the west. Embedded in the accounts of Sindbad the Sailor and Prince Aladdin are garbled references to the orangutan apes of Borneo and other strange creatures that seemed more mythical than real to the professional storytellers of Cairo and Baghdad.

Of greater concern to the sea captains who voyaged to southeast Asia and China were the Indian Ocean's seasonal monsoon winds that enabled their ships to sail far out of sight of land for weeks on end. In addition to the monsoons these mariners also relied on a primitive form of sextant called a *kamal*, and Chinese nautical inventions such as the magnetic compass and the hinged stern rudder.

Even before these new inventions became

868	**897**	**c.900**	**c.900**	**909**	**911**	**929**	**934**
Abbasid officer Ahmad Ibn Tulun governs Egypt, later controls Palestine and Syria	A Shi'a Muslim dynasty, the Zaydi Imams, is established in the Arabian highlands	The Abbasid caliphate dominates trade in the Old World	Arab tribes unite under the Shi'a Qarmatians and rebel against Abbasid rule	Shi'a Fatimid caliphate siezes Tunisia; two rival dynasties now claim caliph status	Death of Ishaq Ibn Hunayn, translator of Aristotole, Euclid, and Ptolemy into Arabic	Ruler of al-Andalus assumes title of caliph; now three rival dynasties in the Islamic world	Genoa is sacked by an Islamic fleet

available, Arab captains used books called *rahmanis*. These contained information about the positions and movements of the stars, astronomical tables, the latitudes of seaports, information about winds, dangerous reefs, currents, coastal landmarks, and useful natural features like the shoals of sea snakes that were found off the Indian coast.

Given the sophistication of trans-oceanic trade, it is not surprising to find that an Arabian port like Sohar in Oman, traditionally the home of Sindbad the Sailor, flourished. Until the ninth century Sohar was of little importance, but it rose to prominence as Oman won independence from the Abbasid caliphate.

In addition to peaceful trading voyages, fleets from Sohar even attacked Basra and obliged the rival port of Siraf to build a defensive wall. Meanwhile, Sohar sent merchant fleets to east Africa and Madagascar, bringing back cargoes of ivory, tortoiseshell, leopard skins, and ambergris which were in demand not only within the

Islamic world but also in India and China.

This period of greatness was short, however, and in the later tenth century Sohar's maritime independence was crushed by the Buwayhid rulers of Iran. Other ports further south took over, though the pattern of oceanic trade hardly changed at all.

The main ports and sea-trading routes used by Omani merchants from Sohar during the eighth to tenth centuries

Glassware like this Karakhanid bottle from Kuva in modern-day Uzbekistan were prized in many other parts of the Arab trading world.

935	945	965	969	970	971	975	980–1037
A Turkish governor establishes a second dynasty in Egypt, the Ikhshid	Shi'a Buwayhids are recognized in Baghdad by the Sunni Abbasid caliphs	The Volga Bulghars gain independence from the Khazars and ally with the Abbasids	General Jawhar takes Egypt from the Ikhshids on behalf of the Shi'a Fatimid caliph	Foundation of al-Azhar in Cairo, considered the oldest university still in existence	The Fatimids take Palestine and Syria from the Abbasids	The Fatimids drive Carmathian Muslims from Egypt, Palestine, and Syria	Life of Ibn Sina, Persian philosopher and medical doctor

The Disappearance of Arabia

Although not isolated, Arabia had rarely been a significant player. With the coming of Islam, Medina was briefly the capital of the expanding Muslim state, while the peninsula enjoyed a renaissance for several centuries, before declining into a warlike, tribal backwater.

Even after the caliphal capital was moved first to Syria and then to Iraq, Arabia remained a vital part of the new superstate. Its two main towns, Mecca and Medina, were the goal of Muslims making their pilgrimage. The Red Sea and Persian Gulf coastal regions also remained within the mainstream of international trade, while further south Yemen and Oman similarly flourished.

Central Arabia was a different matter. In this largely nomadic region, groups alienated from current Islamic politics and culture often found a refuge. As early as 661 the Kharijis, who wanted Islam to be a divinely guided theocracy, attempted to assassinate three Muslim leaders including Ali, the fourth caliph. Ali was murdered, and the Kharijis continued to be a problem for the subsequent Umayyad caliphs. On the other hand this movement was stronger in

Iran and North Africa than Arabia.

Most Arabian tribes remained largely loyal to the Umayyads and their Abbasid successors until the rise of another but very different revolutionary movement at the end of the ninth century. These were the Qarmatians, a radical Shi'a movement with its roots in the less violent but still revolutionary Isma'ili branch of Shi'a Islam. The Fatimid caliphate that installed itself in Egypt was of this persuasion.

QARMATIAN RADICALS

The Qarmatians were named after a missionary named Hamdan Qarmat who is said to have preached in Iraq, but the Qarmatian uprising actually erupted among the Bedouin of northeastern Arabia. Here, in an area called Bahrayn, which included coastal regions of on each side of the Qatar peninsula, a formidable principality emerged. It soon dominated most of Arabia, including Oman, while raiding deep inside Iraq, Syria, and even Egypt.

Experiments with an almost communist form of society came to nothing, but the Qarmatians remained radical in religious matters. They even attacked the Holy Cities

Right: The pre-Islamic and Islamic fortress of Qala'at al-Kisra at Rustaq, Oman.

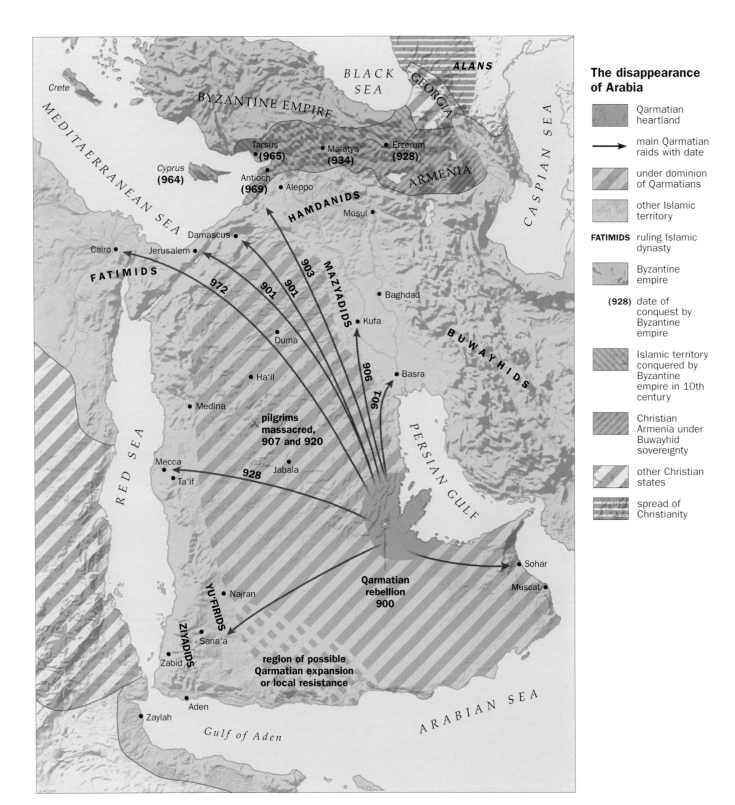

The disappearance of Arabia

	Qarmatian heartland
→	main Qarmatian raids with date
	under dominion of Qarmatians
	other Islamic territory
FATIMIDS	ruling Islamic dynasty
	Byzantine empire
(928)	date of conquest by Byzantine empire
	Islamic territory conquered by Byzantine empire in 10th century
	Christian Armenia under Buwayhid sovereignty
	other Christian states
	spread of Christianity

and carried off the sacred Black Stone from the Ka'aba in 930, which they continued to regard as a symbol of superstition. It took 20 years of pleading by their occasional ally, the Fatimid caliph in Cairo, before they replaced the Black Stone.

Gradually, however, these Qarmatians became more moderate, while their state continued as a republic. The Persian traveler Nasir-i Khusraw, who visited Qarmatian eastern Arabia in the 11th century, reported that towns like Yamamah and Lahssa still had strong fortresses and large, warlike populations. Only a few decades later the Qarmatian state was overthrown by a joint Abbasid and Seljuk Turkish campaign in alliance with a local Arab chief.

Yet the fall of the Qarmatians did not end the relative isolation and increasing backwardness of much of Arabia. The region did not play a major role in the political affairs of the Islamic world until the discovery of oil in the 20th century once again placed Arabia in the forefront of world affairs.

CHAPTER SIX

The Caliphate of Cordoba

Islamic conquest of Iberia

Recently, some historians have questioned whether the Muslims really conquered the Iberian peninsula. Instead, some explain the sudden appearance of Islamic rule in what are today Spain and Portugal as a political takeover, or a coup resulting from infiltration of the fatally weakened Visigothic kingdom by newly Islamicized North Africans. Clearly, the "conquest" of the Iberian peninsula was a complicated and little documented sequence of events.

This is unfortunate, since the Arab invasion was of major significance for the future of western Europe. It led to the creation of a powerful, wealthy, and sophisticated Islamic civilization on the continent. This culture endured for eight centuries, and its legacy remains strong, not only in Portugal and Spain themselves but also in the lands these two countries colonized from the 15th century onward, most notably in the Americas.

The true situation in Visigothic Iberia at the start of the eighth century is far from clear (*see map*), but there was much unrest that also affected Morocco. Into these volatile territories came a small number of Arab-Islamic frontiersmen who were pushing westward across North Africa; sometimes with the express authority of the caliph, but sometimes as freelance raiders.

The most extraordinary such campaign was led by Uqbar Ibn Nafi in 680–3. He actually reached the Atlantic in southern Morocco but was killed by a Berber tribal army at Tehuda on his way home. A generation later, after much hard fighting to consolidate Arab-Islamic authority in what is now Tunisia, Musa Ibn Nusayr, the Umayyad governor of North Africa, extended Islamic authority across northern Algeria and northern Morocco.

It is now that legend and history become almost inextricably mixed. In 711 a small but largely Berber force crossed the straits from Sabta in Morocco under the leadership of Tariq Ibn Ziyad. They are said to have been given ships by Count Julian of Sabta, whose daughter had supposedly been abducted by the Visigothic King Roderick. If it is true that Tariq needed Julian's ships, this would suggest that Tariq's followers were raiders rather than serious invaders. They may even have been acting unofficially, since the Islamic caliphate now had its own highly effective Mediterranean fleet. Whatever the precise background, Tariq's name lives on in the modern name Gibraltar—derived from Jebel Tariq (Tariq's rock or mountain).

ASTOUNDING SUCCESS

Whether this was a reconnaissance in force or merely a search for plunder is unknown, but it clearly defeated a substantial Visigothic army. Roderick was killed in the battle and the Visigothic kingdom plunged into confusion. Perhaps taking advantage of the unexpected success of Tariq's raid, Musa Ibn Nusayr undertook a proper invasion. Most of the troops involved were still Berber tribesmen, including those recently and only superficially converted to Islam, plus large numbers of pagans, Jews, and Christians. Arabs formed the majority of the leadership plus, presumably, a small elite of professional soldiers.

By 716 virtually the entire peninsula was under Islamic control except for a strip of mountainous coastal territory in the far north. This remained autonomous rather than strictly independent under local Visigothic leaders, while in the southeast of the country a Visigothic prince named Theodomir was allowed to remain as a vassal of the Umayyad caliph in a region subsequently known as Tudmir.

Between 716 and 721 al-Hurr al-Thaqafi and al-Samh al-Khawlani, two of the Umayyad governors of what the Muslims called al-Andalus, extended Islamic authority over the previously Visigothic enclave around Narbonne in southern France. Their men also raided further north, penetrating far up the Rhône valley and also through Bordeaux toward the Loire. As a result the large, wealthy, and effectively independent Duchy of Aquitaine in southwestern France briefly accepted Islamic suzerainty. This would change after the French victory over a substantial Islamic army near Poitiers in 732, but for a while many in western Europe feared that the Muslim Arabs were going to overrun western Christendom, just as they seemed set to overrun Byzantine Christendom.

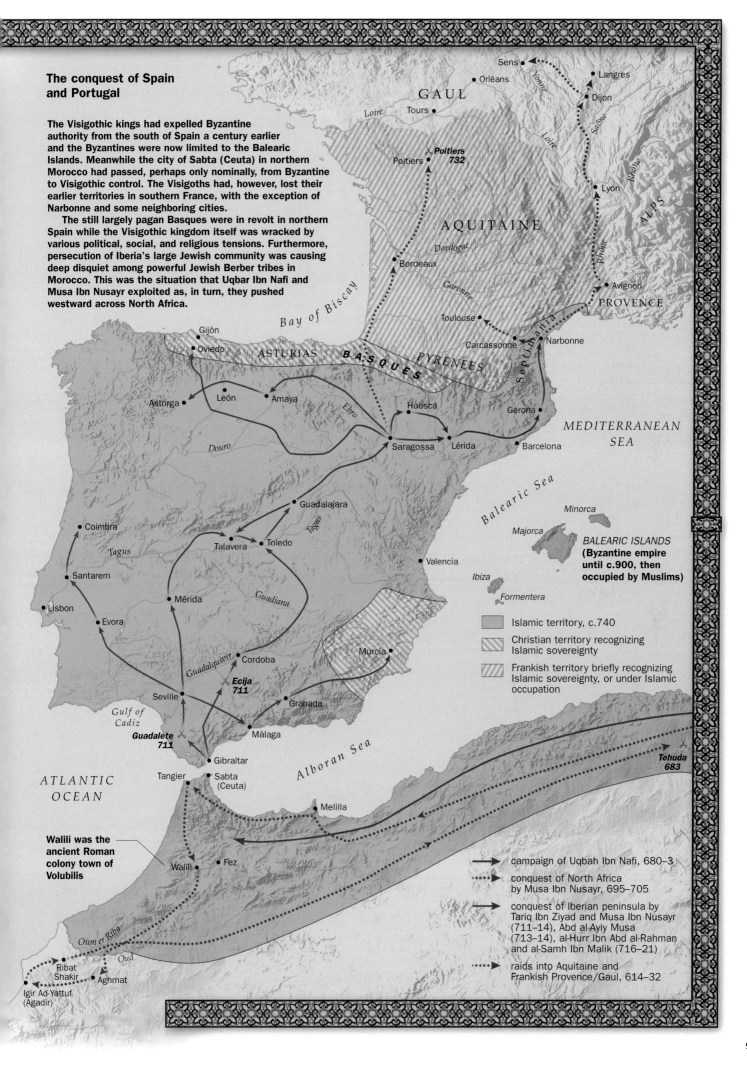

The conquest of Spain and Portugal

The Visigothic kings had expelled Byzantine authority from the south of Spain a century earlier and the Byzantines were now limited to the Balearic Islands. Meanwhile the city of Sabta (Ceuta) in northern Morocco had passed, perhaps only nominally, from Byzantine to Visigothic control. The Visigoths had, however, lost their earlier territories in southern France, with the exception of Narbonne and some neighboring cities.

The still largely pagan Basques were in revolt in northern Spain while the Visigothic kingdom itself was wracked by various political, social, and religious tensions. Furthermore, persecution of Iberia's large Jewish community was causing deep disquiet among powerful Jewish Berber tribes in Morocco. This was the situation that Uqbar Ibn Nafi and Musa Ibn Nusayr exploited as, in turn, they pushed westward across North Africa.

GAUL

Sens
Orléans
Langres
Dijon

Loire
Tours

✗ **Poitiers 732**
Poitiers

AQUITAINE

Dordogne

Bordeaux

Garonne

Lyon

Avignon

PROVENCE

Toulouse

Carcassonne — Narbonne

Bay of Biscay

Gijón
Oviedo
ASTURIAS
BASQUES
PYRENEES
Septimania

Astorga
León
Amaya
Ebro
Huesca
Gerona

Douro
Saragossa
Lérida
Barcelona

MEDITERRANEAN SEA

Balearic Sea

Minorca

Majorca

BALEARIC ISLANDS
**(Byzantine empire
until c.900, then
occupied by Muslims)**

Ibiza

Formentera

Guadalajara

Tagus

Coimbra

Talavera
Toledo

Valencia

Tagus

Santarem

Mérida

Guadiana

Lisbon

Evora

Islamic territory, c.740

Christian territory recognizing
Islamic sovereignty

Frankish territory briefly recognizing
Islamic sovereignty, or under Islamic
occupation

Murcia

Guadalquivir
Cordoba

Seville
Ecija 711

Granada

Gulf of
Cadiz

Guadalete 711

Málaga

Gibraltar

Alboran Sea

✗ **Tehuda 683**

Tangier
Sabta
(Ceuta)

ATLANTIC
OCEAN

Melilla

**Walili was the
ancient Roman
colony town of
Volubilis**

Walili
Fez

campaign of Uqbah Ibn Nafi, 680–3

conquest of North Africa
by Musa Ibn Nusayr, 695–705

conquest of Iberian peninsula by
Tariq Ibn Ziyad and Musa Ibn Nusayr
(711–14), Abd al-Ayiy Musa
(713–14), al-Hurr Ibn Abd al-Rahman
and al-Samh Ibn Malik (716–21)

raids into Aquitaine and
Frankish Provence/Gaul, 614–32

Oum er Riba

Ribat
Shakir
Aghmat

Oud

Igir Ad-Yattuf
(Agadir)

Cordoba: City of Light

The most obvious change that the Islamic rulers brought to the Iberian peninsula was to shift the regional capital from Visigothic Toledo to Cordoba in the south. The city flourished, becoming the largest in western Europe.

Right: Mihrab of the Great Mosque of Cordoba, dating from the 10th century.

Below: A view of Cordoba looking north over the Guadalquivir toward the Mezquita (Great Mosque), with its much later Christian cathedral thrusting through the center of the mosque's lower roofline. The Mezquita itself was built on the remains of an earlier Visigothic church. In the foreground stands the Roman bridge, its carriageway having been reconstructed by the Muslim conquerors.

Christian fears that the Muslims would conquer western Europe proved unfounded, since the Arabs had reached almost as far as their manpower and resources would stretch. This was particularly true in the west. Furthermore, the caliphate's strategic and cultural priorities were already turning eastward, and in Iberia their main aim was to consolidate and exploit territorial gains. The cities of the region became major centers of culture and trade.

The suggestion that the Arabs and Berbers, on reaching cold, misty, and damp northern lands, had no wish to occupy them is, however, a myth. In the east Muslim-Arab armies continued to press forward into the far harsher regions of Afghanistan and central Asia. What actually happened in the Iberian peninsula mirrors what had previously happened in Iran. In both regions the Muslim-Arabs took over existing states; the Visigothic kingdom in Iberia and the Sassanian empire in Iran. In both cases they ruled as successors to the previous kings or shahs, leaving most of the existing administrative framework, communications network, and frontiers intact.

In the east the Arabs pressed on further, but the new conquests were generally regarded as new entities. In the west the Muslims soon abandoned their brief suzerainty over Aquitaine, but fought hard to retain the ex-Visigothic province of Septimania, the region around Narbonne in southern France.

In many ways, Muslims' movement of the capital from the sparsely populated center to the richer, more fertile, and much more densely populated south was a return to the pre-Visigothic situation. Much of southern Iberia had also been ruled and colonized by the Semitic Phoenicians or Cathaginians in pre-Roman times, and had retained close links with both North Africa and the Middle East. It was this area that the Byzantine

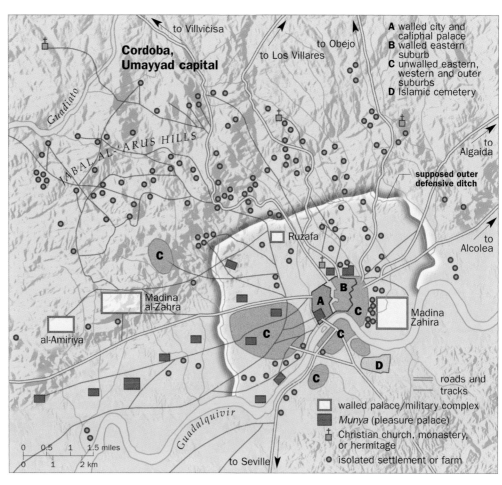

empire had been most keen
to recover. Above all, it was
the region in which urban
life had survived to a greater
extent following the fall of
the western Roman empire
in the fifth century. Southern
Iberia remained culturally
and economically part of the
Mediterranean world that the early Islamic
caliphate had inherited.

RAPID DEVELOPMENT

Of course all the Iberian provinces which
remained under Islamic rule for more than a
few decades would benefit from the
astonishing economic and cultural progress
that characterized medieval Islamic
civilization. Even the Christian enclaves in
the north, which soon regained their
independence from Islamic overlordship,
would benefit to some degree.

Yet it was the urbanized south and east
that really flourished. In fact the fertile
valley of the Guadalquivir, the
Mediterranean coastal strip, and the
similarly fertile valley of the Ebro in
northeastern Iberia became the three
cultural, economic, and population
heartlands of Islamic al-Andalus.

Cordoba now grew steadily, and it was
already the biggest city west of
Constantinople by the end of the eighth
century. Cordoba was eventually home to
around half a million people, including
Muslims, Christians, and Jews. Beyond the
original roughly rectangular walled city
known as al-Madina lay extensive suburbs,

and areas of orchards or market gardens to
supply the inhabitants with fresh food. At
one time, according to Arab geographers,
Cordoba had over 470 mosques, the most
important of which was, of course, the
superb Great Mosque overlooking the river
Guadalquivir.

In addition there were over 200,000
houses for artisans and merchants, 60,000 for
officials and other government employees,
and over 80,000 assorted shops. Cordoba
was still dwarfed by some of the great
Islamic cities of the Middle East, although in
comparison Aix-la-Chapelle (Aachen), the
contemporary capital of the Carolingian
empire in what is now western Germany,
was little more than a country town.

The countryside beyond Cordoba, its
suburbs, and market gardens was dotted
with villages, farms, and the *munya* country
residences of the Islamic aristocracy of al-
Andalus. There were also several large
palace enclosures which served as military
and administrative bases for the ruling *amir*
or, as he later declared himself, caliph.

Meanwhile, much of the rural population
remained Christian, as it did elsewhere in al-
Andalus, and there were several important
monasteries in the hills around Cordoba.

*Above left: The
Andalusian ivory pyx
made for al-Mughira
in 968.*

Mystical Islands and Whales

Medieval Islamic navigation in the Atlantic extended over greater distances than is generally realized. The Vikings were not the only contemporary people who routinely sailed out of sight of land—the Andalusians also traversed the waters of the Sea of Darkness.

Right: Illustration showing the ship Argo *in an early 13th-century manuscript of the* Kitab al-Sufar *from Ceuta, now in the Vatican Library.*

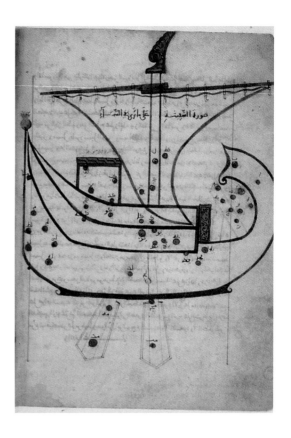

Islamic seamen sailed in the waters around the Iberian peninsula, the northwestern coast of Africa, and the Canary Islands; perhaps even the Azores and Madeira. Some of these islands were well known, while others were little more than sailors' legends. The seas within this zone have been called the Mediterranean Atlantic, because seafaring here was so closely linked technologically, economically, and historically with the Mediterranean.

Roman vessels had plied coastal waters from the Straits of Gibraltar and Iberian peninsula to the English Channel and British Isles. After the collapse of the western half of the Roman empire a maritime link appears to have survived between the Visigothic

Above: Illustration of a Great Flood, showing drowning figures and sunken galleys, in a copy of the Beatus Commentaries, AD *922–52.*

kingdom in Iberia and the Celtic fringes of Britanny, the British Isles, and Ireland.

Perhaps this survived after the Arab-Islamic conquest of Spain and Portugal, since it is clear that Britain remained the main source of tin for al-Andalus well into the ninth century. It is worth noting that the famous terror stories about the Atlantic, or Sea of Darkness as it was known in much of

the Islamic world, stem from the Middle East rather than Morocco or al-Andalus.

The best known seafarers of the early medieval Atlantic were the Celtic Irish and the Scandinavian Vikings. However, only two peoples habitually sailed the eastern Atlantic during the early medieval centuries; the Vikings and the Islamic Andalusians. The latter may not have ventured as far as the Scandinavians, but they remained the Vikings' only real rivals. Furthermore, Viking raids prompted the Umayyad rulers of Cordoba to send at least one official embassy to the far north to discover the source of this sudden outburst of naval aggression.

The Viking threat soon became serious enough for an Umayyad naval squadron to be created in the mid-ninth century, specifically to patrol the Atlantic coast. The first Umayyad Andalusian naval bases had been on the Mediterranean coast but in the mid-tenth century additional facilities, including shipbuilding arsenals, were constructed on the Atlantic side of the Iberian peninsula. The resulting Islamic Atlantic fleets then proved themselves fully capable of defeating major Viking raids.

OVER THE HORIZON

Most voyages by Muslim sailors in the Atlantic were undertaken for commercial, diplomatic, or military reasons, though some were the result of that intellectual curiosity which characterized the golden age of medieval Islamic civilization. A commander of a naval patrol that fought Vikings in 889 was named Khashkhash ibn Sa'id of Pechina. One of the so-called "Adventurers of Lisbon" was also named Khashkhash and was probably the same man.

This Khashkhash made several expeditions far into the Atlantic before disappearing, along with his companions. Their first voyage north proved dangerous and won little reward, though it seems to have reached Viking settlements in Ireland. The adventurers' subsequent voyages headed south and found greater reward in Bilad al-Sudan, "the land of black people" beyond the Canary Islands. It is possible that they even reached the Cape Verde Islands.

The large fishing fleets of Lisbon and the Algarve in what are now Portugal also ranged far out into the Atlantic and ventured down the western coast of Africa in search of good catches. Meanwhile, the Atlantic coast of Morocco saw considerable economic expansion in the 12th century and the Muwahhidun ruler Ali Ibn

Yusuf even planned a naval expedition, later aborted, to conquer the Canary Islands. In the early 13th century a mariner named Ibn Fatima and his crew were wrecked off Ras Nu'adhibun, much further south in what is now Mauritania.

Taken together, such fragments of information give a distinct impression that voyages were normal and almost commonplace. Yet perhaps the most surprising account tells of an attempt by the Muslim ruler of early 14th century Mali, south of the Sahara, to seize the "western islands," presumably the Cape Verde Islands. The very fact that such an expedition could be considered not only indicates knowledge of the objective but also the availability of ships and crews to undertake such an expedition.

Islamic territory in the 9th century

Islamic Mali in the early 14th century

coasts patrolled by Umayyad naval squadrons against Viking raids, mid-9th–10th centuries

center of Islamic naval and geographical knowledge (including spherical world), later influencing Portuguese navigators of the 15th century

⚓ shipbuilding naval arsenals

✇ fishing gounds used by Andalusian fishermen (possibly including whaling)

⊗ Viking defeat by Ummayad fleet

✗ Castilian defeat by Moroccan fleet, 1340

········▸ maritime link between Ireland, western Britain, Brittany, and pre-Islamic Visigothic Iberia

──▸ export of Cornish tin, 8th–9th centuries

──▸ Viking raids, 843–972

──▸ Andalusian naval assault on Santiago, 997

········▸ Islamic embassy to the "King of the Majus" (probably Turgeis, Viking leader of Dublin, 845)

──▸ voyages by Khashkhash and the "Adventurers of Lisbon," mid-9th century

········▸ Abortive attempt to seize Canary Islands by Ibn 'Ali Yusuf (Murabit ruler of Morocco, 1107–42), and Cape Verde Islands by early 14th-century ruler of Mali

········▸ coastal traffic between Al-Andalus–Maghrib and Ras Nu'adiban, and perhaps as far as Senegal or Gambia, by 13th century

SCANDINAVIA

IRELAND

ENGLAND

Brittany

FRANCE

"SEA OF MISTS" (ATLANTIC OCEAN)

Azores

Lisbon

AL-ANDALUS

Cordoba

MEDITERRANEAN

Sala

Fez

MAGHRIB

Madeira

Marrakesh

Sijilmassa

Taurirt

"Eternal Islands" (Canaries)

Ras Nu'adhibin

SAHARA DESERT

desert trading routes

Timbuktu

Cape Verde Islands

slaves

Kumbi Saleh

Gambia

MALI

gold

slaves

slaves

gold

gold

The Tiny Kingdoms

Al-Mansur ruled al-Andalus with an iron hand, but soon after his death Islamic Spain splintered into myriad tiny states. Although these prospered, their lack of unity made them the targets of Christians states in the north.

Right: Bab Mardum Mosque (now the church of San Christo de la Luz) in Toledo was built between 980 and 1000.

During the late tenth century a grand *wazir* (vizier) named al-Mansur became the virtual dictator of al-Andalus, while the Umayyad caliph of Cordoba was a mere puppet within his own palace. Al-Mansur's armies were the terror of the Iberian peninsula, and the small Christian kingdoms of what is now northern Spain seemed incapable of resistance. Yet within a year of the death of al-Mansur's successor, everything seemed to fall apart. Islamic al-Andalus suddenly fragmented into an astonishing array of tiny states, some of them no more than one city and its immediate surroundings. These were the Ta'ifa or "party kingdoms."

In the center and south-center, senior officers of Berber origin seized power. Along the Mediterranean and at Lérida in the foothills of the Pyrennees dynasties emerged which claimed descent from European Slavs—former slaves (from which the word derives). Other dynasties with varied ethnic or cultural origins sprang up elsewhere.

Above: An Andalusian brass celestial globe of c.1085 attributed to Ibrahim Ibn Sa'id al-Sahli.

The largest Ta'ifa states emerged along the border with the Christian kingdoms, the three biggest based on existing *thughur* militarized frontier provinces. With few exceptions, the smallest were found in the urbanized and more densely populated south. This fragmentation seems like an act of political suicide by the Muslim Andalusians, yet this was not how it was seen at the time. The Andalusians were confident in their own civilization and generally regarded the northern Christians as little better than barbarians. Nor did most of the early 11th-century Ta'ifa rulers feel particularly threatened—some of the smallest states had virtually no army.

THRIVING BUT UNDEFENDED

Within a few decades the threat would become painfully apparent, but in the meantime Andalusian-Islamic civilization flourished as rival rulers tried to attract poets and scholars to their courts. Poetry, geography, mathematics, medicine, and horticulture all thrived. Several of the leading scholars were Jewish, proving that the inclusiveness that had characterized earlier Islamic-Andalusian civilization remained strong. Some of the more ambitious rulers like those of Seville attempted to take over other Tai'fa states, perhaps hoping to recreate the unity of al-Andalus.

Unfortunately, the prosperity that supported this flowering of culture also attracted the predatory interests of poorer Christian states to the north. Although the culture, art, architecture, and military organization of these northern kingdoms had been deeply influenced by those of Islamic al-Andalus, they had frequently fought the Muslim southerners and now realized that the once-feared Andalusians were much weaker than before.

The Islamic collapse began when the strongest of the Christian kings, Alfonso VI of León and Castilla (1065–1109), forced his Islamic neighbors to pay tribute. Then in 1085 the largest of the Andalusian states, Toledo, fell to King Alfonso VI. This sent ripples of alarm throughout Andalusia, and al-Mutamid, the ruler of Seville, turned to the rising power of the Murabitun in North Africa for help.

However, the Murabitun's origins lay on the other side of the Sahara desert, and their armies included large numbers of African tribesmen who had only been superficially converted to Islam. As a result many among the sophisticated elite of al-Andalus saw these African newcomers as a greater threat than the northern Christians, especially as the aristocracy of the Christian Iberian states had so much in common with their Muslim neighbors. Many of the Christians could speak Arabic, while a majority of Andalusians probably spoke a Latin-based language, an early form of Spanish or Portuguese, when at home. Arabic, it seems, was the language of culture, commerce,

diplomacy, and religion, but not necessarily the mother tongue of Muslim Andalusians.

The confusion that followed the first Murabitun expedition in support of their fellow Muslims in 1086 seems to have convinced the Murabit ruler, Yusuf Ibn Tashfin, that Andalusian Islam would only be saved by being conquered by the Murabitun themselves.

In 1090 he began to take over the small Ta'ifa states and by the end of 1102 all that remained of the mosaic of independent Andalusian kingdoms were the Balearic Islands and Sarragossa in the far north.

Above: Ruins of the castle of Gormaz, Andalusian 10th century.

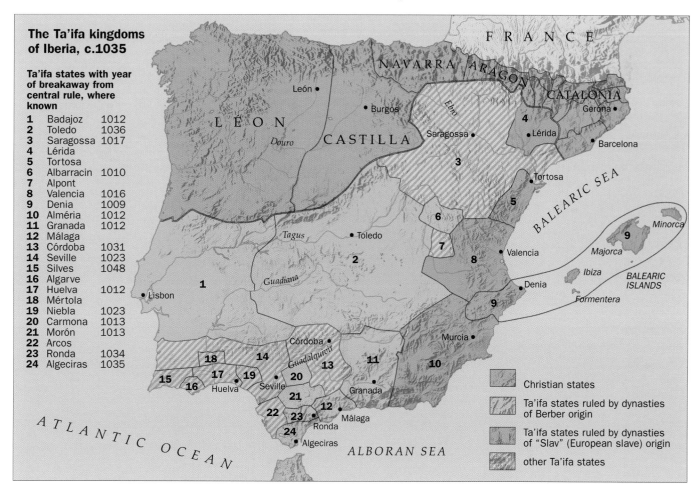

The Ta'ifa kingdoms of Iberia, c.1035

Ta'ifa states with year of breakaway from central rule, where known

1	Badajoz	1012
2	Toledo	1036
3	Saragossa	1017
4	Lérida	
5	Tortosa	
6	Albarracin	1010
7	Alpont	
8	Valencia	1016
9	Denia	1009
10	Alméria	1012
11	Granada	1012
12	Málaga	
13	Córdoba	1031
14	Seville	1023
15	Silves	1048
16	Algarve	
17	Huelva	1012
18	Mértola	
19	Niebla	1023
20	Carmona	1013
21	Morón	1013
22	Arcos	
23	Ronda	1034
24	Algeciras	1035

Christian states

Ta'ifa states ruled by dynasties of Berber origin

Ta'ifa states ruled by dynasties of "Slav" (European slave) origin

other Ta'ifa states

Saragossa: City on the Frontier

Under Islamic rule, Saragossa became a cosmopolitan city, home to Muslims and also large numbers of Christians and Jews. As a frontier town it witnessed almost ceaseless conflict, and in the early 12th century it finally fell into purely Christian hands.

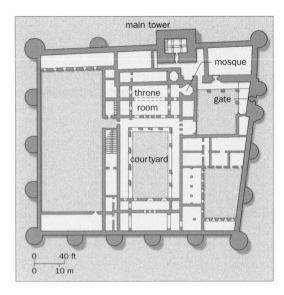

Right: Ground-plan of al-Ja'fariya palace, built in the mid-11th century for Ahmad I al-Muqtadir, the Ta'ifa ruler of Saragossa. Off the throne room is the position of the tiny mosque, or musalah.

Saragossa was known to the Arab-Andalusians as Sarakusta and as al-Madina al-Bayda, "the white city." Under the Umayyad rulers of Cordoba, Saragossa had been the main city of the Upper March or northeastern frontier province of al-Andalus. During the 11th century it became the capital of a relatively large and powerful Ta'ifa kingdom under the Banu Hud.

These Hudids were not, however, the first independent rulers of Saragossa since, as early as 1017, the local governor al-Mudhir

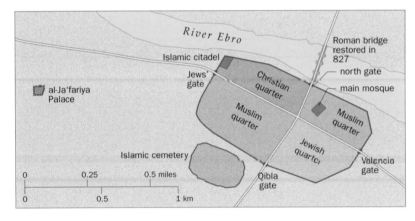

al-Tujibi had followed other local Andalusian leaders and declared his independence. His family held Saragossa until 1040, when Suleiman Ibn Hud al-Judhami took over. The resulting Hudid dynasty stemmed from a long established Arab family who regarded themselves as part of the true aristocracy of al-Andalus.

Known as al-Musta'in I, Suleiman Ibn Hud was the first of a dynasty which at various times ruled Saragossa, Huesca, Tudela, Lérida, Denia, Tortosa, and Calatayud. It clung to some territory in central Spain even after losing Saragossa. Far to the south a later member of the Banu Hud briefly ruled Murcia in the mid-13th century, between the Muwahhidun collapse and the Christian conquest.

Facing: The north-facing main tower of al-Ja'fariya Palace

Saragossa flourished under the Hudids, despite being almost surrounded by enemies. The medieval city remained inside the restored Roman walls on the southern bank of the Ebro. Its two main streets linked the four gates and divided the city into quarters; one largely inhabited by Christians, one by Jews, and two by Muslims.

In the northeast quarter stood the main mosque built in the eighth century, probably on the site of an earlier church. It had been considerably enlarged since then and would eventually be replaced by a cathedral after Saragossa fell to the King of Aragon.

During the ninth century the Muslims had restored the battered Roman bridge over the Ebro following a terrible flood that also swept away much of Saragossa's fortified wall. This Puente de Piedra still exists, but the most remarkable surviving structure from the Islamic period is the Ja'fariya Palace, near the western or Jewish gate. It was built between 1046 and 1081 for the rulers of this prosperous Ta'ifa kingdom.

FINE ARCHITECTURE

Within an irregular rectangle of stone and brick walls and towers is the brick palace of Ahmad I al-Muqtadir (1049–82). It is decorated with stucco, some of which includes exceptionally complex floral and geometric patterns. Next to the throne room of the palace is a small and unusual eight-sided mosque whose interior is entirely covered with decorative stucco work.

Ahmad I al-Muqtadir of Saragossa was an open-minded and practical ruler. He paid tribute to King Ferdinand I of Castilla, the self-proclaimed emperor of Spain, because Castilla was stronger than Saragossa. Three years later, when King Ramiro I of Aragon invaded his territory, Ahmad I marched against him with an army that included a contingent of Castillian knights. Ahmad's combined Islamic and Christian force was successful and King Ramiro was killed in the subsequent battle.

When the famous Spanish Christian hero El Cid was banished from Castilla by King Ferdinand's son, Alfonso VI, he and 300 knights found refuge with Ahmad I al-Muqtadir in Saragossa. Ahmad gave El Cid an important command when Saragossa made war on the neighboring and fellow Islamic Ta'ifa state of Lérida. In turn the Christian King of Aragon supported the Muslim ruler of Lérida, resulting in two mixed Islamic and Christian armies fighting each other.

By skillful diplomacy and occasional warfare, the Hudid rulers kept their Christian neighbors at bay and preserved their independence from the Murabitun,

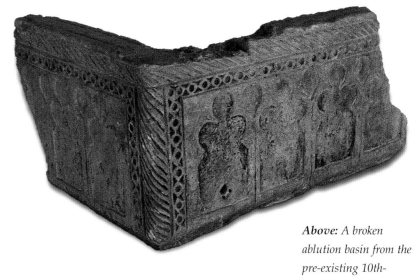

who had taken over the rest of mainland al-Andalus. In 1110, however, the Murabitun finally seized Saragossa, only to lose it to Alfonso the Battler of Aragon eight years later.

Above: A broken ablution basin from the pre-existing 10th-century mosque stands in the cloisters of Tuleda Cathedral.

Union with Morocco

From the late 11th to mid-12th centuries, al-Andalus formed part of the huge realm of the Murabitun. In 1121 this remarkable African empire was challenged by an Islamic teacher in the mountains south of Marrakesh in Morocco.

Right: Gilded and enameled buckle-plate from a sword-baldric from Gibraltar, Andalusian 12th century.

The Muwahhidun empire

maximum extent of the Muwahhidun state, late 12th century

Banu Ghaniya (ex-Murabitun)

other Islamic territory

Christian states of northern Iberia

other Christian states

Mohammed Ibn Tumart was a Berber who had studied in the Middle East before returning home to preach against the moral laxity and theological conservatism of the later Murabitun. Ibn Tumart's followers became known as the Muwahhid, or "those who proclaim God's unity." The Unity of God was, of course, always a fundamental Islamic doctrine but the Muwahhid focused on this primary belief and were also reformers.

Ibn Tumart's followers then proclaimed him to be the Mahdi or promised charismatic leader who would lead Islam to triumph. Many orthodox Muslims now declared the Muwahhid to be heretics, especially as Ibn Tumart encouraged the translation of religious and legal texts from Arabic into Berber.

The Muwahhidun movement has sometimes been seen as a reaction by the Berber tribes of the mountains against the dominant and by now largely Arab cultural elites of the lowland cities. Certainly the Berber warriors who formed the first Muwahhidun armies were fierce and dedicated. They gradually took Morocco from the weakened Murabitun until, in 1147, Ibn Tumart's lieutenant and successor, Abd al-Mu'min, captured the Murabitun capital of Marrakesh.

The collapse of Murabitun power in North Africa caused something of a power vacuum in al-Andalus. There was a second though briefer Ta'ifa period when several local leaders seized control. Some of these formed alliances with the advancing Christian kingdoms of the north and a few even tried to hand their kingdoms over to the Christians rather than see them fall into African hands again. This almost inevitably led to them being driven from power by their own people, yet such political gambles show how close the Andalusian Islamic aristocracy felt to the Christian feudal nobility during the 12th century.

BETWEEN TWO WORLDS

In 1145 Abd al-Mu'min sent a powerful army to the Iberian peninsula and, after hard

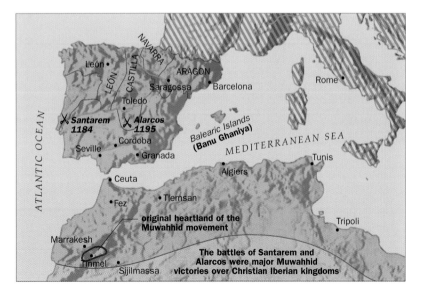

The battles of Santarem and Alarcos were major Muwahhid victories over Christian Iberian kingdoms

998	c.1000	1005	1006	1012	1018	1037	1038
Ghaznavid territory expands into Afghanistan and Persia	Al-Mansur is virtual dictator of al-Andalus, the caliph of Cordoba a puppet ruler	Samanids are succeeded by the Qarakhanids (Ilig-Khans) in central Asia	Sunni Mahmud of Ghazna invades Multan and incorporates it into his state by 1010	Appearance of first Ta'ifa or party kingdom ruler during break up of al-Andalus	Mahmud of Ghazna breaks power of Hindu states in northern India	The Christian kingdoms of León and Navarre ally against Muslims in the south of Spain	Seljuk Toghril Beg takes Nishapur; proclaims himself champion of Sunnis

campaigning and the foundation of a strategic naval base that became the city of Gibraltar, the Muwahhid took over what remained of Islamic al-Andalus.

All that was left outside their control and that of the Christian kingdoms were the Balearic Islands. These were held by the Banu Ghaniya who were descended from the last Murabitun governor, and retained their independence until 1203. One member of this family took his followers to Tunisia where they continued to fight the Muwahhid until finally defeated in 1236.

The unorthodox Muwahhid ruled al-Andalus and North Africa for over a century and were responsible for some of the finest Islamic monuments in these regions. The few illustrated manuscripts that survive from the medieval Islamic west largely date from the Muwahhidun period and there was also a late flowering of Arabic poetry.

The Muwahhidun court in Seville became a center of learning and philosophy, patronizing such scholars as Ibn Tufayl (known in Europe as Abubacer), and Ibn Rushd (known in Europe as Averroes). The later Muwahhidun rulers even assumed the title of caliph, although this was only recognized within their own territory.

Meanwhile the supposedly protected Peoples of the Book—Jews and Christians—suffered persecution of a type never before seen in al-Andalus. This led to a migration of Christians to the north, where their suffering reinforced the growing ideology of Reconquista, and of xenophobia and anti-semitism in Christian Europe. Among those who left was the Jewish physician and philosopher Maimonides, who settled in Cairo.

The series of sophisticated castles that the Muwahhid built to halt the Christian onslaught failed. Despite victories like that at Alarcos in 1195, the main Muwahhidun army was crushed by a combined Christian army at Las Navas de Tolosa in 1212. This was followed by a rapid decline in Muwahhidun authority in the Iberian

Left: The Muwahhid Torre de Oro (Tower of Gold), a fortified riverside structure of about 1220, stands in Seville.

peninsula and North Africa.

In 1277 the town of Tinmel, cradle of the Muwahhidun movement in Morocco's Atlas Mountains, was finally conquered by the Banu Marin, who moved the capital of Morocco to Fez.

Below: An illustration in the Bayad wa Riyadh, an Andalusian manuscript of the 13th century, shows a lover sleeping beside a water-wheel.

Collapse of al-Andalus

The collapse of al-Andalus during the 13th century offers a striking example of how history is written by the winning side, the most dramatic in the sequence of events known as the Reconquista. This process supposedly began with a skirmish in 718, recalled as the Battle of Covadonga.

Below: Mihrab and interior of the Ziyyanid Mosque, 1296, Tlemsan, Algeria.

By the 13th century the Christian states of northern Iberia had adopted the myth of the Reconquista, an ideology that had much in common with that of the Crusades. This maintained that the aggressive Christian rulers of Portugal, Léon-Castilla, Navarra, and Aragon were merely regaining southern territories that had been illegally held by Islamic rulers since the Moorish conquest of the early eighth century.

At this stage, however, the ideology of the Reconquista was focused on the supposed illegality of Islamic rule, not the actual presence of Islam within the Iberian peninsula. Indeed, several Christian kings had proclaimed themselves protectors of both Christianity and Islam, implying that there was no problem with Muslims living in what is now Spain and Portugal, as long as they accepted rule by a Christian monarch. King Alfonso VII of Castilla (1126–57) had not only proclaimed himself emperor over all the states of the Iberian peninsula, both Christian and Islamic, but also "King of the Two Religions."

Alfonso VII was premature in his ambitions, but as Muwahhidun control fragmented in al-Andalus in the wake of the battle of Las Navas de Tolosa in 1212 there was a third very brief Ta'ifa period. It began when Muwahhidun authority collapsed 12 years after Las Navas.

Local leaders and commanders now took over in Valencia in the east, Niebla in the west, Murcia in the southeast and, with greater success, Granada in the south. Only in Murcia and Granada did ruling dynasties emerge, that of Murcia being founded by another member of the Banu Hud named Mohammed Ibn Yusuf. Nevertheless it only lasted from 1228 to 1266.

In almost all cases such local Islamic Andalusian rulers had to accept Christian overlordship until they finally fell under direct rule. The Nasrids or Banu'l-Ahmar clung on in Granada for a further two and a half centuries, however. This dynasty was founded by a relatively minor Islamic leader named Mohammed al-Ghalib who claimed to be descended from one of the original Companions of the Prophet Mohammed.

BITTER STRUGGLE
Elsewhere the great cities of al-Andalus fell to the Christians of the north one by one; Cordoba in 1236 and Seville 12 years later. Yet these conquests were by no means a walkover for the armies of Portugal, Castilla, and Aragon. They involved several separate

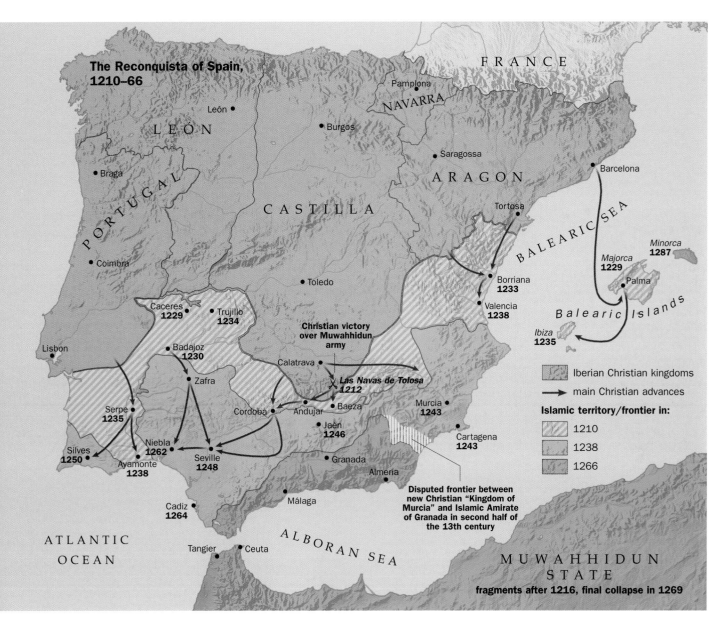

The Reconquista of Spain, 1210–66

FRANCE

NAVARRA

Pamplona

León

Burgos

LEÓN

Braga

Saragossa

ARAGON

Barcelona

PORTUGAL

CASTILLA

Tortosa

Coimbra

Toledo

BALEARIC SEA

Minorca **1287**

Majorca **1229**

Palma

Borriana **1233**

Valencia **1238**

Balearic Islands

Caceres **1229**

Trujillo **1234**

Christian victory over Muwahhidun army

Ibiza **1235**

Lisbon

Badajoz **1230**

Zafra

Calatrava

Las Navas de Tolosa **1212**

Cordoba

Andujar

Baeza

Murcia **1243**

Serpe **1235**

Jaén **1246**

Cartagena **1243**

Niebla **1262**

Seville **1248**

Granada

Silves **1250**

Ayamonte **1238**

Almeria

Disputed frontier between new Christian "Kingdom of Murcia" and Islamic Amirate of Granada in second half of the 13th century

Cadiz **1264**

Málaga

ATLANTIC OCEAN

Tangier

Ceuta

ALBORAN SEA

MUWAHHIDUN STATE
fragments after 1216, final collapse in 1269

- Iberian Christian kingdoms
- → main Christian advances
- Islamic territory/frontier in:
  - 1210
  - 1238
  - 1266

---

invasions, as well as the ravaging of huge tracts of the richest and most fertile regions of the Iberian peninsula. There were also some long and bitterly contested sieges. Cadiz remained Islamic until 1264 and the isolated island of Minorca held out until 1287.

In many regions the Islamic population was expelled, especially from the cities, and Christians settlers were encouraged to take their place. In many areas cattle ranching took over from intensive agriculture, and southern Spain would never again achieve the level of irrigated fertility that had been seen under Islamic rule.

For many years the conquered cities remained little more than shells, with small populations who were in turn more concerned with defense than trade or manufacture. Elsewhere huge tracts of land were handed over to the crusading Military Orders, whose sole reason for existence was warfare against their Muslim neighbors.

Left: The so-called Minaret of San Juan, built in 930, Cordoba.

105

CHAPTER SEVEN

Threats from West and East

The Seljuks, Crusaders, and Mongols

By the early 11th century the Islamic world had reached a pinnacle of cultural and artistic achievement. Paradoxically it was also in a state of political fragmentation, confusion, and weakness, as internal strife and external aggression tore at its very fabric. Yet the situation was not entirely gloomy, as a new Muslim force, the Seljuk Turks, arrived in the Islamic heartlands of the Middle East and radically altered the balance of power in Islam's favor.

In the Iberian peninsula the Christians had seized regions that had been under Islamic rule for centuries. Elsewhere in the Mediterranean Italians took control of Corsica and Sardinia while Norman adventurers would soon conquer Sicily.

In the Middle East the Byzantine empire had already occupied much of eastern Anatolia where they replaced Islamic suzerainty and, in a shortsighted move, disarmed the existing military elites of Armenia. Byzantine armies even dominated parts of Syria, but the Byzantine empire then returned to a policy of static defense, confident that its Islamic neighbors no longer posed a serious challenge.

Meanwhile in the northeastern provinces of the Islamic world the Seljuk Turks had started to play an important role. Their name was that of a noble family in a clan forming part of the Ghuzz Turkish tribe, which dominated the steppes north of the Caspian and Aral Seas. After most of the Ghuzz converted to Islam, the Seljuks and their followers served as soldiers for various eastern dynasties including the Samanids, Qara Khanids, and Ghaznavids, the latter two of which were themselves Turkish.

During the first half of the 11th century, however, the Seljuks reached Khurasan and, campaigning on their own behalf, took control of Nishapur in 1038. Toghril Beg, the

Seljuk leader, proclaimed himself champion of Sunni Muslims and of the Abbasid caliph. With his highly effective and largely Turkish army, Toghril Beg swept aside resistance by the Shi'a Buwayhids and entered Baghdad in 1055, where he was proclaimed sultan by a grateful Abbasid caliph.

BYZANTINE COLLAPSE

Within a few years the Seljuks controlled Iran, Iraq, and much of Syria. Meanwhile other bands of adventurers, not necessarily Seljuk or even Turkish, started raiding deep into Byzantine territory in eastern Anatolia. Some of these raiders may have been over-enthusiastic troublemakers whom the Seljuk sultan was happy to send against Islam's ancient Byzantine foe. By the start of the 1070s the most significant attacks clearly had Seljuk authorization and in 1071 a substantial

Map legend:
- Great Seljuk sultanate
- Great Seljuk tributaries with Islamic majority population
- Great Seljuk tributaries with non-Islamic majority population
- other Islamic region
- Islamic community under non-Islamic rule
- disputed between Seljuks and Fatimids
- Byzantine empire
- other Christian state

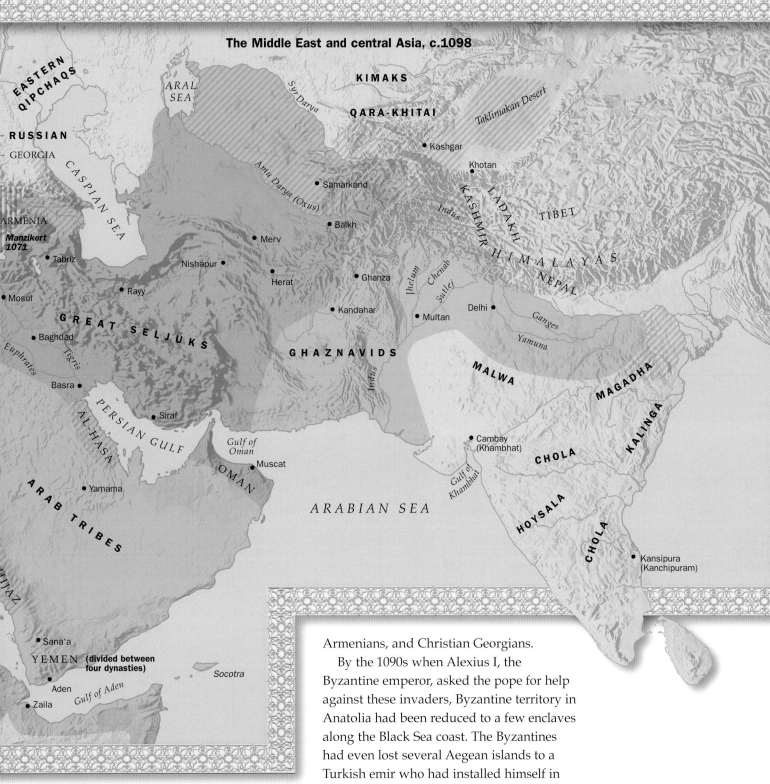

The Middle East and central Asia, c.1098

EASTERN QIPCHAQS

ARAL SEA

KIMAKS

QARA-KHITAI

Taklimakan Desert

RUSSIAN

GEORGIA

CASPIAN SEA

Syr Darya

• Kashgar

Khotan

Amu Darya (Oxus)

• Samarkand

Indus

KASHMIR

LADAKH

TIBET

ARMENIA

Manzikert 1071

• Tabriz

• Balkh

• Merv

• Mosul

Nishapur •

• Herat

• Ghanza

Jhelum

Chenab

Sutlej

HIMALAYAS

NEPAL

• Rayy

Delhi •

Ganges

G R E A T   S E L J U K S

• Kandahar

• Multan

Yamuna

Euphrates

Tigris

• Baghdad

GHAZNAVIDS

Indus

MALWA

MAGADHA

Basra •

P E R S I A N   G U L F

• Siraf

KALINGA

A L - H A S A

Gulf of Oman

• Muscat

• Cambay (Khambhat)

CHOLA

A R A B

• Yamama

O M A N

Gulf of Khambhat

HOYSALA

T R I B E S

A R A B I A N   S E A

CHOLA

CHOLA

• Kansipura (Kanchipuram)

HIJAZ

• Sana'a

Y E M E N **(divided between four dynasties)**

Socotra

Aden

• Zaila

Gulf of Aden

Armenians, and Christian Georgians.

By the 1090s when Alexius I, the Byzantine emperor, asked the pope for help against these invaders, Byzantine territory in Anatolia had been reduced to a few enclaves along the Black Sea coast. The Byzantines had even lost several Aegean islands to a Turkish emir who had installed himself in Smyrna (now Izmir).

While the Byzantine empire collapsed, most of the heartlands of the Islamic world were absorbed within the Great Seljuk sultanate, which also competed with the Shi'a Fatimid caliphate of Egypt for control of Palestine and Syria. Back in Transoxania the Qara Khanids accepted Seljuk overlordship but the Ghaznavid rulers of much of what are now Afghanistan, southeastern Iran, Pakistan, and northern India, remained dedicated rivals of the Seljuks.

Seljuk army under Sultan Mohammed Alp Arslan defeated the main Byzantine field army under Emperor Romanus IV.

This was the momentous battle of Manzikert. It was followed by Byzantine civil wars that fatally undermined their authority in Anatolia. Bands of Turks, some led by the Seljuk aristocracy, took territory that earlier Arab-Islamic invaders had never controlled. Non-Turks also seized this opportunity, including Muslim Kurds, Christian

The Fatimids

The ambitious aim of the Fatimid caliphate, which claimed to represent the majority of Shi'a Muslims, was to overthrow the much longer established Abbasid caliphate. However, the Fatimids are mainly remembered for their patronage of art and architecture.

Right: Decorated entrance to the Fatimid Mosque of Aqmar, 1125, Cairo.

The Abbasids' spiritual authority was, of course, recognized by the majority of Sunni Muslims. During this period the Abbasid caliphate in Baghdad was politically dominated by the Shi'a Buwayhid dynasty from Iran. Under such circumstances the Fatimids' political ambitions must have seemed a serious possibility. Unfortunately for the Fatimids, however, the Buwayhids were not willing to abandon their power. Instead the Buwayhids proclaimed themselves the protectors of the Abbasids—despite being Shi'a, though of a different sect to the Fatimids.

The Fatimids' bid to replace the Abbasids was further hampered by limitations on their political, military, and economic power. The Fatimid state had been founded in Islamic North Africa, which was relatively backward, weak, and even isolated when compared to the Islamic

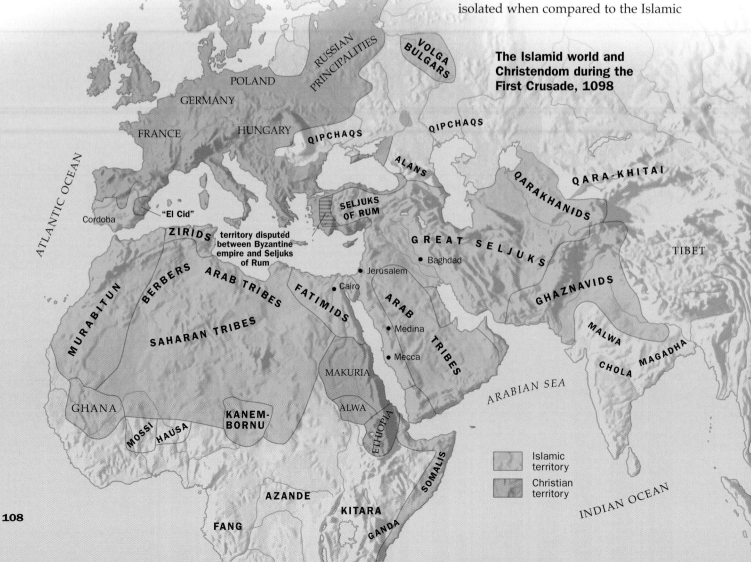

The Islamid world and Christendom during the First Crusade, 1098

POLAND
RUSSIAN PRINCIPALITIES
VOLGA BULGARS
GERMANY
FRANCE
HUNGARY
QIPCHAQS
QIPCHAQS
ALANS
QARAKHANIDS
QARA-KHITAI
SELJUKS OF RUM
ATLANTIC OCEAN
Cordoba
"El Cid"
ZIRIDS
territory disputed between Byzantine empire and Seljuks of Rum
GREAT SELJUKS
TIBET
BERBERS
ARAB TRIBES
FATIMIDS
Baghdad
MURABITUN
Jerusalem
Cairo
ARAB TRIBES
GHAZNAVIDS
SAHARAN TRIBES
Medina
MALWA
Mecca
CHOLA
MAGADHA
GHANA
MAKURIA
ARABIAN SEA
ALWA
ETHIOPIA
MOSSI HAUSA
KANEM-BORNU
SOMALIS
AZANDE
Islamic territory
Christian territory
KITARA
FANG
GANDA
INDIAN OCEAN

heartlands of the Middle East. The bulk of the Fatimid army had been drawn from Berber tribesmen, who remained rather primitive in their military techniques, organization, and armaments throughout the Middle Ages. This was especially true when Fatimid armies were compared to the professional Turkish military elites of central and eastern Islamic dynasties.

The Fatimids were aware of such problems, of course, and attempted to hire Turks and purchase slaves for military training. But their eastern rivals largely controlled the sources of such troops, so the Fatimid caliphs generally had to rely on sources that were considered second best. These included Sudanese and other Africans, western European mercenaries, or slave recruits, and large numbers of Armenians who, despite their military effectiveness, largely remained Christian and thus not wholly reliable.

Above: A stone carving on a wall from Kubachi in the Caucasus Mountains depicts a Turkish horseman of the 12th to 13th centuries.

Ismaili Shi'a Islam became the Fatimids' most effective weapon in their rivalry with the Sunni Abbasids.

Unfortunately the impact of such missionaries was often diluted by splits within the religious movement. These eventually resulted in the emergence of an extreme sect in Syria known as the Druze, who were eventually declared to be outside the community of Islam altogether.

Another split led to the so-called Assassin sect of Iran and Syria, while a more moderate Isma'ili sect developed in India, the community led today by the Agha Khan. This third Isma'ili sect's adherents are largely found in India and Yemen.

Despite these seemingly negative factors, Egypt and its new Fatimid capital of Cairo enjoyed a cultural flowering and economic prosperity that overtook that of Iraq, which was in decline by then. Trade with Europe flourished across the Mediterranean, as it did with India to the east. Egypt's Jewish community similarly flourished both economically and culturally. So did Egypt's Christians, although to a lesser degree and interrupted by occasional persecutions.

It was, however, Islamic art and architecture that became the jewels of the Fatimid period. Some of the finest examples of metalwork, ceramics, textiles, glassware, and carved ivory were made under Fatimid patronage.

MINORITY SECT

The bulk of the Fatimid caliphate's Islamic population was Sunni, especially in Egypt, which became the Fatimid powerbase from the mid-tenth century. Furthermore, the majority of the population of Egypt and perhaps of Syria was still Christian rather than Muslim. Egypt remained a poor base from which to dominate the Middle East, a geopolitical factor that had been true ever since the time of the pharaohs.

Perhaps the Fatimid caliphs soon realized that their ambitions were unlikely to be achieved by military or political means. Certainly they became active patrons of culture, art, architecture, and religious scholarship. The *da'is* or missionaries of

Left: Musician and female dancer are shown in this carved wooden panel from the Fatimid caliphal palace, Cairo.

Barbarians from the West

Before the First Crusade, the Muslims of the Middle East had faced only one Christian foe, the Byzantine empire. They were unprepared for a ruthless and genocidal onslaught from the west, and several years passed before its origins, motivation, and aims were understood.

Right: Painted paper fragment showing an Islamic soldier with a shield and javelins, 11th–12th century, from Cairo.

European forces had made several assaults on Islamic territory closer to Catholic western Europe during the 11th century. Although Christian invasions of al-Andalus had been largely reversed by the Murabitun, raiders from the Italian maritime Republic of Pisa had driven Islamic outposts from Corsica as well as the more established settlements in Sardinia. They also raided North Africa and Sicily.

Most dramatic of all was the invasion of Islamic-ruled Sicily by Norman adventurers from southern Italy. By 1090 they had conquered the entire island, although they left most of its Muslim population and previous elites in place. The Normans then seized Malta, which had been Arabic-speaking and largely Muslim since the ninth century. Here the indigenous population retained its Semitic language, which is still spoken today.

When hordes of crusaders suddenly appeared on the frontier of the Islamic world in 1098, they were at first regarded as an extension of the Byzantine army. It was assumed they had been recruited by the Byzantine emperor to regain territory his predecessors had lost to the Seljuks and other Turks in Anatolia.

Even when the First Crusade crossed the mountains into Syria it was still assumed to be fighting on behalf of the Byzantine empire. The emperor's own Byzantine forces were, after all, currently mopping up in western Anatolia. Meanwhile, the crusaders were campaigning in areas that the Byzantine empire had held only a few decades earlier.

Several local Christian communities, such as the Greeks in Antioch, the Armenians in Edessa, and even the largely non-military Syrian Christians rallied to support the crusaders. Similarly, many indigenous Arab-Muslim leaders saw the crusaders as potential allies against the dominant Seljuk Turks. At first the Fatimid caliphate regarded the crusaders in the same way and attempted to form an alliance against the Seljuks. Even when the crusaders moved south and seized Jerusalem, the Fatimids still seemed to regard these aggressive newcomers as an extension of Constantinople.

Gradually, however, the surrounding Islamic countries realized that they were facing an entirely new and dedicated foe. The crusaders' massacre of a large part of the Muslim

Below: An Arab tower built between the 12th and 13th centuries stands beside remains of the great Roman temple of Bacchus in the Bekaa Valley at Baalbek, Lebanon.

and Jewish populations of Jerusalem, and their "ethnic cleansing" of Islamic elites within those regions that they occupied, betrayed an intolerance that the Byzantines had rarely shown.

RAISING EXPECTATIONS

Once established, the new Crusader States—the County of Edessa, Principality of Antioch, County of Tripoli, and Kingdom of Jerusalem—continued to attack their neighbors. They rarely sought alliances and soon made it clear that they would like to dominate Egypt. An unsuccessful and unnumbered crusade of 1101 may even have been heading for Baghdad, the seat of the Abbasid caliphate. At the same time, the traditionally well-informed Islamic governments were soon aware of tensions between the crusaders and the Byzantines.

It would probably be wrong to attribute clear-cut strategic ambitions to the earliest crusaders. The First Crusade probably saw itself as little more than an armed pilgrimage, dedicated to reaching Jerusalem and expelling the "infidels" from the Holy Land. Additional ambitions apparently developed during the latter part of the crusade and more particularly after the conquest of Jerusalem.

Nevertheless, the remarkable success of the First Crusade does seem to have raised western Christian expectations. For a while it even seemed possible that Christian armies might conquer the entire Islamic heartland of the Middle East, overthrowing both the Abbasid and Fatimid caliphates as well as destroying the Islamic Holy Cities of Mecca and Medina. Some crusader enthusiasts even anticipated digging up and destroying the body of the "false prophet" Mohammed.

Given the traditionally efficient intelligence systems available to major Islamic states, such ambitions are likely to have been known by neighboring Islamic governments. If this is so, such knowledge probably contributed to a steady revival of the spirit of *jihad* in the region. In the event, the high-flying crusader ambitions proved wholly unattainable.

Above: The Bab Wastani Gate of 1123, Baghdad, Iraq.

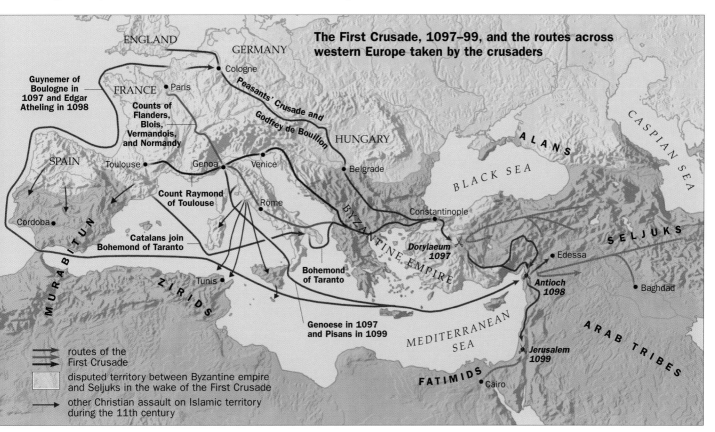

The First Crusade, 1097–99, and the routes across western Europe taken by the crusaders

ENGLAND
GERMANY
Cologne
Guynemer of Boulogne in 1097 and Edgar Atheling in 1098
FRANCE • Paris
Peasants' Crusade and
Godfrey de Bouillon
Counts of Flanders, Blois, Vermandois, and Normandy
HUNGARY
ALANS
CASPIAN SEA
SPAIN
Toulouse
Genoa
Venice
Belgrade
BLACK SEA
Count Raymond of Toulouse
Rome
Constantinople
SELJUKS
Cordoba
Catalans join Bohemond of Taranto
Dorylaeum 1097
Edessa
MURABITUN
Bohemond of Taranto
BYZANTINE EMPIRE
Antioch 1098
Baghdad
ZIRIDS
Tunis
ARAB TRIBES
Genoese in 1097 and Pisans in 1099
MEDITERRANEAN SEA
Jerusalem 1099
FATIMIDS
Cairo

routes of the First Crusade
disputed territory between Byzantine empire and Seljuks in the wake of the First Crusade
other Christian assault on Islamic territory during the 11th century

Holding the Line

The first Islamic peoples, governors, and rulers to resist the crusader onslaught were those directly attacked in the First Crusade. As the Crusader States extended their frontiers and reduced those coastal cities that had defied them, the Muslims realized that these invaders intended to stay.

It became clear to the Islamic world that the crusaders were not simply striking to subdue a perceived threat to Europe, but they intended to maintain a permanent presence in the region. Neither were they campaigning in the name of the Byzantine emperor. Instead they were representatives of a more

immediately threatened by the crusader invasions seemed willing to do anything about them. Most other Islamic governments continued to focus on their own rivalries, usually with fellow Islamic rulers, while doing little more than express pious horror at the crusader assault. They occasionally contributed contingents of soldiers to fragile alliances, but these were all too often defeated by crusaders on the battlefield.

Within two or three decades, Muslim preachers and scholars were working to revive a spirit of *jihad* to combat the crusaders, but for many years this had little

Above: The surviving arch of the 12th–early 13th-century bridge that originally crossed the Tigris at Ayn Diwar in Syria now stands isolated in a field after the river course changed.

fanatical form of Christianity, and a less civilized society than the Byzantine Greeks, who had been Islam's neighbors for centuries.

Yet the relatively primitive culture that the crusaders brought to the Middle East went hand-in-hand with undoubted military effectiveness. Small numbers of knights and soldiers, plus a hardly greater number of settlers, priests, merchants, and others, had created small states, while the supposedly more powerful surrounding Islamic governments seemed unable to stop them.

The reasons soon became obvious. The Muslims were politically, religiously, and socially fragmented. Only those Islamic rulers

effect. The Islamic concept of *jihad* is complex and cannot be translated simply as "holy war." It was based on the idea of struggle against evil; the highest form of *jihad* being an individual's lifelong attempt to resist temptation and live a moral life.

Jihad as a form of communal effort to defend Islam, especially if it was expressed in military terms, had always been seen as secondary, both in importance and in spiritual merit. Nevertheless, the concept of this "lesser jihad" as a means of mobilizing Islamic opinion and action in defense of territory remained. Although moribund for centuries, it was present as a religious concept, ready for scholars, preachers, and eventually rulers to use to motivate armies and peoples.

A number of early 12th-century Islamic rulers in the Middle East used such *jihad* propaganda to justify their own political and military actions. Yet it is impossible to know how seriously they took the idea as individuals. Some were presumably genuine in their call for *jihad*, while others clearly tried to take advantage of the concept's ability to motivate the masses.

UNLIKELY SAVIOR

Paradoxically, the first Islamic ruler to achieve real success against the Crusader States can hardly be described as a fine example of Islamic motivation and morality. He was Imad al-Din Zangi, a hard fighting, hard drinking, and rather brutal Turkish soldier with varied sexual preferences. The son of a *ghulam* or slave-recruited soldier

who rose to high rank under the Great Seljuk Sultan Malik Shah, Zangi (sometimes known as Zengi) was made governor of Aleppo in 1127. He was also *atabeg*, or "father figure" advisor to two of the sultan's sons.

By this time several other Turkish governors and *atabegs* in the Fertile Crescent had effectively become independent of the Great Seljuk sultanate. This not only enabled Zangi to do the same but also allowed him to extend his own territory at the expense of such local rulers and governors.

In addition, Imad al-Din Zangi campaigned against the Byzantines and the crusaders. He did so with such success that, in 1144, Zangi reconquered the city of Edessa and effectively destroyed the crusader County of Edessa. What remained of the county west of the Euphrates fell later, but the retaking of Edessa made Zangi the hero of the Islamic world. It also led to a second crusade, but this proved to be a fiasco.

	Crusader State
	Crusader State border at maximum extent, 1144
	Zangid territory, c.1145
	crusader territory lost to Zangi
	crusader territory lost to other Islamic leaders
	other Christian territory
	other Islamic territory

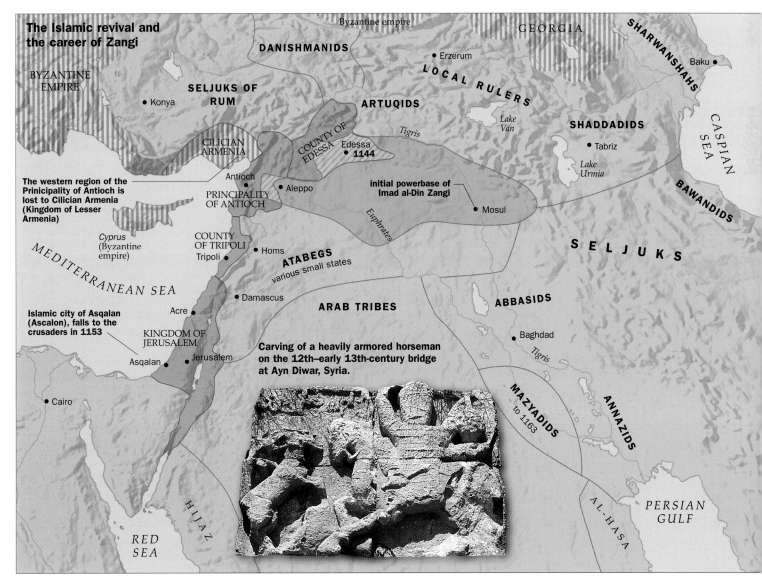

The Islamic revival and the career of Zangi

BYZANTINE EMPIRE

Byzantine empire

GEORGIA

SHARWANSHAHS

Baku

DANISHMANIDS

Erzerum

LOCAL RULERS

SELJUKS OF RUM

Konya

ARTUQIDS

Lake Van

SHADDADIDS

Tabriz

CASPIAN SEA

CILICIAN ARMENIA

COUNTY OF EDESSA

Edessa 1144

Tigris

Lake Urmia

The western region of the Principality of Antioch is lost to Cilician Armenia (Kingdom of Lesser Armenia)

Antioch

PRINCIPALITY OF ANTIOCH

Aleppo

initial powerbase of Imad al-Din Zangi

Mosul

BAWANDIDS

Cyprus (Byzantine empire)

COUNTY OF TRIPOLI

Tripoli

Homs

Euphrates

SELJUKS

MEDITERRANEAN SEA

ATABEGS various small states

Islamic city of Asqalan (Ascalon), falls to the crusaders in 1153

Acre

Damascus

ARAB TRIBES

ABBASIDS

Baghdad

Tigris

KINGDOM OF JERUSALEM

Asqalan

Jerusalem

MAZYADIDS to 1163

ANNAZIDS

Cairo

Carving of a heavily armored horseman on the 12th–early 13th-century bridge at Ayn Diwar, Syria.

HIJAZ

RED SEA

AL-HASA

PERSIAN GULF

An Islamic Hero

Saladin was the most famous leader against the crusading invaders of Palestine and Syria. A gifted commander, his earlier posts in Damascus and Egypt were overshadowed by his battlefield successes against the crusaders.

Facing below: Saladin's tomb in Damascus was restored early in the 20th century.

Salah al-Din Yusuf Ibn Ayyub, or Saladin as he is better known in Europe, was born at Tikrit in Iraq in 1137 or 1138. Saladin's family, the Ayyubids, was of Kurdish origin but his father and uncle both served Zangi, the Turkish ruler of northern Iraq and northeastern Syria (*see previous page*). Together they later arranged the surrender of Damascus to Zangi's son and successor, Nur al-Din, thus making him the most powerful Islamic ruler in the region.

The prestige of Saladin's father and uncle clearly helped his career in the service of Nur al-Din. Educated as a soldier, courtier, and administrator, Saladin must have done well because in 1156 he was placed in command of the Damascus garrison.

However, Saladin's own bid for power resulted from his participation in Nur al-Din's attempts to take over Fatimid Egypt. He played a leading military role in a successful third expedition, and when his uncle Shirkuh died in 1169, Saladin was proclaimed leader by Nur al-Din's senior

Below: The western end of the Islamic aqueduct constructed in the late 13th–early 14th centuries, which originally took water from the Nile to the Citadel of Cairo.

officers in Egypt.

Saladin's appointment as vizier (chief minister) to the impotent Fatimid caliphate was a mere formality and when, in 1171, the last Fatimid caliph died, Saladin abolished the Shi'a caliphate and restored Egypt's allegiance to the Abbasid caliph in Baghdad. Saladin became governor, although under the suzerainty of Nur al-Din.

Increasing tension with Saladin's nominal overlord would probably have resulted in military action had Nur al-Din not died in 1174. Saladin now declared himself Nur al-Din's successor and steadily extended his authority over Syria and northern Iraq. This inevitably led to military action against Nur al-Din's descendants, who regarded themselves as his rightful heirs.

Meanwhile Saladin generally observed a truce with the Crusader States but by 1183 he had created a sufficiently united Islamic front to challenge them. Although his first attacks failed, he launched another major campaign in 1187 that culminated in his great victory at the battle of Hattin. It was closely followed by the liberation of Jerusalem and the overrunning of almost the entire Kingdom of Jerusalem and County of Tripoli. The Principality of Antioch was largely excluded from this astonishing campaign because it had a truce with Saladin.

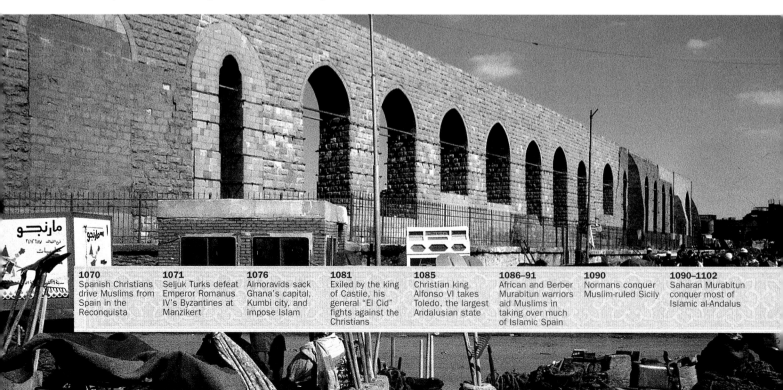

1070
Spanish Christians drive Muslims from Spain in the Reconquista

1071
Seljuk Turks defeat Emperor Romanus IV's Byzantines at Manzikert

1076
Almoravids sack Ghana's capital, Kumbi city, and impose Islam

1081
Exiled by the king of Castile, his general "El Cid" fights against the Christians

1085
Christian king Alfonso VI takes Toledo, the largest Andalusian state

1086–91
African and Berber Murabitun warriors aid Muslims in taking over much of Islamic Spain

1090
Normans conquer Muslim-ruled Sicily

1090–1102
Saharan Murabitun conquer most of Islamic al-Andalus

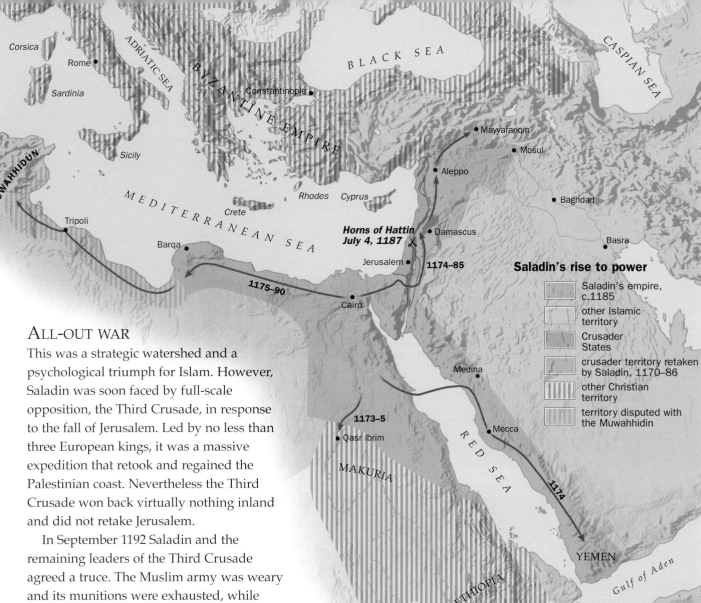

Horns of Hattin
July 4, 1187

1174–85

1173–5

1175–90

1174

Saladin's rise to power

	Saladin's empire, c.1185
	other Islamic territory
	Crusader States
	crusader territory retaken by Saladin, 1170–86
	other Christian territory
	territory disputed with the Muwahhidin

ALL-OUT WAR

This was a strategic watershed and a psychological triumph for Islam. However, Saladin was soon faced by full-scale opposition, the Third Crusade, in response to the fall of Jerusalem. Led by no less than three European kings, it was a massive expedition that retook and regained the Palestinian coast. Nevertheless the Third Crusade won back virtually nothing inland and did not retake Jerusalem.

In September 1192 Saladin and the remaining leaders of the Third Crusade agreed a truce. The Muslim army was weary and its munitions were exhausted, while Saladin may himself have already been mortally ill. He died on March 3, 1193, and was buried in Damascus. Although the Muslims now had the upper hand in relation to the Crusader States, Saladin's successors did not press their advantages. Instead these Ayyubid rulers made political alliances with what remained of the Crusader States and developed commercial relations.

What Saladin had left was a system of collective family rule in which authority was delegated to his relatives and descendants in the major cities of six large but disparate states. These formed a confederacy, with the ruler of Cairo usually at its head. It proved to be a remarkably successful system, only breaking down when faced with the far more dangerous Mongol invasions in the middle of the 13th century.

1094–5	1098	1099	1100	1119	1123	1123-4	1144
Byzantine Emperor Alexius appeals to Rome for help against the Seljuk Turks	Crusaders take Antioch, gateway to the Holy Land	Crusaders gain control of Jerusalem (July)	Baldwin of Edessa becomes King of Jerusalem, head of the Crusader States	A combined army of Aleppo and Damascus defeat crusaders at Ager Sanguinus, Antioch	Death of Umar Khayyam, Persian poet and mystic	Baldwin II of Jerusalem is held by Seljuk Turks led by Balak of Mardin	Joscelin II, Count of Edessa, loses the city to Seljuk Turks led by Zangi

A New Catastrophe

It was his campaigns in the Muslim world that gave Genghis Khan the reputation as one of the world's great destroyers. The Mongols' march of conquest was umcompromisingly brutal, cities obliterated with impunity.

Genghis Khan's unification of Mongolia and eastern Turkestan involved considerable bloodshed but relatively little material damage. His raids on China caused devastation, but nothing out of the ordinary for a nomad invasion. The Mongols' eruption into Transoxania, Afghanistan, and Iran was quite different.

The havoc that the armies of Genghis Khan and his successors brought to the Middle East could be seen to imply that the Mongols had a particularly vindictive attitude toward Islamic civilization. Yet Khan's kindly treatment of Muslims in what had been the Qara-Khitai realm in central Asia, and the presence of Muslim Turks among his soldiers, show that he had no special hatred for Islam. The carnage resulted from political and military considerations, not religious ones.

After overthrowing the last Qara-Khitai ruler, Genghis Khan found himself facing a man as warlike as himself. This was Ala al-Din the Khwarazmshah, who similarly planned to dominate central Asia. Late in 1219 the Mongols advanced on three fronts, followed a few months later by Genghis Khan himself. The Khwarazmshah's garrison in Bukhara was butchered and the leader's confidence seemed to collapse.

What followed was a series of sieges in which outnumbered garrisons were overwhelmed by the Mongol horde. Almost everywhere the defenders were slaughtered, while civic and religious leaders were put to the sword. Prolonged resistance resulted in entire populations being massacred.

The destruction that the Mongols wrought on Afghanistan and eastern Iran grew ever more savage. The Mongols even emptied the graves of Islamic rulers who had helped these regions flourish. Near Tus they obliterated the tomb of the famous Caliph Harun al-Rashid.

DESTROYING HORDES

Genghis Khan's death in 1227 diverted Mongol attentions for a while, but they returned to the Islamic world 53 years later, led by Khan's grandson Hülegü. Like his grandfather, Hülegü was a leader who conquered one Islamic power after another; notoriously destroying Baghdad and killing the last Abbasid caliph to hold real power. Moving into Syria he took Aleppo and Damascus, the triumphant progress of his army halted by an Egyptian army.

On the other hand, Hülegü was also a builder. The Il Khan dynasty which he established in Iran and Iraq would, after it converted to Islam, play a significant role in shaping the history of the Middle East. Furthermore, Hülegü's successors did much to re-establish a sense of Iranian national identity, although presumably without intending to do so. The Il Khan rulers were no longer mere governors of Islamic provinces in the name of another more distant authority such as the Abbasid caliph. They now ruled a state that—for the first time since the fall of the Sassanian empire in

the seventh century—entered into direct and independent diplomatic relations with Europe and China. The Il Khans' centralizing policies also paved the way for the Iranian nationalist attitudes of later rulers such as the 16th-century Safavids.

Nevertheless, the Mongol conquest remained a cultural and economic disaster. Not only was the Il Khan dynasty relatively short-lived but the Mongols, unlike their Arab-Islamic predecessors, proved incapable of creating a Mongol-Iranian civilization comparable to that of the Islamic Arab-Iranian-Turkish civilization that they had devastated. The Mongol empire fell apart in less than a hundred years and left little except destruction in its wake.

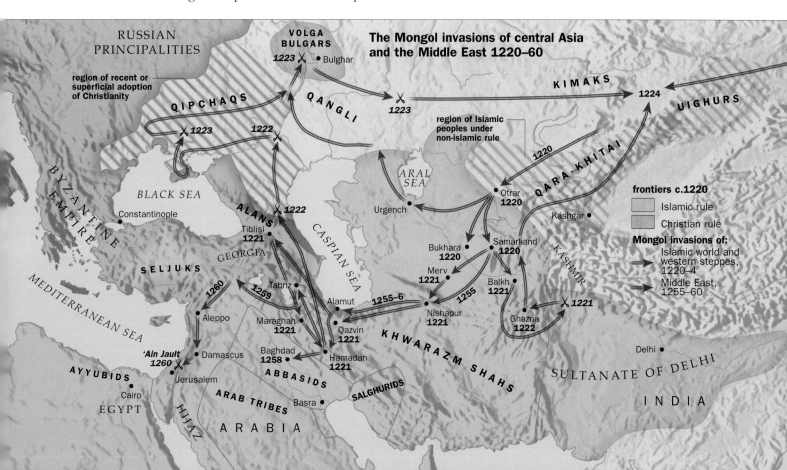

The Mongol invasions of central Asia and the Middle East 1220–60

Slaves Victorious: Rise of the Mamluks

The Mamluk sultanate of Egypt and Syria was ruled by men who, with few exceptions, had once been slaves. One of their greatest achievements was to expel the last crusaders from the Middle East.

Right: A mounted and armored huntsman decorates a silver-inlaid bronze basin of the Mamluk period; Egypt, c.1300.

The slave-recruited military elite of the mamluks held the reins of power and dominated the Egyptian army. The Mamluk sultanate lasted for over 250 years, and remained the dominant Islamic power for most of that time. Maintenance of a powerful army was the primary objective of the Mamluk political system, this army being the culmination of a military tradition that stretched back to the eighth century. The Mamluks provided the model for the Ottoman empire, whose armies reached the gates of Vienna only 12 years after conquering the Mamluks themselves.

In Arabic the word *mamluk* meant a

Above: Heraldic lions adorn the bridge built at Shubra, Egypt in 1266 for Sultan Baybars I, conqueror of the great Syrian crusader castle Crac des Chevaliers.

soldier recruited as a young slave, then trained, educated, and released as a full-time professional. Most mamluks, or *ghulams* as they were also known, were of Turkish origin, having been recruited from the pagan tribal peoples of the central Asian steppes.

In earlier centuries they had formed the core of most Middle Eastern armies as well as several in the western part of the Islamic world. By the 12th century mamluks provided the elites and, very often, the

officer corps of armies facing the crusaders. This included the army of Saladin and his Ayyubid successors.

SECURITY IN NUMBERS

The Mongol invasions of what are now southern Russia and the Ukraine uprooted the Qipchaq Turks of these regions, resulting in far greater numbers of slaves becoming available for purchase as military recruits. Partly as a result of this, the last Ayyubid ruler to wield real power, al-Salih, tried to reunify the fragmented Ayyubid states by purchasing even greater numbers of such Turkish mamluks. They formed the Bahriyah regiment, as well as the Sultan's *Jamdariyah* personal guard. However in 1250, during the campaign that defeated an invasion of Egypt by the Sixth Crusade, Sultan al-Salih died.

His Bahriyah regiment seized control and proclaimed their leader Aybak as the *atabeg* or "father figure" of al-Salih's young son. A short while later Aybak was proclaimed sultan, but the first years of mamluk rule were confused and it was not until the reign of Baybars (1260–77) that the new dynasty became firmly established.

However, the term "dynasty" is potentially misleading, since there were only

Left: The Mamluks adapted and modified many of the crusader castles in Jordan, Lebanon, and Syria, including the massive Crac des Chevaliers. Here, at Shawback castle in Jordan, an Arabic inscription runs around the main tower surrounding the former Christian fortress.

a few occasions when members of the same family actually held power. In many ways the Mamluk political system was anti-dynastic. Furthermore the Mamluks, as "men of the sword," did not feel inferior to the freeborn, largely Arab "men of the pen" who provided the administrative, legal, religious, and other civilian elites who ran the Mamluk empire.

Cairo remained the center of Mamluk cultural life and their place of identity, with cities like Damascus, Aleppo, and Jerusalem coming a poor second. Although the Mamluk elite became patrons of religious architecture and other arts in all these major centers, few seem to have learned Arabic and they usually married women of comparable Turkish slave origin or the daughters of other Mamluks.

Perhaps most remarkable, from a modern point of view, was the Mamluk insistence that their own sons should not achieve senior military rank, instead being directed toward civilian careers. The best soldiers and the best officers, it was agreed, should continue to be of slave-recruited origin.

The Mamluks remained a paradox in several ways, scandalizing more traditional Muslims by their love of elaborate pageants and extravagant costume, as well as public and private entertainments. The latter often left little to the imagination and provided the models for several exotic episodes in the *Arabian Nights* tales. This famous collection of stories achieved its final form in Mamluk Cairo.

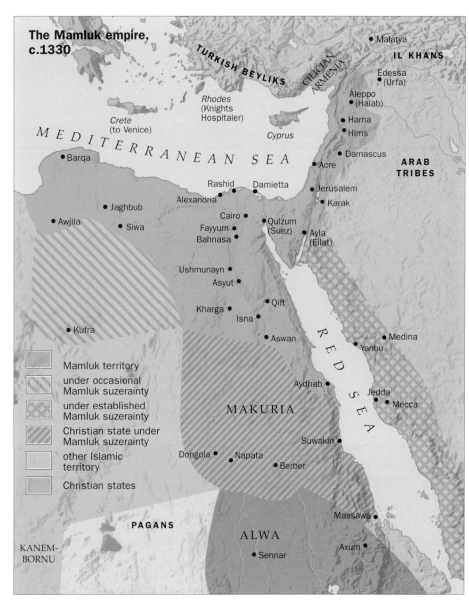

The Mamluk empire, c.1330

- Mamluk territory
- under occasional Mamluk suzerainty
- under established Mamluk suzerainty
- Christian state under Mamluk suzerainty
- other Islamic territory
- Christian states

CHAPTER EIGHT

Age of the Mamluks

Militaristic rule of a slave caste

PRINCIPALITY OF
NOVGOROD

Novgorod

MUSCOVY

· Moscow

TEUTONIC KNIGHTS

BALTIC SEA

KHANATE OF THE GOLDEN HORDE

Volga

ARAL
SEA

LITHUANIA

POLAND

· Kiev

Dnieper

Sarai

Dniester

Vienna ·

Danube

MOLDAVIA

Tana

CASPIAN SEA

HUNGARY

SEA OF
AZOV

Belgrade ·

WALLACHIA

Kaffa
to Ottomans,
1475

Venice

Danube

GEORGIA

Bosnia

Serbia

BLACK SEA

TREBIZOND

Ragusa

Trebizond

Rome ·

NAPLES

OTTOMAN EMPIRE

Albania

Constantinople
to Ottomans,
1453

TURKISH
EMIRATES

QARA QOYUNLU

Athens

Tigris

Morea

Aleppo ·

Baghdad ·

Rhodes

Euphrates

Cyprus
to Mamluks, 1424–26
to Venice, 1489

MEDITERRANEAN SEA

Crete

Damascus ·

MAMLUK SULTANATE

Alexandria ·

Damietta

Cairo ·

Nile

RED SEA

	Mamluk sultanate
	Ottoman empire
	Mongol Golden Horde and vassal khanates
	Byzantine empire (including "Empire of Trebizond")
	Lithuania
	Genoese trading outposts
	Republic of Venice and Venetian trading outposts

······▶ main trade routes supplying
──────▶ mamluk slave recruits to Egypt

Medieval Islamic civilization had a different attitude toward slavery than that seen in western Europe. Not only were slaves better treated in Islamic society, but their status was generally quite honorable. Even the use of the word *abd* or "slave" differed, and Muslim men often included various ways of saying "slave of God" in their own names. In Islamic society, being a slave did not necessarily mean a lifetime of drudgery and mistreatment.

The career opportunities open to a skilful mamluk or military slave were different from those open to a domestic slave, and traditionally included senior command and even political leadership. These factors, and the widely recognized higher standards of living in the Islamic Middle East, meant that there was often little resistance to being taken as a mamluk among the pagan Turks of central Asia. By the later medieval period there were even cases of individuals, including Muslims, volunteering to become mamluks.

Usually the slave merchant was a new recruit's first master. He assessed their potential and took them to a market such as that in Cairo's huge Citadel. The price of individual men varied considerably, but by the 15th century it was generally four times higher than that of a good warhorse.

Training was hard and campaigning was dangerous, yet epidemics of plague seem to have caused the greatest numbers of deaths in mamluk ranks. Many young Qipchaq Turkish women, both slaves and free, also arrived in the wake of mamluk recruits, bringing with them some of central Asia's traditions of sexual equality. At least one Mamluk Sultan's wife gave advice not only on political matters, which Islamic women had done ever since the days of the Prophet Mohammed, but even on details of military recruitment.

TRAINING ACADEMIES

The best opportunities were open to those young slaves who were purchased by the ruler himself. They became *kuttub* students and were sent to *tabaqah* schools for religious, literary, and military education.

Discipline in the *tabaqahs* was strict, but once the students reached adulthood they were freed and became the Sultan's own mamluks. At the end of their training each *kuttub* also received an *'itaqah*

certificate of freedom, and a uniform, horse, bows, arrows, quivers, armor, and some swords.

During the late 13th century this training system led to attitudes of leadership and loyalty similar to those expected from graduates of today's most prestigious military academies. For example, casualties suffered during the final siege of crusader-held Acre in 1291 reveal a ratio of 13 officers killed for every 83 men—much higher than the actual ratio of officers to men.

The survival of several military manuals means that more is known about the training of mamluk forces than any other medieval army. It was based on a number of *maydan* training grounds whose number and state of repair reflected the country's military readiness. Sultan Baybars himself trained in such a *maydan* daily from noon until evening prayer. In fact the *furusiyah* military exercises of the mamluk army became almost a spectator sport for people of the main cities.

Furusiyah itself was not, however, a code of military conduct like the chivalry proclaimed by western Europe's knightly elite. Nor was it merely an ideal of courage. Instead *furusiyah* was a system of physical fitness and military skills based on the use of specific weapons. It also included horsemanship and hunting skills, which were considered vital for cavalry's cohesion and their ability to cooperate as military units. Archery is generally regarded as the mamluks' most important military skill. To conserve their horses, especially when campaigning against Mongols who had far larger reserves of horses, mamluks practiced archery "at rest" with a very high rate of shooting.

To counter the greater mobility of the Mongols a mamluk archer was also expected to hit a target no wider than three feet at a range of 220 feet. He should also be capable of shooting three arrows in one and a half seconds—much faster than that attributed to the much vaunted English medieval longbowman.

Later mamluk training manuals describe exercises using crossbows on foot and on horseback, this weapon being regarded as suitable for a small or inexperienced cavalryman. The sword seems to have been seen as a secondary weapon for a horseman, who relied more on his bow and spear.

Not Mere Soldiers

The Mamluk sultanate maintained the best trained and equipped army in the Islamic world, while their military and governing elite regarded themselves as the true defenders of Islam. Nevertheless, Mamluk society was more than just a professional army.

Below: Abu Zayd pretending to be a holy man, in a copy of the Maqamat *of al-Hariri, Mamluk, 1334. The* maqamat, *which loosely translates as "assemblies," were individual stories linked by the person of the narrator and the likeable rogue he keeps meeting. In the case of al-Hariri (1054–1122), Abu Zayd is a wandering scholar who lives by his wits.*

Mamluks were well educated and generally more literate than their counterparts in Europe, and were highly regarded patrons of Islamic culture. On the other hand the mamluks themselves were not intellectual or scholarly leaders. These roles were filled by the Men of the Pen who were civilians; the Mamluks remaining Men of the Sword. This did not hinder the elite from competing as patrons of the arts. In addition to architecture, the sultan and his senior officers spent huge sums on highly decorated furnishings for their palaces, including some of the finest metalwork ever produced by Islamic craftsmen.

A school of manuscript illumination flourished in the Mamluk sultanate,

although its finest works were largely religious. The illustration of collections of stories like the *Maqamat* of al-Hariri became more impressionistic and some of their best miniature paintings seem to have more in common with 20th century Western art than with that of later medieval or Renaissance Europe.

Cultivated tastes were expected of a senior mamluk, especially during the later 14th and 15th centuries when the most powerful mamluks were recruited from the Caucasus and eastern Europe rather than the Turkish steppes. Many of their leaders were men of culture and fond of learned society. Some had a taste for Turkish history, others for Greek philosophy. Sultan al-Mu'ayyad (1412–21) was a good Arabic poet, fine musician, and public speaker.

INCREASINGLY SOPHISTICATED

There was also a Turkish literature for the class, while Turkish itself served as a common language for the military elites of most of the Middle East and the steppes states to the north. Turkish-Arabic dictionaries were produced, apparently for use by Arab speakers in their dealings with the class.

Several senior mamluks were at the same time leaders of political factions, supported by lesser mamluks who occasionally settled their leaders' quarrels in street brawling. Loyalty between a leader and his followers was, however, fragile and needed regular payment. If a leader died or was exiled his followers simply looked for a new employer, the whole system being based on political calculation rather than abstract concepts of loyalty. On the other hand, political battles tended to be brief and were frequently settled at a "peace feast."

1145	1147	1147–8	1154	1155–1194	1157	1167	1169
Abd al-Mu'min's Muwahhidun army controls Islamic al-Andalus	The Muwahhidun take Marrakesh and oust the Murabitun from North Africa	Second Crusade defeated outside Damascus	Al-Idrisi makes an atlas of the known world for King Roger of Sicily	Seljuk Turks lose some parts of Mesopotamia to a new Abbasid caliphate	Alfonso VII of Castille and León invades Muslim Spain but is killed at Muradel	A combined Seljuk-Fatimid force defends Egypt from crusaders on the Day of Al-Babein	On the death of Shirkuh, Salah al-Din (Saladin) becomes vizier of Egypt

Some feasts were clearly in a Turkish rather than Arab tradition, involving large quantities of horse meat and mare's milk. Much of the latter was fermented to make a typically Turkish alcoholic drink called *kumiss*.

Despite their military traditions, casualties tended to be low, and detailed information about one early 15th century faction shows

Below: Qubbat tomb of an unknown Muslim saint, 14th–15th centuries, stands in old Ramlah.

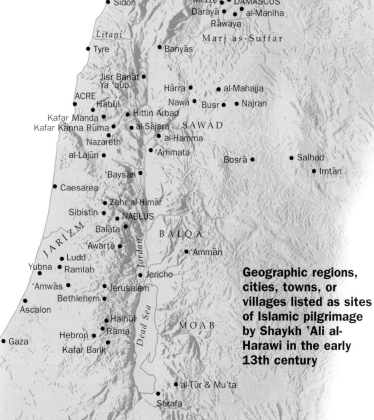

that the majority died of natural causes, including strokes, hernias, and gout. Meanwhile promotion and advancement tended to be on the basis of age, experience, and available vacancies, not by plotting, coups, or street fighting.

By the 15th century, links between the military and civilian elites in the Mamluk sultanate were very close, perhaps because by this time so many Men of the Pen were descended from Men of the Sword. Although the free-born sons of mamluks were excluded from the military elite, they and their descendants often became notable Men of the Pen.

Having been brought up in a thoroughly Islamic and Arabic-speaking environment, a few of them emerged as significant scholars or cultural leaders. In fact the 15th century has been described as the most prolific period in Egyptian literature, rivaled only by Syria during the same period and under the same Mamluk sultans.

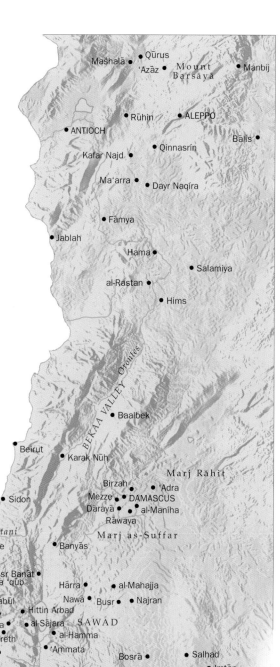

Geographic regions, cities, towns, or villages listed as sites of Islamic pilgrimage by Shaykh 'Ali al-Harawi in the early 13th century

1170–80	1174	1176	1180	1187	1192	1192	1206
The Danishmandid states of Anatolia are conquered by the Seljuks of Rum	Saladin seizes Damascus after deaths of Nur ed-Din and the king of Jerusalem, Almaric	Byzantines under Emperor Manuel defeated by Seljuks of Rum at Myriokephalon	Baldwin IV of the Crusader States makes peace with Saladin, but it is broken in 1181	Saladin defeats the crusaders at Hattin and takes much of Palestine, including Jerusalem	Ghudid ruler conquers Delhi	Richard the Lionheart thwarts Saladin at Jaffa (August); a three-year truce follows	The sultanate of Delhi, north India, is established

The Army is the State

Pressed on all sides, the Mamluks' military prowess was tested in the 13th and 14th centuries. Government, law, and administration were strictly organized too, structured in a similar fashion to an army.

Right: Carving of a Mamluk heraldic insignia and inscriptions on the wall of the Citadel of Damascus, Syria, 14th–15th centuries.

In the late 14th century the Mamluk sultanate was threatened by the rampaging army of Tamerlane (or Timur), and during the final decades of Mamluk power Syria again became a frontier zone, facing the rising power of the Ottoman empire. Of the two main geographical divisions of the sultanate—Syria and Egypt—Syria was the most militarized. In the second half of the 13th century it faced what was left of the Crusader States, as well as the threat from Mongol- and Il Khan-ruled Iraq and Iran. External threats had never been on such a daunting scale.

Syria was divided into the same *mamlaka* administrative units which had existed under the previous Ayyubid sultans. Each *mamlaka* had a smaller version of the administrative system seen in Egypt; these being headed by a *nayib al-sultana* or viceroy of the ruling sultan. He was in charge of the Men of the Sword, the Men of the Pen, the religious establishment, and a provincial army.

Officers of the Men of the Sword in each *mamlaka* were themselves mamluks, as were administrative officers in smaller territorial units such as *niyabas* and *wilayas*. The most important such Men of the Sword supervised the army, the collection of taxes, and the government postal system.

Officials in the provincial government council or *diwan* included both mamluks and civilian Men of the Pen, while the head of this diwan was usually a civilian. The *nayib al-saltana*'s duties as viceroy meant that he was responsible for maintaining law and order in his *mamlaka*, in addition to which he waged war, ensured that the northern frontier fortresses were in good repair and properly garrisoned, was responsible for a local fleet if his *mamlaka* had a coast, and also administered justice.

Both Damascus and Aleppo, as the main cities of Syria, had another senior officer called the *nayib al-qala'a*. They were

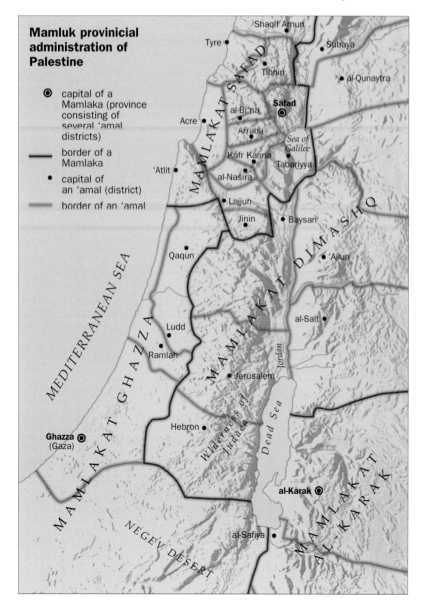

Mamluk provinicial administration of Palestine

- ◉ capital of a Mamlaka (province consisting of several 'amal districts)
- — border of a Mamlaka
- • capital of an 'amal (district)
- — border of an 'amal

MEDITERRANEAN SEA

Shaqif Arnun
Tyre
Subaya
Tibnin
al-Qunaytra
MAMLAKAT SAFAD
Acre
al-Bi'na
Safad ◉
Affaba
Sea of Galilee
Kafr Kanna
'Atlit
Tabariyya
al-Nasira
Lajjun
Jinin
Baysan
MAMLAKAT DIMASHQ
Qaqun
'Ajlun
al-Salt
MAMLAKAT GHAZZA
Ludd
Ramlah
MAMLAKAT
Jordan
Jerusalem
Wilderness of Judaea
Dead Sea
Hebron
Ghazza ◉ (Gaza)
al-Karak ◉
MAMLAKAT AL-KARAK
NEGEV DESERT
al-Safiya

independent of the local *nayib al-sultana* and were responsible for the great citadels of Damascus and Aleppo.

Other senior positions included the *Shadd al-Dawawin* who looked after the financial revenues of the Syrian *mamlakas* and the *Shadd al-Muhimmat* who looked after the special needs of the Mamluk sultan when he visited Syria. The Diwan provincial government council included several other officers, one of the most important being the *Nazir al-Juyush* who looked after the needs of soldiers stationed in Syria.

The size and composition of the Mamluk army in Syria varied according to current circumstances but was often very mixed. It included professional mamluk soldiers, locally recruited Arabs, Turks, and Kurds, various mercenaries including Greeks and Russians, and tribal auxiliaries.

EFFICIENT COMMUNICATIONS

Another important aspect of Mamluk administration in Syria and Palestine was the *barid* or government postal service. Comparable high-speed message systems had been known since pre-Islamic times and had been a feature of the richest and most efficient Islamic governments.

The Mamluk sultanate's *barid* mostly used horses, though camels were vital in some desert areas. There was also a pigeon-post and a system of beacon fires. Warnings of a coastal attack by Christian pirates could, for example, get from Beirut to Damascus in one night. This remarkable system was staffed by carefully selected couriers who wore distinctive insignia. However, it seems to have declined in the later 14th century, being virtually destroyed during Tamerlane's invasions.

Smaller towns had their own *wali* or *nayib*, responsible for local government and security. Those in coastal towns had to ensure that local "men of the sea" had their ships and weapons ready in case of need, as well as looking after visiting European merchants. Each *wali* had a *shurta* or police force to help him, and most towns also had locally recruited nightwatchmen under their own *ra'is* or chief. At village level a local *ra'is* was responsible for law, order, and security, while also being regarded as the representative of the Mamluk state.

Left: A Mamluk horseman armed with a crossbow decorates the top and neck of this early 14th-century enameled glass lamp.

Beauty Without Gold

Until the emergence of the tradition of manuscript illustration in the later Middle Ages, Islamic artists excelled in metalwork, glass, textiles, and ceramics. A wide range of glazes and techniques innovated decorative ceramics, influencing artists in other and later cultures.

Right: Minai-ware ceramic cup illustrated with scenes from the Shahnamah, Iran, 12th–13th centuries.

One of the chief characteristics of medieval Islamic art and architecture was the use of bold but relatively simple shapes whose surfaces were then decorated with increasingly complex patterns. This was as apparent on the domes of mosques and palaces as it was in metalwork and ceramics. Compared with China, pre-Islamic ceramics of the Middle East are primitive. Early Islamic pottery continued in the simple traditions of Byzantium and Sassanian Iran for many years.

During the Umayyad period ceramics were utilitarian rather than luxury ware, and fine Islamic ceramics did not appear in any quantity until the ninth century. This may have been a result of the importation of Chinese porcelain, which Middle Eastern potters tried to imitate. It may also have reflected a metals crisis during which even the Islamic heartlands began to run short of the gold and silver previously used to make luxurious tableware. This shortage was almost certainly responsible for the development of techniques that used small quantities of precious metals to decorate the

surfaces of vessels made of much cheaper bronze or brass. These inlay techniques were so successful that they were eventually used to decorate entire metal doors of some important buildings, including mosques.

The Islamic world did not have access to the fine clay required to make real porcelain, so Islamic craftsmen imitated Chinese porcelain by covering ordinary ceramics with opaque white or off-white glazes. This they sometimes decorated using tin oxide.

Since they could not compete with the quality of the ceramic itself, Islamic potters now experimented with various forms of

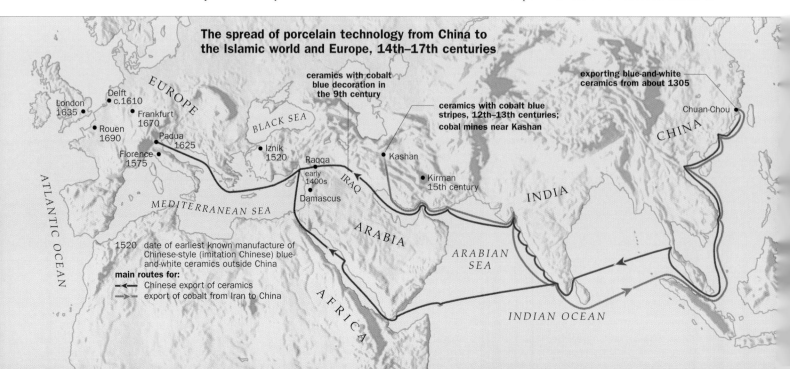

The spread of porcelain technology from China to the Islamic world and Europe, 14th–17th centuries

ceramics with cobalt blue decoration in the 9th century

ceramics with cobalt blue stripes, 12th–13th centuries; cobal mines near Kashan

exporting blue-and-white ceramics from about 1305

London 1635

Delft c.1610

Frankfurt 1670

Rouen 1690

Padua 1625

Florence 1575

Iznik 1520

Raqqa early 1400s

Damascus

Kashan

Kirman 15th century

Chuan-Chou

EUROPE

BLACK SEA

IRAQ

MEDITERRANEAN SEA

ARABIA

AFRICA

ARABIAN SEA

INDIA

CHINA

ATLANTIC OCEAN

INDIAN OCEAN

1520 date of earliest known manufacture of Chinese-style (imitation Chinese) blue-and-white ceramics outside China

main routes for:
◄— Chinese export of ceramics
—► export of cobalt from Iran to China

decoration, including carved or embossed surfaces and the development of dramatic new glazes. These were soon in advance of anything seen before in the Middle East and were often technologically ahead of the Chinese, who were admired as the greatest potters in the world. These techniques then filtered into Europe, most notably into Renaissance Italy with its *majolica* ceramics.

The most striking of these new techniques were luster and the use of cobalt to produce brilliant blue patterns. Ironically, the cobalt needed to manufacture the famous Chinese blue and white ceramics came from Islamic Iran, having first been used as a glaze in ninth century Iraq. Luster, which gave a humble clay plate the appearance of polished metal, was also developed in Iraq in the ninth and tenth centuries during the golden age of Abbasid civilization. It used silver and copper oxide during a second low temperature firing of the ceramic. Several metallic colors could be made, although gold was most popular. The technique then spread to Syria, Egypt, and Iran.

Another technique that allowed greater control when drawing on the surface of a piece of pottery was called slipware. Here slightly raised lines of very wet clay were added to the surface to stop the colors running. The entire pattern was fixed beneath a clear glaze.

INNOVATION AND EXPERIMENTS

In the 12th and 13th centuries, under the rule of the Seljuk Turks, other new glazes were invented that permitted potters to draw or color very detailed patterns and realistic scenes on their ceramics. They also incorporated a greater variety of colors.

This *minai* ware sometimes represented well-known stories like the Persian *Shahnamah* epic and were probably influenced by an established tradition of wall-painting, although on a much smaller scale. It is interesting to note that book illustration from this period and later seems to have been similarly influenced by wall-painting.

Kashan ware was the last major development during the medieval period, appearing in the 13th and 14th centuries. It combined multi-colored glazes and luster, being used not only for portable ceramics but

also for architectural tiles. As a result large areas of a building could appear to have a metallic surface. Meanwhile in later medieval Granada, far to the west, Málaga became a significant center for the manufacture of luster, much of it exported to western Europe. A rival center then developed in Valencia, in the Christian Kingdom of Aragon, although the majority of its potters were either Muslims or recent converts from Islam. It was here that a tradition of European luster ceramics really began.

Back in the Middle East, some of the Turkish states of Anatolia emerged as centers of fine ceramics manufacture. Their earliest designs incorporated strongly Mongol-Iranian and Chinese patterns, and it was from these that the superb school of early Ottoman Turkish ceramics subsequently developed.

Above: Silver-inlaid bronze doors of the Mosque of Hassan, 1356–9, Cairo, Egypt.

Cairo, Mother of the World

Although the Islamic conquerors moved the capital of Egypt from Alexandria to the area of Cairo, they left Old Cairo to the Coptic Christians and Jews, constructing a new town for themselves to the northeast.

Below: The Khanqah of Baybars II, dating from 1310, stands amid modern street markets.

A settlement had existed in what is now Cairo since before the Arab-Islamic conquest of Egypt in the seventh century. The southern quarter now known as Old Cairo was a fortified Byzantine town containing many churches, several of which

Right: Old Cairo with its teeming, narrow streets often hides its treasures from the visitor. Here, the Mosque of al-Mu'ayad, built 1415–21, towers above the smoke of numerous workshops.

still exist. Cairo in the Mamluk period was the true "City of the Arabian Nights." It was here that the extraordinary collection of stories called *The Thousand and One Nights* was written in the form known today. Many of these stories date back hundreds of years but the *Tales of the Arabian Nights* beloved by children and adults are mostly set in a world that reflects that of Mamluk Cairo and the surrounding countries.

The *Arabian Nights* were scorned by the educated elite of their day and are still not regarded as worthy of serious study by most Muslims. Yet they provide a clearer picture of everyday life, attitudes, costume, and customs in Mamluk Egypt than is available for practically any other medieval country.

When the Islamic conquerors constructed their new city, they called it al-Fustat, "The Tent," or Misr, the modern Arabic name for Egypt itself. Over the following centuries new settlements extended this city north and east. In 1168 the suburb of al-Fustat itself was burned to deny it to invading crusaders, and today most of it remains a dusty wilderness of interest only to dogs and dedicated archaeologists.

Triumphant city

While Old Cairo remained as a largely non-Muslim southern extension of the city, the heart of medieval Cairo eventually filled the area between an aqueduct running from the Nile to the Citadel, the Citadel itself, the fortified northern wall of the 10th–11th century Fatimid Palace-City of al-Kahirah (Cairo, meaning "the triumphant"), and the old bed of the Nile to the west.

Nevertheless, even before the Fatimids created al-Kahirah their predecessors had already founded suburbs north of al-Fustat. For example al-'Askar or "the Cantonments" was created after the Abbasid caliphs overthrew the Umayyads in 750, while al-Katai or "the Ward" was founded in 870. Al-Kahirah itself was laid out in 969.

Thus Cairo gradually grew in a northeasterly direction, as it continues to do today. Several monuments survive from these earlier periods, some of them wonderful pieces of architecture, but medieval Cairo owes its skyline and general character to those Mamluk sultans who ruled from the mid-13th century until 1517.

Meanwhile something else was happening to the west, where the bed of the Nile gradually shifted away from the medieval city. During the early 14th century a large pool left by the retreating river became a sort of pleasure lake surrounded by palm trees and partially covered by yellow water lilies. Charming palaces were built for the rich and powerful around what came to be known as the Ezbekiya Lake. Ordinary people also relaxed on hot summer evenings, in boats and listening to music.

The flat land between Lake Ezbekiya and the new bed of the Nile was often flooded by the rising river and was consequently very fertile, soon being covered with gardens, orchards, and bean fields. Bulaq developed as a bustling river port and some way upstream, facing the island of Rawda, another separate quarter developed, mainly consisting of fine palaces set in great gardens.

Mamluk Cairo, although it had its slums and poverty, was one of the most beautiful cities of the Mediterranean world, and its architecture could compete with the finest to be seen anywhere.

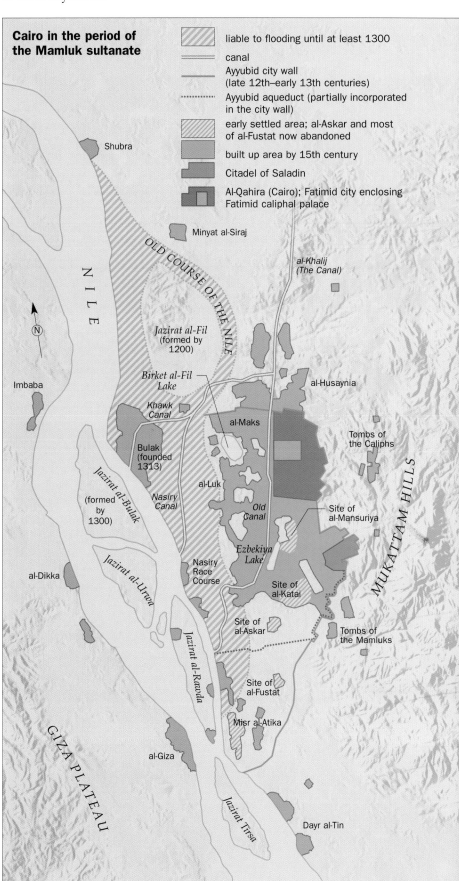

Cairo in the period of the Mamluk sultanate

- liable to flooding until at least 1300
- canal
- Ayyubid city wall (late 12th–early 13th centuries)
- Ayyubid aqueduct (partially incorporated in the city wall)
- early settled area; al-Askar and most of al-Fustat now abandoned
- built up area by 15th century
- Citadel of Saladin
- Al-Qahira (Cairo); Fatimid city enclosing Fatimid caliphal palace

Textiles as Treasure

Textiles and rugs were manufactured in many parts of the medieval Islamic world, Egypt among the most important centers of production. Ironically, Islamic textiles were popularized in the west by crusaders returning home.

Below: Men rinse red-dyed wool hanks next to an old bridge, near Arak in modern-day Iran, where Persian carpet-making remains an important craft.

The making of knotted pile and flat-woven *kilim* type rugs was primarily a Turkish and Iranian artform. Rugs were, after all, very suitable furnishings for nomadic peoples who inhabited regions of the world where temperature and climate swung between extremes of heat and cold.

Within the Islamic world, Transoxania, northern Afghanistan, Iran, and Turkey became most famous for their rugs. All had, of course, been settled by Turkish tribal peoples during the course of the Middle Ages and as these Turks gradually spread westward, so new centers of production developed.

Woven carpets were made in some of these regions in pre-Islamic times; Chinese records mentioned those of Sassanian Iran in the late sixth and early seventh centuries, shortly before the Islamic conquest. However, the oldest surviving rug was found by archaeologists in the Altai Mountains of southern Siberia, close to what is now Mongolia. This is the famous Pazyryk Rug which dates from about 500 BC and is now in the Hermitage Museum in St. Petersburg. Where it was made is a matter of debate, with some experts suggesting that the Pazyryk Rug came from Iran, while others maintain that it was made in central Asia.

Its pale blues, beiges, and yellows are very similar to those of rugs made in the medieval period. Even today, woolen rugs using traditional or natural dyes include a similar color range. More remarkably, perhaps, the overall design concept of the Pazyryk Rug is similar to much later carpets. In fact rug-making was a conservative artform in which the technologies available to Turkish tribal weavers inhibited major changes.

REFLECTING NATURE IN FABRIC

Many Islamic peoples and their non-Islamic neighbors saw the carpet as a way of bringing the image of a garden indoors or into a tent. The technique of weaving using brightly colored wools also lent itself to this idea. Persian poets in particular combined the image of the colorful carpet and the garden, as well as shady trees,

Persian and Turkish carpet manufacture in the Middle Ages

Urganj
Isfijab
Bukhara
Samarkand
Badakhshan
Balkh
Kabul
Ersinjan
Nishapur
Konya
Rayy
Mosul
Hamadan
Qayin
Baghdad
Isfahan
Damascus
Tustar
Kirman
Istakhr
Cairo
Shiraz
Medina

● major center of rug or carpet-making

running water, fruit, and the company of beautiful women, to conjure up a picture of paradise—or at least of its approximation here on Earth.

Images of gardens and flowers were incorporated into the designs of many rugs, particularly Persian carpets when compared to those made by Turkish peoples. Although there is no clear demarcation line between the Persian and the Turkish carpet, Persian weavers tended to use more flowing and sometimes more naturalistic designs. The more traditional Turkish weavers generally relied on abstract or highly stylized patterns and geometric shapes. To some extent this reflected differences in taste, but they were also rooted in available technology. A weaver working in a city could, for example, have a larger and more sophisticated loom than a tribal weaver working outside a tent. Nevertheless, such an argument must not be overstated.

Highly stylized and abstract designs were used by urban Turkish weavers in the great centers of Bukhara and other Transoxanian cities, and also by Persian weavers in the cities of Iran. Different attitudes toward naturalistic representations of living things among Sunni and Shi'a Muslims are unlikely to have had any impact during the medieval period, although this may have been significant in later centuries when Shi'a

Islam became the state religion of Iran.

Carpets are believed to have been taken back home by crusaders in the 12th and 13th centuries, although it seems unlikely that these armed pilgrims were the first to carry such items to western Europe. Nevertheless the crusader period was characterized by a growing taste for Islamic novelties and designs in Europe, and several aspects of Islamic art and architecture influenced European tastes during this period.

By the later 14th and especially the 15th century, Islamic rugs had clearly become fashionable. They were still very expensive luxury items and their incorporation in Italian Renaissance painting symbolized the importance of the scene or the person portrayed. In fact the Turkish or Persian rugs shown beneath the feet of the Virgin in Italian and Dutch Renaissance painting, and in many other scenes, provide evidence for the designs and colors of such textiles when very few medieval rugs have survived to the present day.

Above: Decorative patterning on the interior surfaces of the early 15th-century Mausoleum of Barquq in Cairo bear a strong resemblance to those used in many Islamic carpet designs.

Above left: A late 9th–early 10th-century textile fragment depicts a seated man with a cup, a very traditional and ancient Turkish motif.

Failure of an Elite

Following the Ottoman conquest of Constantinople in 1453, the sultan Mehmet the Conqueror sent news of his victory to Islamic rulers. His message to the sultan in Cairo included a coded challenge to the Mamluks' assertion that they were the primary defenders of Islam.

Above: "The Arrival of the Venetian Ambassadors at Mamluk Damascus" by the school of Bellini was painted in the 16th century. Having encountered Ottoman hostility, the mercantile republic of Venice had good reason to make common cause with the Mamluks.

Right: The fort of Sultan Qayt Bay stands on the shore at Alexandria.

In his message to the sultan in Cairo, Mehmet the Conqueror described himself as the "Defender of the Islamic Frontier," addressing the Mamluk ruler merely as the "Defender of the Islamic Holy Places"—namely Mecca and Medina in Arabia. In 1481 Cem, son of Mehmet, arrived in Mamluk Syria, seeking sanctuary after an unsuccessful bid for the Ottoman throne.

Mamluk Sultan Qayt Bay invited Cem to Cairo, and the following year he returned to Ottoman territory at the head of a small army of supporters. Again Cem was defeated and this time he sought refuge with the crusading Knights Hospitaler on the island of Rhodes. It was an episode that did nothing to improve relations between Mamluks and Ottomans.

Meanwhile, as the effectiveness of the Ottoman Turkish army steadily improved, that of the Mamluk army declined. In 1483 young mamluk recruits rioted in Cairo, as their predecessors had done ten years earlier. These revolts were partly a result of non-payment of salaries by a government that was seriously short of money, and partly reflected a breakdown of both discipline and morale. By then, the Mamluk state was facing challenges on its exposed northern

frontier. This area had traditionally been where the Mamluks concentrated their greatest effort, first against the Mongols in the 13th and early 14th centuries, then against Tamerlane, and now against troublesome local Turkish rulers.

In 1483 the small state of the Dhulghadir Oghullari in southern Anatolia attacked Mamluk-held Malatya, supposedly having been urged on by the Ottoman sultan in revenge for Mamluk support of his brother Cem. A Mamluk relief army was defeated but after hard campaigning the Dhulghadir Oghullari were driven back. In the process some Ottoman troops and their regimental flags were captured, proving that the Dhulghadir Oghullari had Ottoman support.

Efforts to re-establish peaceful relations failed and in 1487 an Ottoman army invaded the Mamluk frontier province of Cilicia. Despite the ramshackle state of the Mamluk military, and its clinging to outdated tactics, an army under Grand Emir Uzbek was victorious. It was to be almost the last success enjoyed by a Mamluk army.

CHANGING TIMES

Within a few years the Mamluk sultanate was facing a completely new threat from a totally different direction. In 1498–9 Vasco da Gama sailed around South Africa and made his epic voyage to India. Seven years later Portuguese pirates started attacking Islamic merchant ships and raiding Islamic trading outposts around the Indian Ocean. In 1506 they struck the island of Socotra off the Horn of Africa, then won naval victories off the coast of India. In 1513 they attacked Mamluk territory itself, besieging the port of Suakin.

The Mamluks had long ago given up much interest in naval warfare, although they were not as landbound as sometimes suggested. However, their fleets were not very effective and a large naval squadron was also destroyed off the Cilician coast by the Knights Hospitaler in 1510.

To face this new challenge the Mamluks and Ottomans briefly attempted to co-operate, but achieved nothing. Instead the Ottoman sultan decided that the Mamluks were a spent force. Not only could they be defeated, but they should be toppled from power for the good of Muslims as a whole.

In 1514 the Mamluk garrison in Aleppo mutinied. In 1516 the Ottomans invaded Syria, defeating the Mamluk army and killing the Mamluk sultan al-Ghawri.

The following year the Ottoman sultan Selim the Grim invaded Egypt and destroyed the last Mamluk army at Raidaniya on the northeastern outskirts of Cairo. The Mamluks resisted for over three months but there was no escaping the fact that the end of their era had come, and their defeat marked the end of the Middle Ages for the Islamic world.

Above: Mamluk cannon captured by Ottoman Turks in the late 15th–early 16th centuries are displayed at the Askeri Muzesi, Istanbul.

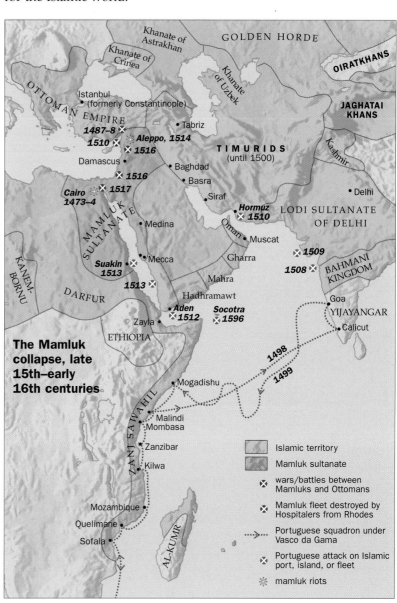

The Mamluk collapse, late 15th–early 16th centuries

Islamic territory

Mamluk sultanate

wars/battles between Mamluks and Ottomans

Mamluk fleet destroyed by Hospitalers from Rhodes

Portuguese squadron under Vasco da Gama

Portuguese attack on Islamic port, island, or fleet

mamluk riots

CHAPTER NINE

Islam in the East

The forgotten frontier

During the early eighth century, as part of the Umayyad caliphate's policy of taking over all the territory which had once formed part of the Sassanian empire, Arab-Islamic armies were sent to campaign in some of the most difficult terrain they had ever faced. These were the huge mountains and plunging valleys of what is now the western part of Pakistan, Afghanistan, and the high eastern provinces of the ex-Soviet republics of central Asia.

One of the most daunting regions of all was the mountainous desert where today Iran, Afghanistan, and Pakistan meet. In addition to the difficulties posed by climate and geography, the Islamic armies were now up against very fierce foes. Whereas the majority of the population of the central and western provinces of the old Sassanian empire were Zoroastrians, those of the east were Buddhists, Hindus, and pagans.

The Zoroastrians, like the mercantile Buddhists of Transoxania, put up stiff resistance but then recognized that the Sassanian empire was a thing of the past, and largely accepted Islamic rule. In the wild eastern frontier zones of Afghanistan, where Sassanian authority had already collapsed before the arrival of Islam, warlike and largely Buddhist tribal peoples fought hard and long against the Muslim Arab newcomers.

One of the most remarkable of these Umayyad campaigns was the invasion of Sind, in the southernmost province of what is now Pakistan, during 712 and 713. It was commanded by Mohammed Ibn Qasim al-Thaqafi and involved an epic march across the deserts of Mukran to the river Indus.

Half a century later the Abbasid caliph launched a naval campaign in the same direction. On this occasion a large fleet sailed down the Persian Gulf from Iraq carrying almost 9,000 troops to destroy a pirate lair at Barabad.

CONVERSION AND ASSIMILATION

Once Islamic rule had been established along the lower reaches of the Indus it seems that the local Buddhist minority of what became the provinces of Multan and Mansura cooperated with their new Arab rulers more willingly than did the Hindu majority. This led to the gradual absorption of the Buddhist population which also disappeared in neighboring Afghanistan. The great traveler al-Biruni could find no trace of Buddhism when he visited Sind in the mid-11th century.

It is interesting to note that Tibet, having recently been converted to Buddhism, also entered a period of belligerent expansion in the seventh century, although in a northerly direction. After a brief confrontation between Tibet and the caliphate, these two powers—Buddhist and Islamic—were generally at peace.

The Arab-Islamic conquest of Sind re-established the ancient link between Iraq and the Indus valley, the two great river-based civilizations of western Asia, but from the eighth to tenth centuries Mansura and Multan seemed to slip into obscurity. In reality, however, they flourished in relative peace as economic, trading, and intellectual centers, avoiding most of the tensions and civil wars that dominated so much of the history of the rest of the medieval Islamic world.

By the ninth century caliphal control had became tenuous and instead of being governed by officials sent from Baghdad, they accepted the leadership of local families of Arab settler origin. Meanwhile Muslims and Hindus generally co-existed peacefully during these centuries.

In the tenth century Isma'ili Shi'a missionaries became active, especially around Multan, and for a brief period the *khutba* or dedication of weekly communal prayers was done in the name of the distant Fatimid caliph of Cairo. This attracted the attention of the ambitious and strictly Sunni Muslim Sultan Mahmud of Ghazna.

His powerbase was in the mountains to the northwest. Eager to prove his loyalty to the Sunni Abbasid caliph in Baghdad, Mahmud of Ghazna seized this excuse to invade Multan in 1006. Four years later he overthrew the local ruler and incorporated Multan into his expanding state.

Some time in the first half of the 11th century the southern province of Mansura fell to a Hindu Indian revival led by a Rajput clan called the Sumeras. It was, however, retaken for Islam by the Ghaznavids' even more warlike successors, the Ghurids, whose powerbase was again in the mountains of what is now Afghanistan.

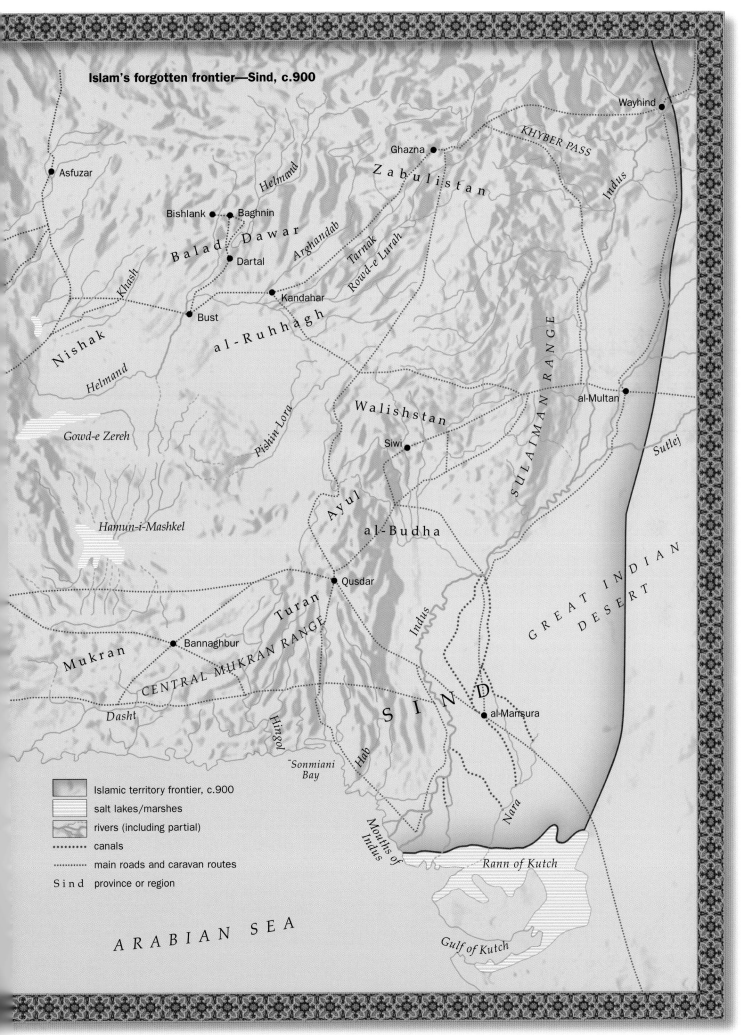

Islam's forgotten frontier—Sind, c.900

Wayhind

KHYBER PASS

Asfuzar

Ghazna

Z a b u l i s t a n

Helmand

Bishlank

Baghnin

B a l a d

D a w a r

Dartal

Arghandab

Tarnak

Rowd-e Lurah

Indus

Khash

Kandahar

Bust

a l - R u h h a g h

Nishak

Helmand

Walishshtan

al-Multan

SULAIMAN RANGE

Gowd-e Zereh

Siwi

Sutlej

Hamun-i-Mashkel

A y u l

a l - B u d h a

G R E A T   I N D I A N

D E S E R T

Qusdar

Indus

Turan

Mukran

Bannaghbur

CENTRAL MUKRAN RANGE

S I N D

al-Mansura

Dasht

Hingol

Hab

Nara

Sonmiani
Bay

Mouths of
Indus

Rann of Kutch

	Islamic territory frontier, c.900
	salt lakes/marshes
	rivers (including partial)
······	canals
······	main roads and caravan routes
Sind	province or region

Gulf of Kutch

A R A B I A N   S E A

Out of Afghanistan

Between the mid-eighth and late tenth centuries, the caliphate's eastern borders, facing Tibet and what would become northern Pakistan and India, remained largely unchanged. Over the centuries, these neighboring cultures and religions of Buddhism and Hinduism had a subtle but lasting effect on the Islamic empire.

Below: Oriental cultural and artistic influences moved westward, as this ceramic elephant of the 12th–13th centuries found at Rayy (Tehran) indicates.

Even the rise and fall of various provincial dynasties within the eastern part of the Islamic world had little impact on the stability of the frontier. Within the Islamic-ruled regions of what is now Afghanistan, however, major changes would take place, although it took a long time for caliphal authority to become more than merely superficial. There then followed a long period during which the warlike local tribal peoples gradually converted to Islam from Buddhism, Hinduism, and various forms of paganism.

During this poorly documented process it seems that various aspects of Buddhist mysticism had a profound impact on the growing phenomenon of Islamic mysticism, especially in the forms generally known as Sufism. In a rather different way, the Buddhist tradition of fortified monasteries and warrior-monks, seen in Tibet and far to the east in Japan, probably contributed to the emergence of the Islamic *ribat*.

Here, religiously motivated volunteers spent time, or indeed their whole lives, in prayer, meditation, and the defense of the Islamic frontier. Such *ribats* were soon seen along the frontier with the Byzantine empire, on the North African coast facing Christian pirates, and in al-Andalus where they faced the Spanish Reconquista.

Back in the east, during the confusion that accompanied the decline of the Samanid dynasty, Alptigin, a senior Turkish military officer of *ghulam* or slave-recruited origin, established himself in Ghazna. From here Alptigin and his followers raided the Hindu Indian principalities further east.

This proved so lucrative that Ghazna and its new Ghaznavid rulers became strong and wealthy enough to challenge neighboring Islamic governors. Although this achieved some success, Mahmud of Ghazna (998–1030) decided that the future of his dynasty lay in India. Having secured his northern frontier with several victories over Islamic rivals, Mahmud launched a series of daring campaigns that earned him the title of Hammer of the Infidels. Ghaznavid armies swept into Kashmir, down to the Indian Ocean coast where they destroyed the famous temple and "idol" at Somnath, and penetrated far across the Ganges plain.

A SLAVE ELITE

Left and below: The Qutb Minar complex is one of the oldest Islamic monuments in the Delhi area, with its tall minaret and the Court of Ala al-din.

By the time Mahmud of Ghazna died, his domain was the most impressive seen in the eastern Islamic world for centuries, while his army was the most efficient of its day. Under Mahmud's son, however, the eastern part of this fragile empire fell to the newly arrived Seljuk Turks.

its military power crumbled, until the last of the Ghaznavids was overthrown by another warlike dynasty, the Ghurids.

Ghur was a poor, remote, and very mountainous region of Afghanistan which had long been famous for exporting fine quality iron armor, and the soldiers to use it. Despite being nominally part of the caliphate, the population of Ghur had clung tenaciously to paganism well into the 11th century.

During the 12th century, as the power of the Ghaznavids faded and that of the Seljuk Turks made little local impact, a local family rose to prominence. These were the Shansabanis. When the Great Seljuk sultanate in Iran in turn declined, the Shansabanis were able to carve out their own independent realm, eventually replacing the Ghaznavids but continuing their tradition of aggressive warfare against the "infidel" Hindu princes of northern India.

After 1059 a peaceful arrangement was achieved with the Seljuks, enabling the Ghaznavids to once again concentrate on their Indian territories. Yet there would not be much more expansion. Instead the Ghaznavid court became a brilliant center of Persian-Islamic culture. This remained while

Again like the Ghaznavids, these Ghurids as they were now known could not resist attempting to expand westward against their fellow Muslims. They largely failed and so focused on India. The last Ghurid sultan was overthrown in 1215 by the same ambitious Khwarazmshah, Jalal al-Din, who would soon be conquered by the Mongols.

Nevertheless, the Ghurid military leadership in northern India remained. These men were of Turkish *ghulam* or mamluk origin and, having survived a subsequent Mongol onslaught, became known as the Slave Kings of Delhi.

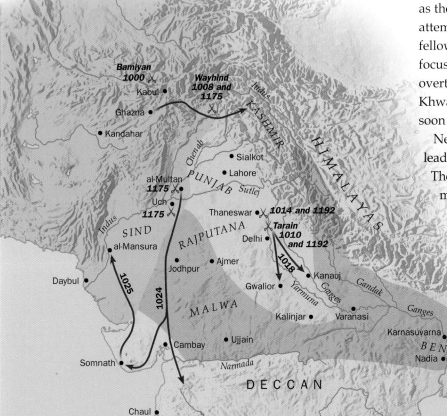

Legend:
- Islamic territory, c.1000
- Ghaznavid conquests, 1000–1186
- Ghurid conquests, 1186–1215
- main raids by Sultan Mahmud of Ghazna

The Mongols Become Muslims

Muslims had no real experience of being ruled by non-believers. Those in the east would have been shocked by non-Muslim conquerors, but the Mongols were not even recognized People of the Book.

Below: A glorious mosaic decoration adorns the drum and dome of the palace of Tughata Beg Khatun at Kunya Urgench, Turkmenistan in c.1370.

When the Mongols conquered the eastern half of the Islamic world in the 13th century they took over regions where people were primarily identified by religion rather than ethnic origin. Here Islam was, of course, the dominant faith, while other Peoples of the Book, such as Christians, Jews, and Zoroastrians, had complete freedom of worship. Although many Mongols were Buddhist and a small minority were Christian, the great majority are believed to have been shamanists, followers of tribal cults, which made them pagan in Islamic eyes.

Islam—Buddhism had a widespread impact. Buddhist monks arrived from as far away as Tibet and China, erected pagodas decorated with religious paintings and statues, and even excavated cave-temples in northwestern Iran. These were later obliterated, almost without trace, but the impact of Buddhist and Chinese art on those of Islamic Iran and some neighboring regions remained. In the late 13th century, Buddhists from India brought the techniques of yoga mysticism and further influenced Islamic sufi mysticism.

Meanwhile Jews and all Christians were favored by the early Il Khan rulers to such an extent that the subsequent conversion of the Il Khanids to Islam was followed by an anti-Christian backlash. In fact the close alliance that developed between several Christian communities, including the Armenians with their Mongol conquerors, would eventually do terrible damage to Christianity in the Middle East.

DIFFICULT TRANSITION

Some Mongols had converted to Islam even before Hülegü, the first of the Il Khan dynasty, invaded Iraq and devastated Baghdad. Hülegü's son Tëgüdur then converted to Islam soon after he came to the throne in 1282, but his Mongol followers were not ready for such a move, and his conversion resulted in civil war.

Not until Ghazan became Il Khan ruler and publicly proclaimed his Muslim faith did Islam become the official religion of the state. This was followed by a fierce anti-Buddhist backlash. Temples were destroyed and idols dragged through the streets, while Buddhist lamas and monks either had to convert or leave the country.

The Mongols went on to rule much of the Islamic world for many decades. During these years their alien culture had a profound influence on many aspects of life in Transoxania, Iran, Iraq, Turkey, the Caucasus, and those parts of the western steppes that had become Islamic by this period.

Under the first Il Khanid Mongol rulers of Iran—before the dynasty converted to

Not all Mongols converted to Islam at once, yet the die had been cast and the gradual assimilation of the invaders into

Islamic-Iranian society became inevitable. Although they remained largely nomadic for many decades, the Mongol elite developed close relations with the urban and agricultural population, just as the Seljuk Turks had done before them, and during the 14th century the Mongols of Iran lost their separate identity. Nevertheless a Mongol tribal or family origin remained a source of great prestige for well over a century.

The Jagatai Mongols, whose Khanate included part of Afghanistan, all of Transoxania, part of Chinese Turkestan, and territory extending to the frontiers of Mongolia, resisted assimilation by Islam despite the fact that most of their subjects had been Muslim for centuries. In fact when the Jagatai Khan Tarmashirin converted to Islam and adopted the name Ala al-Din, the strongly anti-Islamic Mongol tribes in the eastern half of the Khanate rebelled and killed Tarmashirin. This was soon followed by the disintegration of the Jagatai state.

Further west the Blue Horde, which later came to be known as the Golden Horde, was the first Mongol state to adopt Islam. It soon developed close relations with the Mamluk sultanate of Egypt, but the conversion of Blue Horde tribesmen remained only skin-deep for generations, and it was not until the mid-14th century that this westernmost Mongol Khanate could be called Islamic.

The White Horde, whose ill-defined state covered much of western Siberia, also included many nominal Muslims. Again, however, the state itself did not officially become Islamic until after it had been united with the Blue Horde to create a vast late medieval state known as the Golden Horde.

Below: An illustration from a late 14th-century manuscript shows a scene of cavalry combat and infantrymen, probably Mongol or Aq Qoyunlu, in Iraq, Iran, or Azerbaijan.

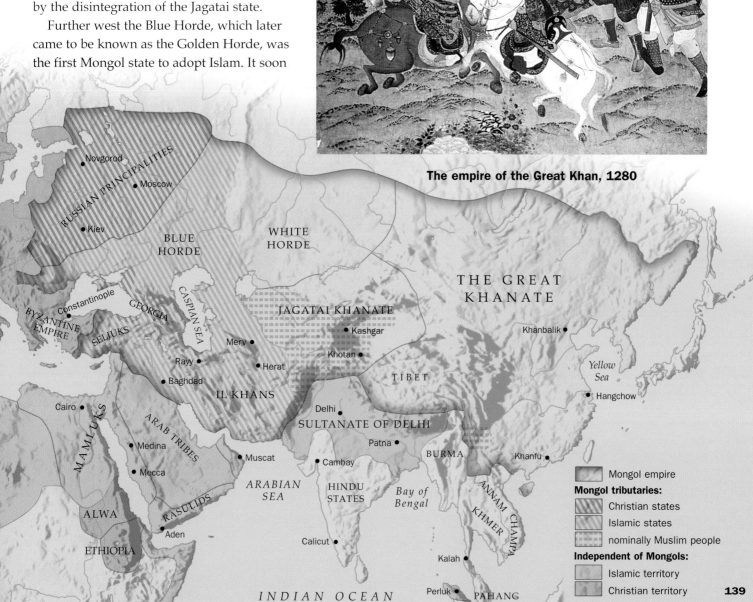

The empire of the Great Khan, 1280

139

Tamerlane

The name became a synonym for cruelty, despite the fact that Tamerlane was a man of considerable culture, genuine intelligence, and supreme skill as a military commander. Known in the Islamic world as Timur-i Lenk, he claimed to be a descendant of Genghis Khan.

Right: A stone quarter arc showing degrees of elevation in a stepped pit at the astronomical observatory of Ulugh Beg, Samarkand, mid-15th century.

Timur's conquests, late 14th–early 15th centuries

Timur's empire at greatest extent

other Islamic territory

Christian territory

campaigns:

→ 1371
┅┅▶ 1375–6
·······▶ 1381–4
→ 1386–8
┅┅▶ 1391–2
→ 1392–6
·······▶ 1398–9
→ 1399–1404

Tamerlane was born in 1336 into the Barlas clan, which dominated a small region south of Samarkand. These Turks or Turko-Mongols were members of the military elite of the Jagatai Khanate. In an extraordinary series of ruthless campaigns, Tamerlane and his army overran large areas of central Asia, Russia, Iran, the Middle East, and India, and only Tamerlane's death in 1404 stopped the Mongols from invading China. These wars were marked by savage massacres and cruelties that even exceeded those of his Mongol predecessors.

Another feature of Tamerlane's epic conquests was the fragility of the state he created. Having been born and risen to power in the borderland between the nomadic steppes of central Asia and the settled, urbanized lands of Transoxania, Tamerlane was a man of both cultures. His state and his highly effective army were similarly mixed. Even when it came to the legal system, Tamerlane relied on two traditions; the Mongol *yasa* of Genghis Khan and the *sharia* religious law of Islam.

The behavior seen in Tamerlane's nomadic but sumptuous court was again a strange mixture of Islamic and pagan Turko-Mongol traditions. For example, only Christians were allowed to drink wine but Tamerlane's courtiers regularly got drunk on other alcoholic drinks not made from grapes.

Although a nomad at heart and wreaking appalling damage to the fragile irrigation-based agricultural systems of his enemies,

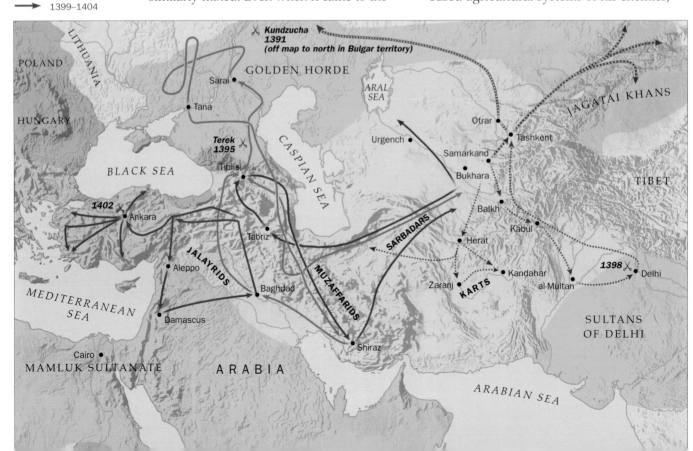

Tamerlane is said to have been interested in farming.

CONSTANT WARFARE

Despite the apparent sophistication of the administration Tamerlane put in place, his empire failed to take root in conquered territories even during his own lifetime. He had to reconquer many provinces more than once and was never able to consolidate his hold much beyond his own homeland of Transoxania. His son, Shah-Rukh, re-established control and may in fact have been a more successful state-builder than Tamerlane himself. Other descendants were also brilliant rulers, fine generals, and famous patrons of the arts, yet they were unable to build anything permanent on Tamerlane's fragile foundations. Nevertheless, the Timurid dynasty survived until the end of the 15th century. It made cities like Herat, Bukhara, and above all Samarkand major centers of late medieval Islamic architecture, arts, crafts, literature, and even scientific discovery.

The Timurid period was similarly impressive in manuscript painting. Little seems to have been left of the rich Il Khanid Mongol school of painting when Shah-Rukh came to the throne. So he sent agents to collect what still existed. This he ordered to be copied and in some cases enlarged to ensure its survival. The true Timurid style of manuscript painting, however, resulted from a different tradition. This was the indigenous Persian school which developed in southwestern Iran and Iraq following the fragmentation of the Il Khanid empire. Inspired by such earlier work, a new school of painting was established in Timurid western Iran. This in turn was followed by another center at Herat in northern

Afghanistan that eventually became the true home of what art historians call the classical Timurid court style.

Less well-known but equally superb were the decorative arts of the Timurid period. They included astonishingly fine leather bookbinding, inlaid metalwork, larger forms of cast bronze metalwork, woodcarving, and a style of jade carving which clearly betrayed strong Chinese influence.

In many ways Timurid art represents the ultimate refinement of a creative tradition that goes back to the dawn of Islamic history. So it is a sad paradox that it was produced for a ruling dynasty founded by a man whose actions showed that he had virtually no understanding of the basic humanity of Mohammed's message.

Above: Although Timurid architecture was influenced by buildings of previous 14th-century eastern Islamic dynasties, what makes it particularly striking is the sheer abundance of surviving monuments, with their brilliantly colored tiles covering both domes and walls. The glazed dome of Tamerlane's mausoleum in Samarkand is a fine example.

The Far North

In 921–2 the Abbasid caliph sent an embassy to the far north, to the ruler of a little-known Turkish state whose capital lay close to the junction of the Volga and Kama rivers. These people were the Bulgars.

The Bulgars were important participants in long-distance trade from northeastern Europe to the Abbasid caliphate and the Byzantine empire. One of the senior men in the Abbasid embassy was named Ibn Fadlan, and his account of the mysterious Volga Bulgars is one of the most detailed to survive. Many if not most of these Bulgars had converted from pagan shamanism to Islam by the early tenth century, perhaps as a way of asserting a separate identity in relation to their nominal overlord, the Khazar Khanate, whose ruling elite was Jewish.

The Volga Bulgars' early history is shrouded in legend, but they were apparently descended from a branch of the Bulgar people who migrated northward from the steppes bordering the Black Sea. This had taken place when the earlier Khanate of Great Bulgaria broke up under Khazar pressure in the seventh century. Other Bulgars had migrated to the Balkans where they established the state now known as Bulgaria, while some had remained under Khazar rule.

The group that traveled north created the Volga Bulgar Khanate, which survived until it was crushed by Mongol invaders in the 13th century. Even then the tradition of an independent Turkish state in this region survived, re-emerging with the Khanate of Kazan. This eventually fell to the Russian Czar Ivan the Terrible in 1552.

Above: An iron face-mask with a small amount of inlaid silver decoration, found in the territory of the Volga Khanate. This sort of protection was used by the elite heavy cavalry horse-archers of several medieval Turkish and Mongol armies. They were also adopted in parts of the Middle East. Similar masks have been found in southern Russia, the Ukraine and in the ruins of the Byzantine Imperial Palace in Istanbul where Turks were recruited as one of the emperor's personal guard regiments.

Muslims were expelled from the city of Kazan and their mosques destroyed, to be replaced by Russian settlers and their churches. Nevertheless a Turkish-Islamic population remained in the region, regaining some autonomy under Russian rule, and today their homeland of Tatarstan is one of several largely autonomous Islamic regions within the European part of the Russian Federation.

TRADERS AND MIDDLEMEN

The old Volga Bulgar state seems to have been a tribal confederation under an overall chief or *yiltuwar*, who was more of a patriarch than a ruler. He in turn was subordinate to the Khazar *khaqan*. The Volga Bulgars also paid tribute to their Khazar overlords in the form of valuable furs and other forest produce that they obtained from their Finn and Slav neighbors or subjects.

When the Khazar state fell apart in 965, the Volga Bulgars achieved independence. This enabled their ruler to win greater authority, to adopt the Arabic title of emir, and to cement an alliance with the Abbasid

caliph. Even so the majority of the population still led a nomadic way of life, raising cattle as the primary source of income.

During the tenth century many Volga Bulgars settled down to become farmers and horse breeders. A number of small towns also appeared, some of which included substantial timber fortresses. According to one Muslim traveler, al-Istakhri, many of the people spent the winter in wooden houses and the summer in tents. Agriculture expanded to such an extent that the Volga Bulgars were soon exporting grain in substantial quantities. On at least one occasion their grain exports saved the Russian town of Suzdal from famine.

The Volga Bulgars were already experienced merchants, trading with forest peoples far to their north and sometimes using the system known as dumb barter because neither side understood the other's language. Also involved, the Russians brought furs, slaves, and iron weapons. Much of this was then re-exported to the Islamic heartlands further south, along caravan routes to the Caspian Sea and Transoxania, or down the Volga to the Black Sea.

According to the famous Palestinian geographer al-Muqaddadi, tenth century Volga Bulgar exports included an exotic variety of items: marten, sable, beaver, fox and squirrel furs, horse and goat skins, leather shoes, hats, arrows, sword blades, armor, sheep, cattle, hunting falcons, fish teeth, birch wood, walnuts, wax, honey, and slaves. In return the Volga Bulgars' most sought-after imports from the Islamic heartlands were textiles, military equipment, ceramics, and various other luxury items.

Above: The remains of a 14th-century hamam *(heated public bath) in the ruins of Bulgar. Most buildings were, however, of wood. Heated bathhouses, often known in the West as Turkish Baths, were copied by the Russians, where traditional steambaths still have much in common with both the Islamic* hamam *and the Scandinavian sauna.*

Facing: The tomb of an unknown religious or political leader is the only structure to survive intact in what had been Bulgar. Its design is similar to the gumbat *tombs of Turkish rulers in the Caucasus, parts of Iran and Turkey itself. Next to the tomb are ruins of the earlier Great Mosque. All that remains are the foundations and the minaret which, although original, has been considerably restored.*

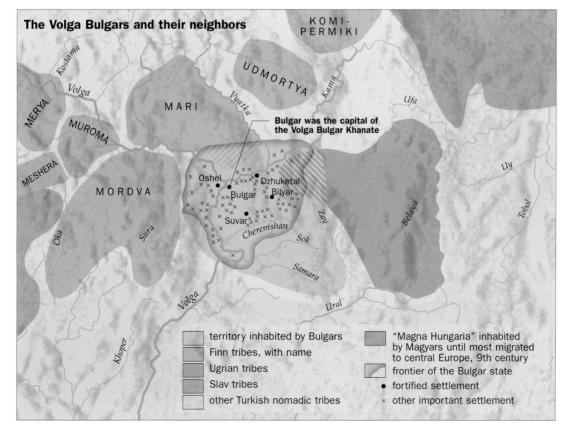

The Volga Bulgars and their neighbors

KOMI-PERMIKI

UDMORTYA

MARI

MERYA

MUROMA

MESHERA

MORDVA

Kostoma
Volga
Vyatka
Kama
Ufa
Uy
Tobol
Belaya
Zay
Sok
Samara
Cheremshan
Suvar
Oshel
Bulgar
Dzhuketal
Bilyar
Sura
Oka
Volga
Khoper
Ural

Bulgar was the capital of the Volga Bulgar Khanate

territory inhabited by Bulgars	"Magna Hungaria" inhabited by Magyars until most migrated to central Europe, 9th century
Finn tribes, with name	frontier of the Bulgar state
Ugrian tribes	• fortified settlement
Slav tribes	× other important settlement
other Turkish nomadic tribes	

Sultans of Delhi

Invasions by Ghaznavids and Ghurids exposed the military and political weakness of India's indigenous Hindu principalities. Even the warlike Rajputs of northwestern India were defeated. Despite continued efforts, the sultans of Delhi could not impose their will on the whole of India.

Following brief but devastating Mongol incursions during the first half of the 13th century, the so-called Slave Kings established their capital in Delhi. They were the first of the sultans of Delhi, who remained a significant force in Indian affairs until the 16th century. These first rulers were mamluks comparable to the slave-recruited sultans who ruled Egypt and Syria for a quarter of a millennium.

The extent of their territory fluctuated dramatically according to the power and personality of each sultan. As early as 1235 Sultan Iltutmish, for example, ruled from Sind to Bengal, although the Rajputs were still resisting Islamic domination not far from Delhi itself. Toward the end of the 13th century another group of Turks took control. They were known as the Khaljis and they were able to annex an even greater part of India, sending armies deep into the southernmost provinces.

Like the Mamluk sultans of Egypt, these Turkish rulers of Delhi dedicated their entire system of government to supporting an army that had in turn become a very effective fighting force. But unlike their Islamic predecessors in Delhi, the Khaljis welcomed Indians who converted to Islam into the administration; some of these men rising to high office.

During this period the Muslims of northern India gradually became Indianized, just as the early medieval Arab settlers had become an accepted part of the population of Sind. Such changes in attitude also had the advantage of making the Khalji sultans more acceptable to their Hindu subjects. The latter, of course, greatly outnumbered the Indian Muslims throughout the Middle Ages.

At the same time the remaining Hindu kingdoms accepted Khalji suzerainty and became the sultans' vassals. The sultans of Delhi were the first Muslims who could be called Indian rulers rather than merely rulers of India. The Khalji dynasty collapsed in 1320 when one of the sultan's favorites, a convert to Islam from Gujarat, briefly seized the throne and was said to have abandoned Islam. Within the year he was overthrown and Islamic control was restored by a Turko-Indian military leader named Tughluq Shah I. His descendants ruled until the early 15th century, and under his son Mohammed Shah II, the Sultanate of Delhi reached its greatest

Sultanate of Delhi
other Islamic areas

1212	1215	1218	1220	1220–4	1228	1236	1236
Combined Christian armies defeat Muwahhidun at Las Navas de Tolosa	Khwarazms overthrow Ghurids, but Ghurid military leadership remains in northern India	Crusaders besiege port of Damietta; Cardinal Pelagius refuses a Muslim peace offer	Crusaders' assault on the Nile ends with their surrender to the Egyptian navy	Mongol invasion of Transoxania and Iran	The Almohads are replaced by the Hafsid dynasty in Tunisia	Cordoba falls to the Christian Spanish Castilians	Mongols control Persia, Armenia, Azerbaijan, and north Mesopotamia

extent. For a few years it even included the very south of India.

POLITICAL FRAGMENTATION

Maintaining such a vast state, and the army needed to keep it under control, required huge sums of money. So taxation increased, causing widespread discontent. The sultan then decided to move his capital, including its entire population, from Delhi to a new city at Dawlatabad in the Deccan. This was a more central location and must have seemed a good idea at the time, but in the event it proved a disastrous failure.

In 1341 the autonomous Islamic rulers of Bengal broke away. Six years later the same happened in the Deccan where the powerful Bahmani kingdom emerged. Other regions followed, then in the early 15th century, the Tughluqid dynasty collapsed and the whole of Islamic India fragmented.

Nevertheless, many of these small regional dynasties remained rich, relatively powerful, and were enthusiastic patrons of art and architecture. These years also saw a coming together of Islamic and Hindu civilizations, not of course in religious terms but in many other aspects of culture. Some

Indian religious thinkers like Kabir (1440–1518) and Nanak (1469–1532) even proclaimed that there were no fundamental contradictions between Islamic and Hindu concepts of God—an idea that would have horrified some earlier religious leaders on both sides, as indeed it would today.

Above: Men rest in the shade of the Multan Fort gate, through which the tomb of Shayk Rukn-i Alam is visible, Multan, Pakistan.

Left: Dawn light silhouettes the tomb of Mohammad Shah (1433–43), third ruler of the Sayyid dynasty, in the Lodi Gardens, Delhi, India.

1237	1243	1244	1248	1248	1250	1258	1259
The Mongols unify as the Golden Horde khanate; Islam is their official religion	The Mongol defeat of Seljuk Turks at Köse Dagh ensures their dominance of Anatolia	Khwarazms sack Jerusalem then ally with Egyptians to defeat crusaders at Gaza	Seville also falls to Christian Spanish	Works begins on the Islamic Alhambra fortress in Granada, Spain	Fatimid rule of Egypt ends when the Mamluks take power	Mongol conquest of Baghdad ends the Abbasid caliphate in Iraq	An observatory is built at Maragha, Iran for the mathematician Nasir al-Din Tusi

New Thrusts

Today Indonesia has one of the largest Islamic populations in the world. Yet although Arab and other Muslim merchants had been visiting the vast archipelago of southeast Asia since the dawn of Islamic history, Islam did not take root there until the late Middle Ages.

Below: Taman Sari (Water Castle) was the place where sultans of Yogyakarta took their rest. Built mostly beneath water-pools in the early 1700s, it has a mosque, pool, and a protective bunker, reflecting the often turbulent times for the Islamic rulers as they expanded control over all of Java.

Hinduism and Buddhism had already been adopted by ruling elites throughout much of southeast Asia in the second and third centuries. This was during an expansionist period when Indian civilization profoundly influenced its northern and eastern neighbors, including China. Following an initial period of great success, Hinduism declined in southeast Asia during the seventh and eighth centuries while Buddhism continued to flourish. It would remain the dominant religion throughout most of southeast Asia, both in the islands and on the mainland, until the 15th century.

Meanwhile, Islam was largely confined to a few coastal enclaves where it remained the religion of merchant-settlers from the Middle East, plus a few local converts. Toward the end of the 13th century, however, Islam took root at the northern end of the huge island of Sumatra, in an area known as Acheh.

Gradually the Sultanate of Acheh extended its authority southward across most of the coastal regions of Sumatra, dominating other local Islamic rulers. By the start of the 16th century Acheh's merchants also seem to have controlled much of the lucrative trade with India and China. This would, of course, bring them into direct confrontation with the newly arrived Portuguese in the 16th century.

A CLASH WITH CHRISTIANITY

Malacca on the Malayan peninsula was the next state to adopt Islam as its official religion. During the 15th century the new Sultanate of Malacca developed into a powerful state on both the mainland, where they warded off Buddhist Thai (Siamese) invasions, and at sea where Malacca's tradesmen proved to be highly effective missionaries. They were probably largely responsible for the spread of Islam to many other islands; notably Java, the Spice Islands or Moluccas, and northern Borneo. In fact the advance of Islam in this part of the world would only be stopped when the Spaniards arrived in the later 16th century, introducing Christianity at the point of a sword.

The expansion of Islam in later medieval central Asia followed a different pattern. Here a Mongol elite ruled vast Khanates and were in several cases actively opposed to the expansion of Islam. Although Islam made little progress among the Mongols themselves, it continued to spread among their Turkish subjects. Many if not most Turkish tribes of the Eurasian steppes west of Lake Balkash had probably adopted Islam by the end of the 14th century—in many cases only superficially. The Uighur Turks of Sinkiang in what is now Chinese central Asia had already converted to Islam by the mid-12th century.

The Mongol flood then halted or slowed further conversion for a while. Then, from the 15th century onward, another two major Turkic peoples, the Kirghiz and Kazakhs north of the Tien-Shan mountains, gradually adopted Islam. The process took several centuries, but they would be followed by other peoples.

Muslims had been trading with and settling in the coastal ports of China since at least the eighth century. Yet these merchant communities remained small and were vulnerable to changes in the attitude of the Chinese imperial government to such "foreign guests."

Following the Mongol conquest of China were particularly numerous in Yunnan, near the southwestern frontiers of China. In subsequent centuries they would increase in number, despite occasional and horrific persecutions, although today the greatest number appear to live in the far northeast of China and Manchuria.

Islam reaches the East Indies

- Islamic, c.1500
- superficially Islamic or converting
- major centers of Islamic minorities
- Hindu, c.1500
- Buddhist, c.1500
- Christian, c.1500
- main trade routes to the East Indies and Spice Islands, along which Islam spread

in the 13th century, however, substantial numbers of Muslims from central Asia and further west arrived in the country, either voluntarily or forcibly settled there by the Mongol rulers. Such Islamic communities

CHAPTER TEN

Islam in Africa

The struggle for the Dark Continent

Sub-Saharan Africa was not isolated from the rest of the world in ancient times, and the Sahara desert, as it appears today, is relatively young. This is not to suggest that the desert was a verdant grassland, but trans-Saharan trade was well established, and iron-working technology probably reached West Africa along such routes.

Archaeological evidence shows that cattle-herding peoples who used two-wheeled chariots roamed the central and western Sahara in the first and even second millennia BC. Trade between such peoples contributed to the development of organized states, and it was this that attracted Arab and Berber merchants when Islamic civilization revived regional trade during the early medieval period. Such merchants may have controlled trans-Saharan traffic and have encouraged the building of towns as commercial centers, but many of the towns themselves had been founded before the Islamic merchants arrived.

Camels were used for transport in Egypt and North Africa before the Arab-Islamic conquests but they were not considered important. During the Islamic period, however, the single-humped camel or dromedary caused a revolution in desert warfare and trade. They became the true "ships of the desert" while the merchant caravans were like convoys that navigated the Sahara as if it were a sea.

Yet this analogy must not be taken too far. Camels and men still needed water, and so merchant caravans had to follow established routes between one oasis and the next. It was dangerous and largely pointless to stray from these established routes. As a result,

control of the vital Saharan oases and their water gave control of the trade that passed through them.

Nevertheless, increasing contact with flourishing and wealthy Islamic regions like North Africa and Egypt gave a huge boost to the towns. Most grew up in the Sahil or

steppe land along the edge of the desert, or in grasslands and open forest further south. As yet none appeared in the dense jungles that bordered the Atlantic Ocean and Gulf of Guinea.

LAND OF GOLD

In addition to considerable wealth, trade also brought new technologies, ideas, and artforms to West Africa, where the Soninke kingdom of Ghana became the dominant power. Its capital was a city also called Ghana, which is believed to have been what is now Kumbi Saleh in southeastern Mauritania.

Ghana occupied a strategic position around the southern terminals of several trans-Saharan routes, controlling access to rich gold-fields where the modern states of Senegal, Guinea, and Mali meet. These gold-fields featured so prominently in Arab accounts of West Africa that some historians have assumed these were all that the Islamic merchants were interested in. In fact trans-Saharan trade involved a great variety of commodities ranging from high value luxury items to slaves and salt—the latter being a vital ingredient for life in the parched desert.

Trade within the sub-Saharan regions was largely in the hands of local African merchants. Meanwhile the Kingdom of Ghana, like other smaller pre-Islamic states in West Africa, had its own highly developed social, political, and religious systems. In several cases these were characterized by the almost god-like status of the king. To some extent such veneration of a ruler would even survive the coming of Islam with its essentially egalitarian and democratic social ideals. Aspects of pagan ancestor worship also survived, despite the disapproval of more orthodox Muslims.

The pre-Islamic kingdom of Ghana was not overthrown as a result of conquest by the Berber Murabitin in the later 11th century, as historians used to believe. Instead Ghana probably declined in the 12th century as a result of pressure from indigenous opposition forces assisted by other Berber tribes from the southern Sahara. There was also a gradual but steady spread of Islam among the peoples of Ghana and neighboring regions during this period.

There were, of course, setbacks. For example, at the start of the 13th century the pagan Soninke (from the same tribe that dominated Ghana but who inhabited the Soso region) captured Ghana's capital. This was soon followed by the defeat of the Soso Soninke by the chief of a powerful clan in the rival Malinke people. It was his successors who then established a powerful new kingdom called Mali, which was an emphatically Islamic state.

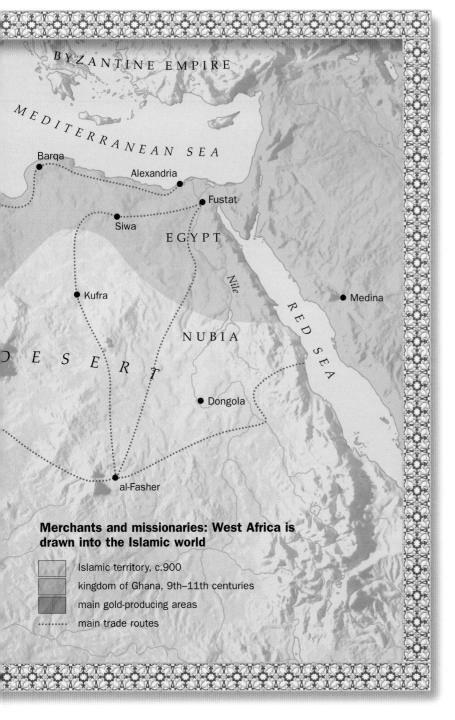

Merchants and missionaries: West Africa is drawn into the Islamic world

Islamic territory, c.900

kingdom of Ghana, 9th–11th centuries

main gold-producing areas

main trade routes

Islam in East Africa

Islamic merchants found East Africa to be a remarkably advanced region, with rich veins of community and commodity to exploit. Islamic trading posts rose and fell, spreading the word as goods and money changed hands.

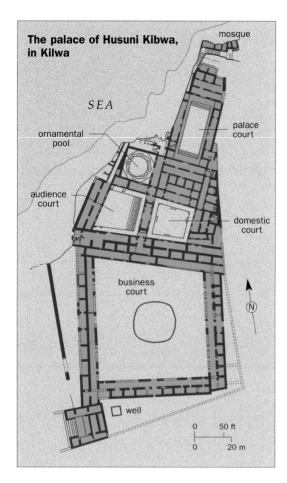

The palace of Husuni Kibwa, in Kilwa

SEA

ornamental pool

audience court

mosque

palace court

domestic court

business court

N

well

| 0 | 50 ft |
| 0 | 20 m |

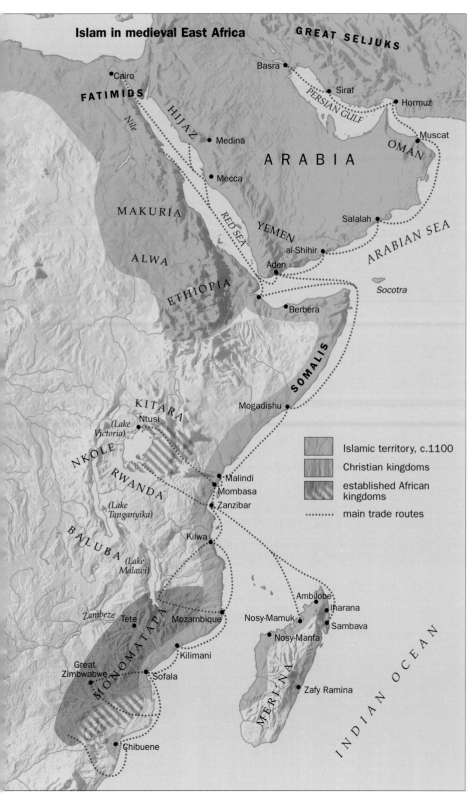

Islam in medieval East Africa

GREAT SELJUKS

FATIMIDS

Cairo

Basra

Siraf

Hormuz

HIJAZ

Nile

Medina

ARABIA

OMAN

Muscat

MAKURIA

RED SEA

Mecca

ALWA

YEMEN

Salalah

ARABIAN SEA

al-Shihir

ETHIOPIA

Aden

Socotra

Berbera

SOMALIS

KITARA

(Lake Victoria)

Ntusi

Mogadishu

NKOLE

RWANDA

(Lake Tanganyika)

Malindi

Mombasa

Zanzibar

BALUBA

(Lake Malawi)

Kilwa

Islamic territory, c.1100

Christian kingdoms

established African kingdoms

.... main trade routes

Zambeze

Tete

Mozambique

Ambilobe

MONOMATAPA

Kilimani

Nosy-Mamuk

Iharana

Sambava

Nosy-Manfa

Great Zimbabwe

Sofala

MERINA

Zafy Ramina

INDIAN OCEAN

Chibuene

When Arab and other Islamic traders arrived on the East African coast, several organized states already existed in this part of the continent. East Africa was in some respects technologically very advanced, high carbon steel having been produced around the Great Lakes and on the coast long before the early medieval period. Islamic explorers found a wealth of raw materials and trading opportunities in the region.

Nor did pre-Islamic East Africa lack contact with the wider world. Ancient Egyptian and other merchants had ventured beyond the Red Sea, while during the Hellenistic and Roman periods merchants from Egypt traveled much further. They reached at least as far as Rhapta, which was somewhere near Zanzibar on the Tanzanian coast. Arab merchants from the Red Sea, Yemen, and the Persian Gulf traded in the same area, probably in larger numbers since there was already an Arab merchant colony or community here in pre-Islamic times. Rhapta itself is even believed to have been ruled by a prince of south Arabian origin.

Even more remarkable were the voyages undertaken by sailors from what is now Indonesia in southeast Asia. They crossed

the huge expanses of the Indian Ocean to Madagascar, whose eastern coast they colonized, and to the mainland where they sold the cinnamon that was so highly valued in the Mediterranean countries.

By the ninth century the most prosperous Arab-Islamic trading post on the East African coast was Manda, close to the modern frontier between Somalia and Kenya. By the 13th century, however, Kilwa, much further south on what is now the Tanzanian coast, had become the most prominent. Here, impressive stone buildings began to replace the traditional local wattle-and-daub structures. They included the palace of Husuni Kibwa which dates from 1245. It is said to have been built for a ruler named al-Malik al-Mansur Ibn Suleiman and contains over a hundred rooms, plus courtyards, terraces, ornamental pools, vaults, and domes. Kilwa also had a large stone mosque dating from the late 12th century, whose roof was made of coral and plaster supported by wooden pillars.

The great Moroccan traveler Ibn Battuta, who visited Kilwa in 1331, described it as one of the most beautiful and well-constructed towns in the world. This was a remarkable claim, since Ibn Battuta also visited most of the rest of the Islamic world, including India and parts of central Asia, as well as China.

TRADING ACROSS A CONTINENT

While the Islamic outposts as far as Kilwa primarily traded with the African peoples between the coast and Lake Victoria, there was another and much more distant group of Islamic settlements. These stood on the coast of what is now southern Mozambique.

The best known was Sofala, beyond the estuary of the Zambeze, although archaeologists have also found evidence of an Islamic trading post near Chibuene not far from present day Maputo. One of the trading routes which linked this, the most southerly medieval Islamic outpost yet discovered, to the interior may even have

gone up the River Limpopo into what is now South Africa.

Gold was again one reason why Arab-Islamic merchants ventured so far south. Inland from their outposts at Sofala and Chibuene a powerful African kingdom had developed on the Zimbabwe plateau. Its main center was probably the extraordinary archaeological site now called Great Zimbabwe and it was presumably the powerful kingdom known at the time as Monomatapa. While this inland African state provided the Islamic communities of the coast with copper, tin, iron, and gold, Monomatapa imported Islamic and Chinese ceramics, various luxury goods, and perhaps weaponry from the coast.

The two communities flourished for centuries. Both then suffered a decline in the second half of the 15th century, Great Zimbabwe being virtually abandoned. Then, only a few decades later, the Arab-Islamic coastal population suddenly found its monopoly of maritime trade challenged by the Portuguese. They had rounded the Cape of Good Hope to reach Sofala in 1497, and from that year everything changed.

Above: During the 12th and 13th centuries, Great Zimbabwe accumulated fortunes through control of the trade routes and became a substantial trading partner with Islamic merchants. The tall walls and conical towers of the citadel were built from shaped granite blocks without the need for mortar.

Below: Coast-hugging Islamic traders used larger vessels similar to these abandoned fishing boats of traditional design and sewn construction, Qurayat, Oman.

From Cross to Crescent

Nubians and Ethiopians were converted to Christianity by the sixth century, but misfortunes on all sides resulted in intermingling with Muslims. Mamluk conquerors spread Islam further, until the Christian kingdoms fought back and the religions clashed.

Right: Early 11th-century wall-painting of a saint from the church of Abd Allah Nirqi, Nubia.

The Ethiopians were converted to Christianity during the fourth century, and the Nubian peoples south of Egypt in the sixth century. Three states then emerged in what is now the Sudan: Nobatia in the north; Makuria (Muqurra), which had its capital at Dongola and dominated the great S-bend of the Nile; and Alwa in the south, whose capital was at Soba not far from modern Khartoum. Nobatia would eventually be absorbed by Makuria to form a powerful kingdom, which remained Egypt's southern neighbor throughout most of the medieval period.

Maps of medieval northwestern Africa give the impression that Makuria, Alwa, and Ethiopia were cut off from the rest of the Christian world by the rise of Islam. In reality, however, the spread of Islam across Arabia, Egypt, and North Africa only isolated these African states from Christian Europe. It did not isolate them from the Christians of Egypt or, indeed, elsewhere in the Islamic world. Their most senior churchmen continued to be recruited from Egypt, since all these states were members of the Coptic Church. In fact for several centuries Makuria remained powerful enough to regard itself—and be regarded by Islamic rulers—as the protector of the Monophysite Church in Egypt.

The power of these Nilotic Christian kingdoms resulted from their control of the Nile as the most important trade route across the eastern Sahara. But when the Nile ceased to be a major artery of trade, the power of Makuria and Alwa declined. Other factors also played their part, including a decline in the demand for African slaves, which undermined Nubia's leading role in the slave trade.

Meanwhile several Arab tribes were virtually forced to migrate from Egypt into the Sudan during the Ayyubid period. There they intermarried with the local inhabitants. Some nomadic peoples who roamed the deserts and steppes of

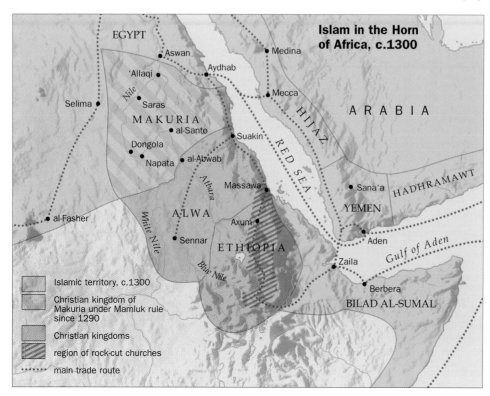

Islam in the Horn of Africa, c.1300

EGYPT
Aswan
'Allaqi
Aydhab
Medina
Selima
Saras
Mecca
MAKURIA
al-Santo
Suakin
ARABIA
Dongola
Napata
al-Abwab
Massawa
Sana'a
HADHRAMAWT
al-Fasher
ALWA
Axum
YEMEN
Sennar
ETHIOPIA
Aden
Gulf of Aden
Zaila
Berbera
BILAD AL-SUMAL
Nile
Atbara
White Nile
Blue Nile
HIJAZ
RED SEA

Islamic territory, c.1300
Christian kingdom of Makuria under Mamluk rule since 1290
Christian kingdoms
region of rock-cut churches
main trade route

central Sudan were also "Arabized" during the later medieval period and similarly converted to Islam.

Finally the new Mamluk rulers of Egypt, recognizing the weakness of the Nubian kingdoms, began to interfere in their internal affairs. Makuria accepted Mamluk suzerainty at the end of the 13th century, and kings with Islamic names soon began to be recorded. The first was Sayf al-Din 'Abd 'Allah Barshambu, a nephew of a previous Christian king named David, who was placed on the throne by the Mamluks in 1316. Nothing was, however, recorded of how the ordinary people of Nubia converted to Islam, although the process took some time.

Meanwhile the southern kingdom of Alwa remained a center of the slave trade and, like Makuria, soon suffered from Mamluk interference. In about 1500 its capital, Soba, fell to an Islamic African people known as the Funj, who subsequently dominated central Sudan.

END OF AXUM

Monophysite Christianity survived in neighboring Ethiopia, though even here it faced many challenges. The most dangerous came not from its increasingly numerous Islamic neighbors, but from an uprising by the largely pagan Agau people in the tenth century. They were led by a fearsome queen named Gudit who was probably a member of the persecuted Falasha Jewish minority. The old Christian Ethiopian kingdom of Axum, whose heartland was in the border regions of what are now Eritrea and Ethiopia, was destroyed. Consequently the center of Ethiopian civilization shifted south to a new capital at Lalibela.

For three centuries the Zagwé dynasty, founded by Gudit's now Christian descendants, dominated the country. This was the period when Ethiopia's extraordinary rock-cut churches were made. In the 13th century the Zagwé were overthrown, to be replaced by yet another Christian dynasty. Meanwhile Islam had spread in and around the Ethiopian kingdom.

In the 14th century relations between Christians and Muslims worsened when King Amde-Siyon (1314–44) embarked on a series of campaigns in an effort to make Ethiopia the dominant regional power and to control trade routes to the Gulf of Aden. In the later 15th century the balance of power changed again, with the Red Sea coastal sultanate of Adal sending raiders deep into the Christian highlands.

This was the general situation when the Portuguese appeared on the scene. The Christians welcomed them as allies, while the Muslims sought an alliance with the Ottoman Turks, who became the leading Islamic power in the Red Sea region after conquering Mamluk Egypt.

Above: A landing place on the side of the Nile at El Khandaq in Nubia is overlooked by an abandoned medieval town.

Below: An abandoned animal-powered mill at Kosha in Nubia was once used to raise the Nile waters into irrigation ditches, as the peoples of the Nile had done from pre-historic times.

An African Empire in Europe

The Sahara desert was an unknown land for early medieval Muslims, despite major changes there and in sub-Saharan West Africa as a result of contact with Islamic North Africa. The sudden emergence of the Murabitun as a powerful military force came as a surprise to their neighbors.

The Murabitun were the first Saharan Islamic movement to establish a large state. It expanded from its birthplace on the lower reaches of the Senegal river, southward toward the West African kingdom of Ghana and northward toward Morocco. The origins of the Murabitun are obscured by pious legends. It is said that the chief of the Berber Gudala tribe, whose territories covered much of modern Mauritania, made the obligatory Islamic pilgrimage to Mecca and on his return was accompanied by a Moroccan religious teacher named Abdallah Ibn Yasin. This man's preaching was so effective that a group of religiously motivated volunteers established a *ribat* fortress near the mouth of the Senegal river. Whether such a *ribat*

Below: Detail from an 11th-century Moorish carved basin showing horsemen in combat.

actually existed or not, the name Murabitun was soon given to Ibn Yasin's followers.

Like other Berbers of the western Sahara, they wore a *litham* or veil across their faces as a protection against the desert dust. The Murabitun's face-covering was a distinguishing feature, and they came to be known in the rest of North Africa and the Iberian peninsula as *al-mutalaththimun*—the "veiled men."

Murabitun armies soon advanced northward, conquering Morocco, much of Algeria, and a huge swathe of the Sahara desert. In 1062 one of their leaders named Yusuf Ibn Tashufin founded the city of Marrakesh in southern Morocco. This became the capital of the Murabitun dynasty, which Yusuf also established.

BULWARKS AGAINST CHRISTIANITY

At this time al-Andalus or the Islamic southern part of the Iberian peninsula was fragmented under numerous local rulers. Being militarily weak they felt threatened by their Christian neighbors, so some of these

1260	1261	1276	1277	1280	1282	1291	1295
New Mamluk ruler Baybars defeats the Mongols at Ayn Jalut, Palestine	Nominal Abbasid caliphate revived in Egypt under Mamluk protection	The Marinid dynasty builds the city of Fez al-Jadid next to the old Fez, Morocco	The Mamluks defeat Mongols in Asia Minor	The Silk Road is re-opened by the Mongol empire	Civil war in the Mongol empire after new Il Khan leader Tëgüdur converts to Islam	Mamluks conquer Acre and other cities; end of the Crusader States	Mongol Il Khan dynasty in Iran converts to Islam

ta'ifa rulers asked the Murabitun for help.

Responding to the challenge, the fierce African and Berber "veiled warriors" of the Murabitun inflicted a crushing defeat on the Christians at the battle of Zallaqa in 1086. Within a few decades they also took over most of the Islamic provinces of the Iberian peninsula. Murabitun African domination of al-Andalus would last until the mid-12th century.

The Murabitun saw themselves as a reformist movement, and religion remained a primary motivating force throughout their history. For example, their troops liked to capture church bells while campaigning against the Christians in Iberia; some of these bells were then converted into mosque lamps. Their armies also included large numbers of black Africans, whose appearance terrified the Spaniards until they became used to their new foes. When the Murabitun were themselves campaigning against West African armies along their southern frontiers, they reportedly suffered severe losses from their enemies' poisoned arrows, as would the first Portuguese to venture into this area in the mid-15th century.

In cultural terms, the Murabitun—despite having originated in one of the most backward and distant frontier regions of the medieval Islamic world—contributed a great deal to the Muslim realm. It was, in fact, under Murabitun and, later, Muwahhidun rule that North African architecture developed its most distinctive characteristics. Surface decoration became very lavish and there was a fascination with various elaborate forms of arch. Other arts were less original, although North African and Andalusian textiles were particularly fine.

During the early 12th century another Islamic reformist movement, based in southern Morocco and bitterly hostile to the African Murabitun, challenged them. These were the Muwahhidun, and the threat they posed in North Africa undermined the Murabitun's inability to resist Christian aggression in al-Andalus.

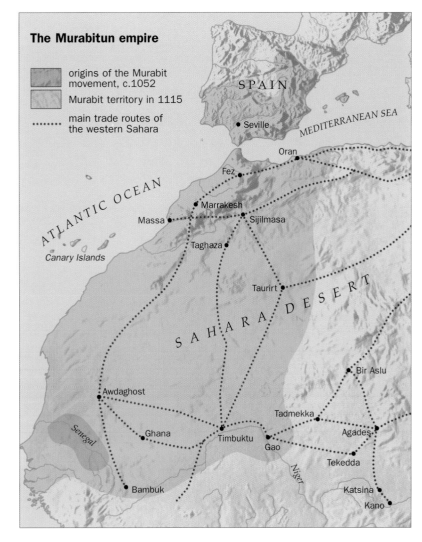

The Murabitun empire

◼ origins of the Murabit movement, c.1052

◻ Murabit territory in 1115

⋯⋯ main trade routes of the western Sahara

SPAIN
MEDITERRANEAN SEA
ATLANTIC OCEAN
Seville
Oran
Fez
Marrakesh
Massa
Sijilmasa
Taghaza
Canary Islands
SAHARA DESERT
Taurirt
Bir Aslu
Awdaghost
Tadmekka
Agades
Ghana
Timbuktu
Gao
Tekedda
Senegal
Niger
Bambuk
Katsina
Kano

In 1147 the last Murabitun ruler of Marrakesh was killed and the Muwahhidun soon crossed into the Iberian peninsula. Here, the descendants of one of the last Murabitun governors retreated to the Balearic Islands where, as the Banu Ghaniya, they clung to power until 1203. Other members of the Banu Ghaniya returned to North Africa, where they continued the struggle against the Muwahhidun until 1236.

Left: Great Mosque of Tlemsen, Algeria built by the Murabitun in the 12th century.

Gold of Mali

Following the fall of the Murabitun, no sub-Saharan Islamic states extended their rule into Europe. Instead they concentrated on controlling regional trade routes, sources of wealth such as the gold-fields, and the fertile lands along the Senegal and upper Niger rivers.

Right: Carved wooden figure of a bowman riding a horse, set on a hollow spherical support. The figure, which has been radio carbon dated to AD 945–1245, came from Djenné in Mali.

Some of the Saharan Islamic kingdoms were extremely rich, powerful, and cultured. The wealthiest was the Keita Kingdom of Mali, which replaced Ghana as the dominant power in West Africa. Its first ruler, Mari Sun Dyata, was a clan leader of the Malinke or Mandinka people who was declared *Mansa* or ruler in 1230. However it was his successors who made the new kingdom of Mali into a powerful state. Unlike Ghana, whose heartland was in the semi-desert Sahil area north of the upper

Above: The Tighanimine Gorge, which connects the Mediterranean coast to the Saharan interior through the Atlas Mountains in Algeria, is typical of the passes used by medieval Islamic traders.

Niger river, Mali's first capital is believed to have been at Niani in a more fertile region south of the Niger.

The capital of Mali moved to different cities at various times, but the kingdom itself developed strong economic, cultural, and diplomatic links with older Islamic lands north of the Sahara. These not only included the traditional links with North Africa but now also an important connection with the

Mamluk Sultanate in Egypt.

Several kings of Mali made the Hajj or pilgrimage to Mecca via Egypt. That of Mansa Musa I, who reigned from 1312 to 1337, was particularly famous because of the astonishing wealth brought by the Mansa and his retinue. This supposedly caused the price of gold to slump in Cairo's market.

TRIBAL TRADITIONS SURVIVE

The organization of Mali was supposedly based on that of Mamluk Egypt, but in reality it was rooted in West African traditions. For example, much of the east was governed by princes of the royal family, this being the heartland of Mali, while much of the west as far as the Atlantic coast remained under the control of local hereditary aristocracies.

Ibn Battuta, who lived in West Africa for some years during the mid-14th century (*see following page*) reported that the Mansa of Mali had an elite bodyguard of 300 slave-recruited soldiers. These *mamluks* are believed to have included Turks and other northerners; perhaps even some Europeans.

Despite increasingly close cultural and religious links with Islamic North Africa and Egypt, Islam was still only a veneer in the countryside of Mali. Traditional animist or pagan practices were widespread, and the local form of Islam seemed highly unorthodox to visitors from other parts of the Islamic world.

The Keita Kingdom of Mali was weakened by several disputed successions in the late 13th century. It lost the vital trading center of Timbuktu and other territories along the Saharan desert fringe, and was threatened by a new power on its eastern frontier—the Songhay, who had only recently been converted to Islam. Deprived of its outlying provinces, Mali shrank to its old Malinke tribal heartland in what are now Guinea and western Mali, where it survived until 1670.

Above: The mosque and minaret of Chinguetti, one of several small towns that sit astride the ancient western trade routes of the Sahara in Mauritania.

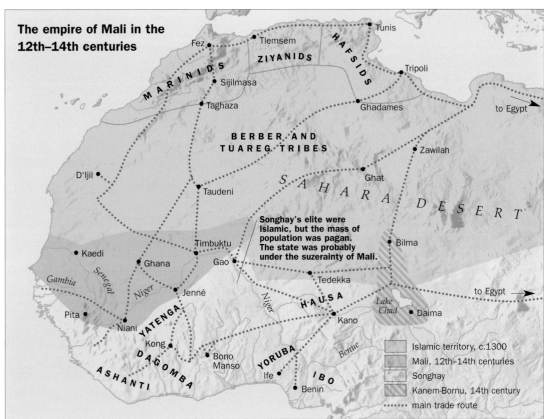

The empire of Mali in the 12th–14th centuries

Songhay's elite were Islamic, but the mass of population was pagan. The state was probably under the suzerainty of Mali.

Islamic territory, c.1300
Mali, 12th–14th centuries
Songhay
Kanem-Bornu, 14th century
main trade route

Ibn Battuta, the Greatest Traveler

Ibn Battuta covered more ground than any previous explorer and would only be outdone when Ferdinand Magellan became the first to sail around the world two centuries later. He made meticulous notes on his journeys, many of which were published in his *Travels* book.

Abu Abdullah Mohammed Ibn Battuta was born in Tangier, on the northwestern tip of Africa, in 1304. Twenty-one years later he began his extraordinary travels, intending only to visit Mecca and Medina. He journeyed far further and spent almost 29 years seeing most parts of the medieval Islamic world.

Ibn Battuta visited the Middle East, the Ukraine, southern Russia, central Asia, India, the East Indies, and even China. He also journeyed down much of the East African coast and, in 1352, set off on another journey across the Sahara to West Africa. Finally, in 1354, Ibn Battuta settled down in the Moroccan city of Fez to write his remarkable *Travels*.

With the exception of his trip to northern China, almost all of Ibn Battuta's journeys were within the Islamic world, since he had little interest in "infidel" peoples. His journeys in Africa similarly focused on the eastern coast, which had been settled by Islamic merchants since the dawn of Islam, and on sub-Saharan West Africa, where Islam was spreading rapidly by the 14th century.

Right: Interior of the Mosque of Sidi Boumedienne, built in 1338/9 in Tlemsen, Algeria.

Below: The mud-brick architecture of medieval Mali is never better exemplified than by the Grand Mosque of Jenné. The first mosque was built in the 13th century by Jenné's first Islamic ruler, although much of its fabric was faithfully restored or rebuilt in 1907. Jenné became a spiritual center for the dissemination of Islam.

In 1330 Ibn Battuta sailed down the eastern coast of Africa as far as Kilwa, where he recalled that "a merchant said that the city of Sofala is a fortnight's march from Kilwa, and between Sofala and Yufi in the land of the Limiin is a further march of a month.... Gold dust is brought from Yufi to Sofala."

Meanwhile the Islamic Kingdom of Mali

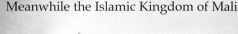

in West Africa (*see previous page*) was a powerful state that controlled the southern end of the trans-Saharan caravan routes along which gold flowed north. Mali also developed a remarkable style of mud-brick architecture which, though rooted in local African traditions, produced mosques and other buildings of extraordinary beauty, several of which survive to this day.

The spread of Islam in these regions had, however, largely been due to Berber peoples from the Sahara desert and missionaries from North Africa, many of whom had themselves been merchants. Mansa Musa I of Mali, whose visit to Cairo in 1324 had caused such astonishment because of the sheer volume of gold which his servants carried (*see previous page*), was also ruler at the time that Ibn Battuta visited Mali. By then Mali's main cities had become centers

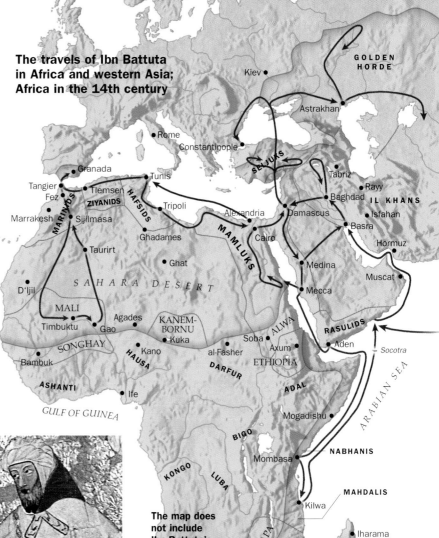

The travels of Ibn Battuta in Africa and western Asia; Africa in the 14th century

The map does not include Ibn Battuta's journeys in central Asia, India, East Indies, or China

of Islamic learning and law as well as major markets for trans-Saharan trade.

FASTIDIOUS RECORD-KEEPER

Ibn Battuta stayed seven months in Timbuktu before moving on to Gao, where he remained for a further month. At each place he noted the appearance and customs of the people, the character of their country, its animals, agriculture, and produce. He also noted how long it took to travel from one place to another (usually by camel caravan), the state and safety of the roads, and the weather he encountered.

For example at Takedda, close to the eastern frontier of Mali, Ibn Battuta stated

Above: A 14th-century painted ceiling in the Sala de los Reys of the Alhambra Palace, Granada, Spain, depicts Qadis, or Islamic judges.

that the town "exports copper to the land of the infidel [non-Muslim] blacks, and also to Zaghai and to the land of the Bornu. It is 40 days' journey from Bornu to Takedda, and the inhabitants of the country are Muslims. They have a ruler named Idris who never shows himself to his people, but speaks to his subjects only from behind a curtain."

All this Ibn Battuta subsequently included in his famous *Travels*, along with other anecdotes about his own experiences. For example he was surprised by the ferocity of a desert snowstorm that greeted him when he finally got back to the Moroccan frontier, writing that; "I have seen much snow in my travels, in Bukhara, in Samarkand, in Khurasan, and in the land of the Turks, but I have never known a more unpleasant route than this!"

The University City of Timbuktu

The Songhay kingdom replaced that of Mali as the dominant power in West Africa in the late 14th century. The Songhay made Islam an "imperial cult" to bolster their prestige among varied subject peoples. Most importantly, Timbuktu was developed as a religious and cultural center.

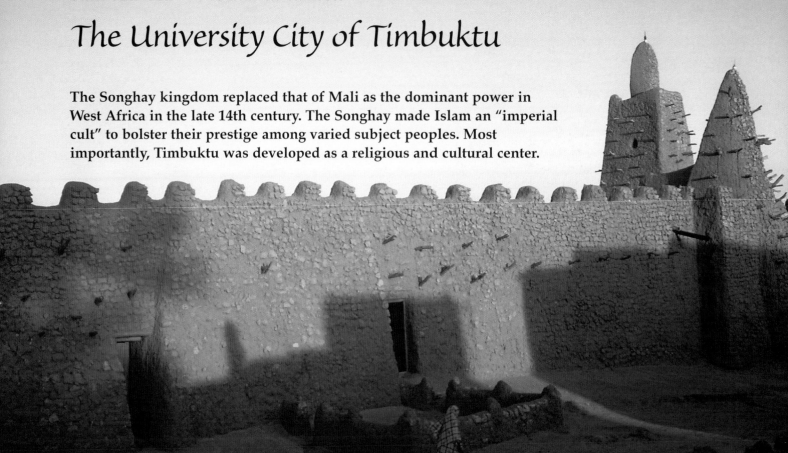

Above: The Sankore Mosque-Madrasa of Timbuktu, built at some point in the 14th–15th centuries, became a university whose fame spread beyond the boundaries of Songhay.
(See also the inset plan, facing:
A *mihrab*
B *minaret*
C *courtyard)*

The city of Timbuktu had long been one of the most important and prosperous southern terminals of the trans-Saharan caravan routes. The Songhay had been a nomadic people of mixed origin inhabiting lands along the River Niger, east of Mali. They were, perhaps, the same people who had established a state which ninth century Arab geographers knew as Gao.

Although the ruling elite of the area may have been converted to Islam as early as the 11th century, the mass of the people were—according to Ibn Battuta—still pagan 300 years later. Whether the Songhay were still subject to Mali is unclear, but within a generation or so they were certainly independent. Under a ruler known as Sonni 'Ali the Great, they built up a powerful army and a remarkable river-based naval fleet.

Some of the most striking and beautiful of the mud-brick and rubble mosques of Timbuktu were enlarged during this period, including the Great or Friday Congregational Mosque and the Sankore Mosque-Madrasa. The latter became a university, and its fame spread throughout the Sudan, Sahara, and beyond. Both buildings are characterized by the poles that protrude from their walls. These are still used as a form of permanent scaffolding so that an outer layer of mud-plaster can be regularly repaired following the sudden concentrated rain storms typical of this part of Africa.

The exploitation of new sources of gold in the Akan region, in what are now the states of Ghana and Ivory Coast, added to the wealth of Songhay. It also led to an eastward shift of the main trading routes and eventually attracted the attention of European adventurers from the coast. Modern Ghana was, of course, known as the Gold Coast under British imperial rule.

SPREAD OF CULTURE

While on pilgrimage to Mecca in 1496–7 the Songhay king Mohammed Ture was officially recognized as ruler over the entire western Sudan—a vast region stretching from Lake Chad to the Atlantic. The Songhay state had expanded at the expense of most of its

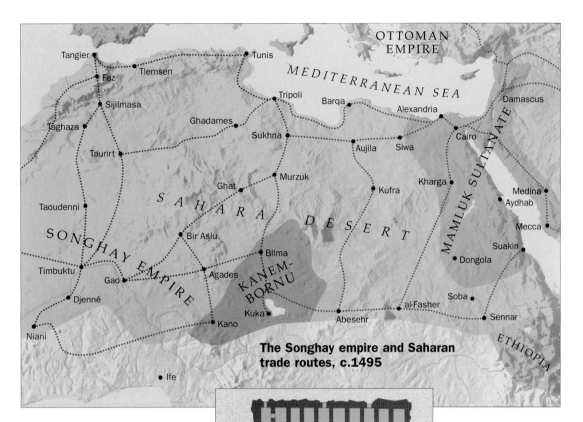

The Songhay empire and Saharan trade routes, c.1495

Below: The minaret of the Djinguerber (Great Mosque or Friday Congregational Mosque) of Timbuktu. The mosque dates from the early 14th century, a period when the city became the cultural and religious center of the Songhay empire.

Sankore Mosque-Madrasa (university)

neighbors, taking control of oases deep in the Sahara and of the caravan routes that linked them. This brought the Songhay frontier into contact with that of Morocco. However, the political situation gradually changed and a century later the Songhay were in turn conquered by a Moroccan army equipped with modern firearms.

East of the Songhay was the much longer lasting Kingdom of Kanem and Bornu, centered around Lake Chad. Here Islam had been introduced as early as the 11th century and the earliest recorded ruling dynasty even claimed descent from a pre-Islamic ruler of Southern Arabia named Sayf Ibn Dhi Yazan. Trading links with Libya and Egypt certainly pre-dated Islam, but were greatly strengthened by the 12th century. In 1237 one ruler, Dunama Dabalemi, sent a giraffe as a present to the sultan of Tunisia.

In the late 14th century the Sayfi ruling dynasty moved from Kanem to Bornu while a rival family took over as the so-called Black Sultans in Kanem. They dominated the country until the late 15th century, when they were in turn ousted by a line of rulers who claimed descent from the previous Sayfi dynasty. Known as the Mais, this ruling family endured until 1846.

CHAPTER ELEVEN

Rise of the Ottomans

Storming into Europe

Facing: The Seljuk-built bridge over the Batman Su river at Silvan, constructed c.1147. Many routes in Anatolia had fallen into decay under Byzantine rule and these were revived by the Seljuks, who also built many new bridges.

By the time the First Crusade passed and the Byzantine imperial armies concluded their campaigns of reconquest in western Anatolia, the Seljuk Sultanate of Rum had been reduced to a small area around the city of Iconium. Yet this provincial town, under its Turkish name of Konya, grew into the capital of one of the most successful and culturally brilliant Islamic states of the Middle Ages.

During the early years of the 12th century it was, however, the Seljuks' rivals, the similarly Turkish Danishmandids who were the greater Islamic power in Anatolia. Having lost much less territory to Byzantine reconquest, the Danishmandids swallowed up a crusade which, marching almost on the heels of the First in the summer of 1101,

proved such a disaster it has not even been graced with a number.

Two lines of Danishmandid emirs emerged in the mid-12th century, the first being based at Sivas, the second at Malatya and Elbistan. Their history remains obscure and they feature more prominently in Turkish folk legends such as the *Danishmand-Name* than they do in factual chronicles. In the 1170s both Danishmandid states were, however, conquered by the Seljuks of Rum or Konya.

Meanwhile the little Seljuk state recovered from its early setbacks. While generally maintaining good relations with the Byzantine empire, it gained territory from the Danishmandids, the Armenian Kingdom of Cicilia, and the Crusader County of Edessa.

In 1176, between the two campaigns that overthrew the Danishmandids, the Seljuks of Rum inflicted a crushing defeat on an invading Byzantine army under the emperor Manuel I. For the Byzantine empire this battle of Myriokephalon was a disaster on the same scale as the battle of Manzikert (1071), and although the Seljuk Turks of Rum did not immediately overrun western Anatolia, Byzantine military power never revived.

The first half of the 13th century was the high point in Seljuk civilization in Anatolia. Most of the magnificent buildings that survive from the Seljuk period date from these years, as do many textiles, carved stucco, ceramics, and metalwork. It was also under the patronage of the Seljuks of Rum that a distinctive new style of Anatolian Islamic art and architecture emerged.

The strongest cultural influences naturally came from Islamic Iran and from the Turks' own central Asian heritage, but the influences of Byzantine and especially Armenian culture can also be seen. Furthermore, this Seljuk Anatolian culture formed the foundation on which Ottoman civilization was subsequently built.

It was a period of striking economic progress, especially in trade. Routes that had fallen into decay under the Byzantines were revived, and many bridges were built along with a network of *khans* or *caravanserais*. These were like fortified "motels" in which merchants and their goods could find shelter from brigands and from Anatolia's harsh climate. The grandest had an enclosed courtyard with a raised prayer room in the center, plus a hall, a *hamam* or public bath, workshops, private chambers, stables for the animals, and storage rooms for goods. The entire concept was in a long-established eastern tradition which could be seen in Iran, in Transoxania, and along some stretches of the Silk Roads to China.

The crusader occupation of the Byzantine capital of Constantinople from 1204 to 1261 enabled the Seljuks of Rum to expand once again, reaching both the Mediterranean and Black Sea coasts. This brought even greater wealth as the Seljuk Sultanate of Rum now controlled a major hub of international trade. However, in 1243 the Mongols turned their attention to the Seljuks and defeated them at Köse Dagh. This battle is interesting because the Seljuk army fought in an almost European manner and did, in fact, include large numbers of European mercenaries. The Mongols were, of course, using much the same central Asian horse-archery and dispersal tactics that the Seljuks' ancestors had used 200 years earlier.

For the last few decades of its existence the crumbling Seljuk Sultanate of Rum was a vassal of the Mongol Il Khans or had a Mongol governor imposed on it. After 1307 Turkish Anatolia fragmented into several small *beyliks*, one of which was to emerge as a power greater even than the Seljuks themselves. These were the Ottomans.

Byzantine "Empire of Trezibond" becomes vassal of Seljuqs in 1243

Trezibond

GEORGIA

ıse Dag 1243

Coruh

can

Erzerum

Aras

Manzikert 1071

Murat

Ahlat

Lake Van

Tigris

MESOPOTAMIA

AYYUBIDS

Mosul

frontier of Seljuk state, c.1243

Seljuk provincial capital

Seljuk territory, 1100

Christian territory, 1240

Byzantine territory lost to Seljuks by 1182

disputed by Seljuks, Danishmandids, Byzantines; annexed by Seljuks by 1180

Danishmandid territory, annexed by Seljuks by 1174

Danishmanid territory, annexed by Seljuks by 1180

Seljuk conquests of Byzantine and Cilician territory, 1182–1240

Seljuk conquests of neighboring Islamic and Crusader States, 1182–1240

Byzantine "Empire of Trezibond"

territory held by Georgia in the early 13th century

other Islamic territory

Who Were the Ottomans?

The origins of the Ottomans are lost in legend. The first Ottomans were probably nomads who fled from the Mongols. From these humble beginnings the Ottoman state would expand to threaten and eventually overrun the ailing Byzantine empire.

The first Ottomans were probably one of many nomadic Turcoman bands that moved westward to the Byzantine frontier following the Mongol invasion of Anatolia in the mid-13th century. The most popular myth that the Ottomans had about their origins says a young warrior named Othman fell in love with Malkhatun, daughter of the saintly Sheikh Edebali but, being poor, his only hope lay in winning military fame. This he did, yet it was only when Othman told the sheikh about a strange dream that he won his beloved's hand.

In this dream Othman saw the moon, symbolizing Malkhatun, rising from Sheikh Edebali's chest and setting in Othman's own. Thereupon a great tree sprang from the young warrior's heart and spread across the sky. From its roots four great rivers flowed; the Tigris, Euphrates, Nile, and Danube. Interpreting this dream as a prophecy of imperial splendor, the sheikh married his daughter to the young conqueror.

Other traditions claim that the Ottomans or Othmanlis stemmed from the noble Qayi

 traditional patrimony of Ertogrul, c.1280

Ottoman conquests:

 before 1300

 1300–26

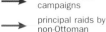 1326–62

by 1362 (probably)

Byzantine empire, c.1362

other Christian territory, c.1362

→ main Ottoman campaigns

→ principal raids by non-Ottoman Turks

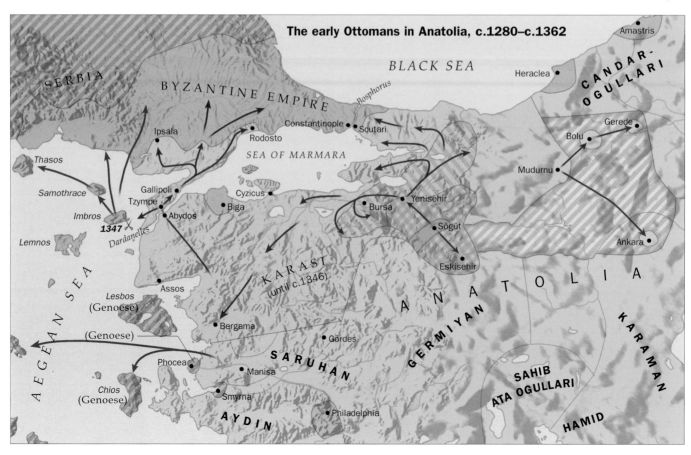

The early Ottomans in Anatolia, c.1280–c.1362

BLACK SEA

SERBIA

BYZANTINE EMPIRE

Bosphorus

Amastris

Heraclea

CANDAR-OGULLARI

Constantinople • Scutari

Ipsala

Rodosto

SEA OF MARMARA

Gerede

Bolu

Thasos

Samothrace

Gallipoli
Tzympe
Imbros
1347
Abydos
Dardanelles

Lemnos

Cyzicus
Biga

Yenisehir

Bursa

Sögüt

Mudurnu

Ankara

Eskisehir

AEGEAN SEA

Assos

KARASI (until c.1346)

A N A T O L I A

Lesbos (Genoese)

Bergama

Gördes

GERMIYAN

KARAMAN

(Genoese)

Phocea

Manisa

SARUHAN

SAHIB ATA OGULLARI

Chios (Genoese)

Smyrna

AYDIN

Philadelphia

HAMID

clan of the Oghuz Turks, who had led a nomadic life in Seljuk Anatolia for many generations. More prosaic evidence has the Ottomans emerging into the light of history in the late 13th century. The legendary Othman probably never existed, but coins naming Ertogrul, the earliest historical leader of the Ottomans, date from the 1270s. His tiny territory was in the mountains around Sögüt and included the battlefield of Dorylaeum where the First Crusade had defeated the Seljuk Turks in 1097.

Events become clearer during the reign of Ertogrul's son, Othman Ghazi (1281–1324). An Ottoman *beylik* or small Turkish state appears as one of several that emerged from the fragmentation of the Seljuk Sultanate of Rum. Being located on the frontier with a weakening Byzantine empire, the Ottomans may have attracted *ghazis* or religiously motivated frontier warriors fighting in defense of Islam. Under existing circumstances, however, clashes between the Byzantines and the *beyliks* were a result of traditional Turcoman raiding rather than Christian aggression.

RISING POWER

Motivation may have been mixed but the results were clear enough. The Ottomans, like other frontier *beyliks*, took over more and more Byzantine territory. Sometimes they left the towns isolated under Byzantine garrisons and governors who only later submitted to Turkish rule.

In many cases these Christian troops and leaders entered Islamic-Turkish service, sometimes converting to Islam at once but often remaining Christian for at least a generation. Such absorption of previous military and aristocratic elites would become a distinctive feature of Ottoman expansion, both in Anatolia and later in Europe. This had a profound impact on the personnel, structure, tactics, weaponry, and costume of Ottoman armies, as well as on the organization of the Ottoman state itself. Similar fusions of new and old, Islamic and Christian, Turkish and Greek, or Balkan Slav would be seen in Ottoman art and other aspects of Ottoman culture.

Although the primary focus of Ottoman expansion was northward, taking over what remained of Byzantine territory along the Asian shores of the Sea of Marmara and the Bosphoros, the Ottomans were also in competition with neighboring Turkish *beyliks*. Several of the latter were pursuing similar expansion against other Byzantine territory. In most case these *beyliks* found nowhere else to go once they reached the Aegean coast, so some took their raiding to sea, becoming what European chroniclers inaccurately called "pirate states." One of these was the Karasi *beylik* in northwestern Anatolia.

The Ottomans' conquest of Karasi in the mid-14th century opened up two new strategic possibilities. The first was offered by the small Karasi fleet, which enabled Ottoman *ghazis* to raid Byzantine islands and coasts in the same way that other *beyliks* were doing. The second was to place Ottoman troops on the Asiatic shore of the Dardanelles. The enfeebled Byzantine rulers were already inviting Ottoman and other Turkish troops to help them in their self-defeating civil wars.

In 1353 Emperor John VI Cantacuzene allowed the Ottoman ruler Orkhan (1324–60) to garrison the little fort of Tzympe (Çimpe) on the Gallipoli peninsula, on the European side of the Dardanelles. From here Ottoman troops raided further afield, imposed Turkish rule and established a bridgehead from which the Ottoman empire eventually spread over the entire Balkans and much of central and eastern Europe.

Above: The Muradiye Mosque, an Ottoman complex of 1426 at Bursa, Turkey.

Facing: Ottoman blue and turquoise ceramic tile decoration in the mosque of Sultan Murad, c.1426, Bursa.

165

Advancing into Europe

The Ottoman conquest of the southern Balkans during the 14th century was one of the most dramatic events in the later medieval period. By the 17th century Ottoman rulers created an empire that stretched from Morocco to Iran, and from the East African coast to Hungary and the Ukraine.

Right: Wall-painting of c.1335 of the Jupan Peter Brajan and his wife in the village church of Karan, Yugoslavia.

Facing: An Ottoman mosque built in 1408 in Stara Zagora, Bulgaria.

Below: Orta Hamam Ottoman public bath, late 14th century, at Bolu in Turkey.

In the decades leading up to 1400 the Byzantine empire consisted only of Constantinople and adjoining coastal areas, southern Greece, and some northern Aegean islands. Similarly little was left of the Crusader States in Greece, while Bulgaria had fragmented into little kingdoms that then fell under Ottoman domination. The fragile Serbian empire had also fallen apart as the Ottomans thrust into the heart of the Balkans.

It had proved almost impossible for the Orthodox Christian Balkan states to join forces with Catholic Christians to the north. In fact, while many of the ruling elites looked northward for help, most ordinary people apparently preferred Ottoman-Islamic domination to that of the Catholic Hungarians who seemed to be the only viable alternative.

Within the fragmented relics of the Byzantine empire confusion reached epidemic proportions. Most of the emperors were now vassals of the Ottoman sultan and everywhere there was hostility between the military and civilians, ruling elites and common people. Furthermore, the crushing of peasant and urban revolts had left large parts of Thrace and Macedonia almost uninhabited except for a few fortified towns.

In contrast, Ottoman expansion was carefully planned and carried out with utter conviction. The first real Ottoman capital had been Bursa in Anatolia but, perhaps after using Greek Didymoteichon as their first European capital during a temporary occupation after 1358–9, the Ottomans made Edirne (the Greco-Roman city of Hadrianopolis, or Adrianople) the base from which the greatest wave of Ottoman conquests was launched.

Most fighting was done by armies based on three frontier *uc* or marches. The first thrust northeast through Thrace was commanded by the ruler himself, while the second marched northwest through Bulgaria and was under Qara Tîmürtash. The third force pushed west into Greece under Gazi Evrenos.

COLONIZING FORCE

During this period the empty plains of Thrace and eastern Macedonia were settled by people from Anatolia, including nomadic groups who became the *yürük* warrior-herdsmen of several mountainous Balkan regions. The role of the Bektashi dervishes who accompanied Ottoman armies was also more important than is generally realized, not only as Islamic missionaries but promoting colonization and the re-cultivation of land devastated by war.

The Ottoman ruler Bayazid I did not, however, feel that the Ottoman position was secure, so in the winter of 1393–4 he summoned his Christian vassals to a conference. Here he selected Stefan Lazarevic of Serbia as his most trustworthy vassal. In turn Emperor Manuel II became convinced that Byzantium was doomed unless he summoned help from the west. The result was another crusade that ended in a crushing Christian defeat by the Ottomans at the battle of Nicopolis in 1396.

Nicopolis was a total victory for the Ottoman army, but it would soon be overshadowed by greater and far more dangerous events. Immediately after the battle Bayazid I chose not to invade further territory but to consolidate the Ottoman position within areas already conquered.

The little Bulgarian kingdom of Vidin was incorporated into the Ottoman state and the entire southern bank of the lower Danube became a frontier zone or *uc* frontier, where the bulk of the population soon became Muslim. Elsewhere Ottoman troops penetrated deeper into Greece, while Bayazid revived his previous siege of Constantinople.

Victory over a full-scale European crusade greatly enhanced Ottoman prestige. As a result administrators and soldiers flocked to enter their service. There were plenty of such volunteers now that the eastern Islamic world was in a state of near anarchy as a result of Tamerlane's devastating campaigns.

However, in 1402 Bayazid I was defeated and captured by Timur

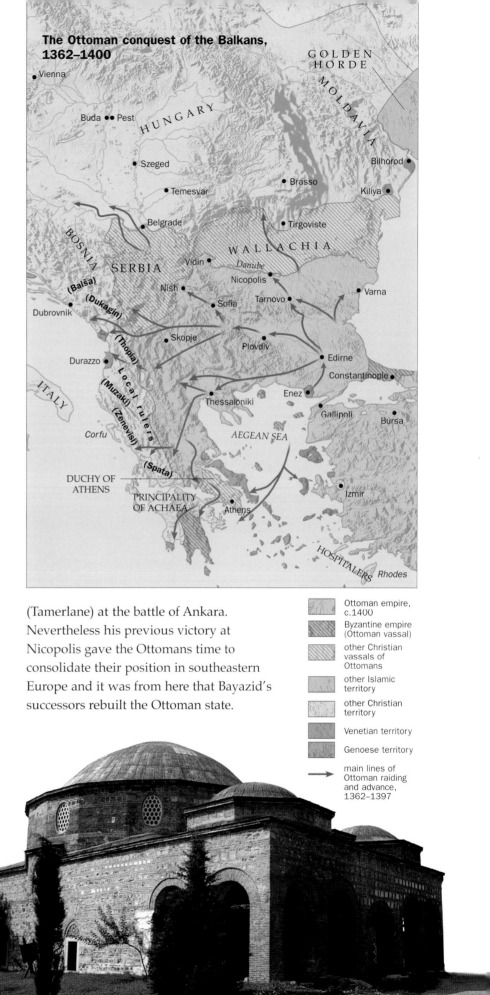

The Ottoman conquest of the Balkans, 1362–1400

	Ottoman empire, c.1400
	Byzantine empire (Ottoman vassal)
	other Christian vassals of Ottomans
	other Islamic territory
	other Christian territory
	Venetian territory
	Genoese territory
→	main lines of Ottoman raiding and advance, 1362–1397

(Tamerlane) at the battle of Ankara. Nevertheless his previous victory at Nicopolis gave the Ottomans time to consolidate their position in southeastern Europe and it was from here that Bayazid's successors rebuilt the Ottoman state.

Edirne, the Jewel City

Following its capture by the Ottomans before 1366, Adrianople was renamed Edirne and became the European capital of the Ottoman state. Its lavish building program continued as the city became a miltary center.

The Byzantine city of Adrianople may have fallen to the Turks as early as 1361. It was certainly in their hands by 1366, following a small but historically significant

Islamic victory over a Byzantine Greek and Bulgarian army between Babaeski and Pinarhisar. Renamed Edirne, the city now became the focal point from which Ottoman Turkish campaigns expanded in four directions within Europe. These lines of advance were along the north coast of the Aegean Sea through western Thrace to Macedonia, up the River Maritza against the Bulgarians toward what are now Plovdiv and Sofia, north toward the eastern end of the Balkan range and the lower course of the River Danube, and east across eastern Thrace toward Constantinople.

Ottoman successes attracted scholars as well as soldiers to their court. Bayazid I already had several noted names in his court before his remarkable victory at the battle of Nicopolis in 1396. They included the historian Ibn al-Jazarî, who finished his famous poetic verse *History of the Prophet and Caliphs* in the Ottoman army camp, three days after Bayazid's soldiers defeated the crusaders at the battle of Nicopolis.

Before Nicopolis Ottoman rulers were addressed merely as emirs, but after Bayazid's victory they adopted the more prestigious title of sultan. This in turn encouraged other scholars to their increasingly wealthy and prestigious court. Not surprisingly, Edirne was soon graced with some fine buildings. The Eski or Old Mosque dates from the start of the 15th century but is rather traditional in design, as is the Mosque of Murad II completed in 1435–6 .

ARCHITECTURAL TREASURES
The Üç Serefeli or "Three Balconies" Mosque was built for Sultan Murad II only a few years later and is regarded as the first major construction in a truly Ottoman architectural style. Its great dome, almost 80 feet across across, would not be surpassed until Mehmet

the Conqueror built his victory mosque in Constantinople (Istanbul). The four minarets of the Üç Serefeli Mosque are each decorated in a different manner. One of them is 220 feet high, with the three balconies that gave the mosque its name. Another has a remarkable spiral pattern on the outside.

Senior military leaders similarly paid for the construction of secular buildings such as the bridge of Gazi Mihail, a convert from Christianity, which dates from 1420, or the Orta Imaret, which was a soup kitchen providing food for the poor. Sadly nothing remains of the great Ottoman palaces built in Edirne in the 15th century, but a huge *bedestan* (covered bazaar) was constructed at the start of the 15th century.

In 1453 Edirne was the hub of a massive military operation and as a result the city ceased to be the capital of the Ottoman empire. In January that year large numbers of volunteers mustered in Edirne for the forthcoming siege of Constantinople. In addition to Ottoman palace contingents and those from Rumelia or the European provinces, there were thousands of camp followers, including merchants to supply the Ottoman army with food and necessities.

Early in 1453 a Serbian vassal contingent arrived, reportedly consisting of 1,500 Christian cavalry plus auxiliaries. Serbian miners arrived rather later. It is also worth noting that, according to the Italian observer Giacomo Tedaldi, Christians in the Ottoman ranks were allowed to worship as they wished.

Meanwhile Karaca, the *beylerbeyi* or governor of Rumelia, sent men to prepare the roads from Edirne to Constantinople so that the bridges could cope with the Ottomans' massive cannon. Fifty carpenters and 200 assistants strengthened the roads where necessary. There was no reported resistance and in February Karaca Bey's troops began to take the remaining Byzantine towns along the Marmara and Black Sea coasts. Next the Ottomans brought their massive guns to the walls of Constantinople, the biggest of the three giant guns requiring 60 oxen to pull it. The final siege of Constantinople had begun.

Above: The mosque and medical complex of Sultan Bayazid II, late 15th century, Edirne.

Facing: Unusually decorated minarets grace the Üç Serefeli Mosque at Edirne.

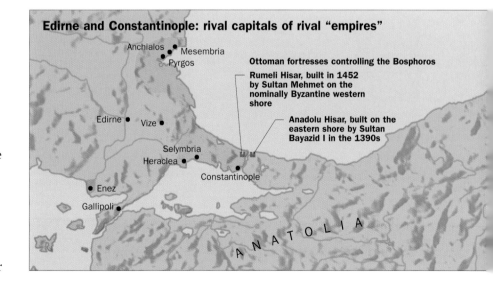

Edirne and Constantinople: rival capitals of rival "empires"

Anchialos
Mesembria
Pyrgos

Ottoman fortresses controlling the Bosphoros
Rumeli Hisar, built in 1452 by Sultan Mehmet on the nominally Byzantine western shore

Anadolu Hisar, built on the eastern shore by Sultan Bayazid I in the 1390s

Edirne • Vize •

Selymbria
Heraclea •
Constantinople

Enez

Gallipoli

A N A T O L I A

1381	1389	1393–4	1399	1400	c.1400	1402	1403
Persia is conquered by Tamerlane	Ottomans defeat the Serbians and their allies at Kosovo	Mesopotamia is conquered by Tamerlane	Tamerlane sacks Delhi and northern India	Tamerlane conquers Syria, defeats Mamluks, and takes Aleppo and Damascus	The Hafsids of Tunisia launch naval raids against pirates	Tamerlane defeats the Ottomans at Ankara; temporary fragmentation of the Ottoman state	Malacca on the Malayan peninsula is established as an Islamic sultanate

Seizing the Red Apple

The fall of Constantinople in 1453 is sometimes seen as the end of the Roman empire or as the final destruction of a redundant relic. In reality the siege and conquest of Constantinople was neither.

Right: Portrait of Sultan Mehmet II, attributed to Costanza da Ferrara, c.1470.

The significance of Constantinople's fall was not in the disappearance of something ancient, but in the birth of something new—namely the Ottoman empire in its fully developed form. Sultan Mehmet and the main Ottoman army left Edirne on March 23, 1453 and assembled $2^1/_2$ miles from Constantinople. Mehmet's artillery was already in position in 14 or 15 batteries, with additional groups of smaller cannon alongside or between the big guns.

The first Ottoman assault was probably launched on April 7, when irregulars and volunteers advanced, supported by archers and handgunners. However, they were met at the outer rampart and driven back with relative ease. In fact the Byzantine artillery was notably effective until their largest cannon exploded, after which Byzantine guns were largely limited to an anti-personnel role.

As the siege progressed, Mehmet had most cannon taken off the Ottoman ships and mounted ashore to bombard enemy vessels that were defending a boom across the Golden Horn. This was when Mehmet was credited with devising a new form of long-range mortar.

Work was also speeded up on the

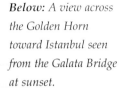

Below: A view across the Golden Horn toward Istanbul seen from the Galata Bridge at sunset.

construction of a wooden slipway from the Bosphoros to the Golden Horn. By April 22 it was complete, and under the cover of an artillery bombardment 72 of the Ottomans' smaller ships were hauled across the hills on rollers before being slid into the Golden Horn. Having lost control of the waterway, troops had to be withdrawn from other areas to man this threatened sector, and the investment of Constantinople was complete.

WAVES OF ATTACK

On May 26, Mehmet called a council of war. The following day he toured the army while heralds announced that a final assault would take place on the 29th. Celebration bonfires were lit and from May 26 onward there was continuous feasting in the Ottoman camp. The defenders saw so many torches that some thought the enemy were burning their tents before retreating.

About three hours before dawn on May

29 there was a ripple of fire from the Ottoman artillery and Turkish irregulars swept forward. Their main attack focused around the battered walls next to the Gate of St. Romanus. Despite suffering terrible casualties, few of them retreated until, after two hours of fighting, Mehmet ordered a withdrawal. Ottoman ships similarly attempted to get close enough to erect scaling ladders.

After another artillery bombardment it was the turn of the provincial troops. These marched forward carrying torches but were hampered by the narrowness of the breaches in Constantinople's defenses. More disciplined than the irregulars, they occasionally pulled back to allow their artillery to fire, and during one such bombardment a section of defensive stockade was brought down. Nevertheless this second assault failed.

The only fresh troops now available to Mehmet were his own palace regiments including the famous Janissary infantry. All sources agree that these advanced with terrifying discipline, slowly and without noise or music. The third phase of fighting lasted an hour before some Janissaries found that a small postern door had not been properly closed after a previous Byzantine counterattack. About 50 soldiers broke in and raised their banner on the battlements. They were, however, in danger of being wiped out when the Ottomans had a stroke of luck.

Giovanni Giustiniani Longo, an Italian soldier who was commanding the most threatened sector of Constantinople's fortification, was mortally wounded. Panic now spread among the defenders, and the Janissaries took the inner wall. Word spread that the Ottomans had also broken in via the harbor, and that the last Byzantine emperor, Constantine XI, had been killed. As a result, the defense collapsed. About noon Sultan Mehmet the Conqueror, as he was thereafter called, rode though the conquered city to the church of Santa Sofia, where he prayed. The huge edifice was then converted into a mosque, which it remained until it was made into a museum in 1935.

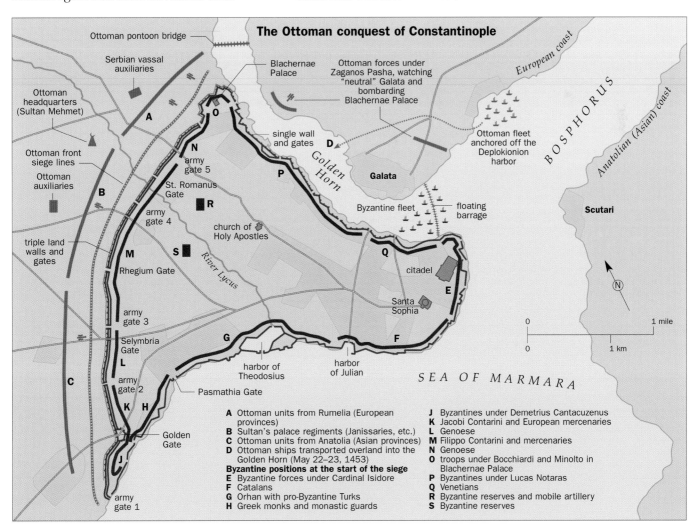

The Ottoman conquest of Constantinople

A Ottoman units from Rumelia (European provinces)
B Sultan's palace regiments (Janissaries, etc.)
C Ottoman units from Anatolia (Asian provinces)
D Ottoman ships transported overland into the Golden Horn (May 22–23, 1453)
Byzantine positions at the start of the siege
E Byzantine forces under Cardinal Isidore
F Catalans
G Orhan with pro-Byzantine Turks
H Greek monks and monastic guards
J Byzantines under Demetrius Cantacuzenus
K Jacobi Contarini and European mercenaries
L Genoese
M Filippo Contarini and mercenaries
N Genoese
O troops under Bocchiardi and Minolto in Blachernae Palace
P Byzantines under Lucas Notaras
Q Venetians
R Byzantine reserves and mobile artillery
S Byzantine reserves

Sultan and Caesar

The relationship between the Ottoman empire and the Islamic Turco-Mongol khanates of southeastern Russia and the steppes was very important. In some ways it mirrored the earlier one between the Romano-Byzantine empire and the pagan steppe states of the medieval period.

Right: An Ottoman **hamam** *of late 14th—early 15th centuries stands next to the Mosque of Sinan Pasha in Prizen, Kosovo Autonomous Region, Yugoslavia.*

Below: A wall-painting of c.1500 on the exterior of the Moldavian Monastery of Voronets, Romania depicts Tartars standing with Turks.

The Ottoman conquest of Constantinople in 1453 and the subsequent mopping up of remaining relics of the Byzantine empire also changed the political, strategic, and economic situation around the Black Sea. The impact on the Ottoman empire itself was profound. The *ghaza* or struggle with neighboring Christian states now focused on the Ottoman sultan's own actions rather than on the autonomous frontier heroes of earlier days.

More immediately, however, Sultan Mehmet II reconstructed his new capital. The fortifications were repaired and Constantinople (hereafter generally known as Istanbul) was repopulated with Christian Greeks, Muslim Turks, and others. Some were encouraged by tax privileges but many were forced to settle in the largely empty city. This rapid growth then led to food shortages, which in turn prompted the Ottoman conquest of grain-producing regions north of the Black Sea.

Mehmet wanted to make Istanbul a multi-faith center for all Peoples of the Book; Muslims, Christians, and Jews alike. This grand imperial statement would create a crossroads where the cultures of east and

west, Europe and Asia, could meet and mingle. Furthermore Mehmet declared himself to be the new *Qaysar* or Caesar, the legitimate heir to the Roman and Byzantine empires, with a claim to territory far beyond the Ottoman empire's existing frontiers. This was widely accepted, not only by the sultan's Turkish and Muslim subjects but by Greek scholars such as George of Trebizond, who wrote to Mehmet in 1466: "No one doubts that you are the emperor of the Romans. Whoever is legally master of the capital of the empire is the emperor, and Constantinople is the capital of the Roman empire."

NEW BALANCE OF POWER

The conquest of Constantinople cut Italian trade through the Dardanelles and Bosphoros to the Crimea, and there was soon a steady emigration away from the Genoese Black Sea colonies. Many Armenians moved to the Ukraine or Poland, some Italian craftsmen went as far as Moscow, and within little more than 20 years Genoa's possessions beyond the Bosphoros had been lost to the Ottomans.

Following the fall of Constantinople a series of other campaigns confirmed Ottoman domination of the Balkans, although a clash with Hungary led to them suffering a reverse outside Belgrade. Wallachia moved firmly beneath Ottoman suzerainty and even Moldavia was theoretically tributary to the sultan after 1456. On the other hand Stefan the Great came to throne of Moldavia the following year and spent much of his reign competing with the Ottomans for domination over neighboring Wallachia.

The consolidation of Ottoman power had already strangled the link between the Mongol Golden Horde and the Mamluk Sultanate of Egypt, having a profound impact on both. The Golden Horde was in decline during the 15th century, having already been defeated and largely absorbed by the Khanate of the Crimea in 1502. The Giray Khans of the Crimea were themselves descended from Genghis Khan's son Jochi. At first they were vassals of the much larger

Golden Horde, but in the early 15th century they achieved independence.

Thereafter the Khans of the Crimea ruled over a substantial part of what are now the eastern Ukraine and southern Russia, as well as the Crimean peninsula itself. Their khanate proved to be the most enduring of all the states that emerged from the fragmentation of the Mongol "world empire."

The Crimean khanate and the Ottoman empire also became natural allies, firstly against the Golden Horde and later against the rising power of Russia. It was, however, a lopsided relationship, with the Ottoman sultans by far the stronger partner. They regarded the khans of the Crimea as their vassals and imposed direct Ottoman rule over the coastal enclaves, which had once been Byzantine, Genoese, or Venetian.

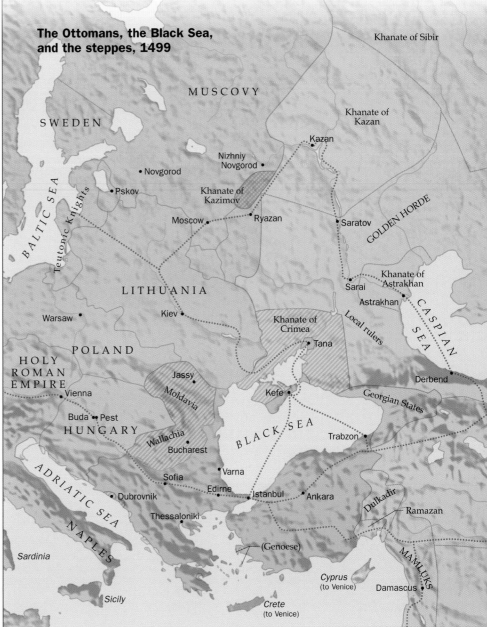

Ottoman empire, 1449:
- Ottoman territory
- Christian vassal
- Islamic vassal

other territories, 1449:
- Islamic
- Venetian
- Christian
- Islamic khanate under suzerainty of Muscovy
- ········ main trade routes

The Ottomans, the Black Sea, and the steppes, 1499

The Ottomans Turn East

European chroniclers naturally focused on the Ottoman empire's rapid and long-lasting conquests in southeastern, eastern, and central Europe. During the same period, however, other Ottoman armies were pressing eastward.

Right: Dervish cell in the Mevlana Convent, Konya, Turkey. The seated figure is a display manikin.

Facing top: Ahi Evren Mosque of the dervishes, dating from the early 16th century, Kirsehir, Turkey.

In the east Ottomans seized territories ruled by rival Turkish dynasties, and eventually penetrated into lands that had been Islamic since the seventh or eighth centuries. Following the crushing defeat of Sultan Bayazid I by Tamerlane in 1405, the Ottoman state used its European provinces as a springboard from which to re-establish its authority across much of Anatolia. Nevertheless it took many years before Bayazid's successors could regain his eastern frontiers.

Several Turkish *beyliks* and emirates had regained their independence as a result of Tamerlane's invasion. Of these the most powerful, and least reliable as an ally against the Europeans, was Karaman in south-central Anatolia. The Karaman Oghullari dynasty was finally overthrown by the

Ottomans in 1475. The neighboring Ramadan Oghullari of Cilicia became Ottoman vassals in 1516, while the Dulkadir Oghullari of Maras and Malatya followed five years later.

Ever since the time of the Seljuks of Rum, Anatolia had been home to several mystical

Islamic movements or *dervish* sects. Some of these reflected the Turks' own pre-Islamic beliefs, including shamanism and Buddhist influences. Some owed more to early Persian-Islamic mysticism, and several clearly included elements of the rather unorthodox Christianity seen in Byzantine Anatolia before the Seljuk conquest.

Shi'a Islam had also been strong in early Turkish Anatolia, especially among *ghazi* or religiously motivated frontier communities. Even the Ottoman rulers themselves, though proclaiming their Sunni orthodoxy, only really became "mainstream" Muslims in the late 15th century. This orthodoxy was then cemented after the Ottomans defeated the Mamluk sultans of Egypt and took over the Middle Eastern heartland of medieval Islamic civilization.

BROAD COALITION

Two *dervish* or *sufi* movements would play a significant role in the conversion of many Balkan people to Islam. They were the Bektashia and the Melamia. It is difficult to separate truth from legend where the origins of the Bektashi dervishes are concerned.

They had a close association with the elite Janissary infantry corps from very early days

The Mystical Orders and Islam in the Balkans

CRIMEAN TARTARS

Buda • Pest
HUNGARY
to Ottoman empire, 1451

Jedisan
Moldavia

to Ottoman empire, 1526

Wallachia

Ottoman vassal, 1504

BLACK SEA

Istanbul

ANATOLIA

Mosul ○

SYRIA

Cyprus
Crete

○ Damascus

MEDITERRANEAN SEA

• Cairo
EGYPT

◆ source of Melami teaching (called Hamyawia after 16th-century reforms)
• Melami teaching recorded between c.145–1560
◆ center of Bektashi movement
• Bektashi centers in Europe and Asia

Ottoman empire, 1451 (excluding vassal states)
Ottoman empire, 1541 (including vassal states)

and were even credited with responsibility for the Janissaries' distinctive tall white felt cap. Hats had been a form of religious identification for many years. The red hats worn by most early Ottoman troops, including the older and even more elite Silahdars, had been worn by revolutionary Shi'a Islamic sects in earlier decades.

First recorded with certainty in 13th century Anatolia, the Bektashis were widely regarded by orthodox Sunni Muslims as heretical. Nevertheless they became very popular among recently converted, ex-Christian, and often only superficially Islamic populations in both Anatolia and the Balkans. Christian influence can clearly be seen in the ceremonial distribution of bread, cheese, and wine when a new member was accepted into the order. The Bektashi movement also developed a remarkable tradition of lyrical poetry.

The original center of the Melami movement was, like that of the Bektashis, in central Anatolia, but they had *tekkes* or meeting places in Üsküdar, on the eastern side of the Bosphoros facing Istanbul, as well as several other major cities. A refusal to be bound by the external forms of religion was a notable feature of Melami belief, and this often got them into trouble with the Ottoman authorities. Perhaps for this reason other major Melami centers were near the European frontiers of the empire, in Albania,

Bosnia, and in Budapest during the relatively short period of Ottoman rule over Hungary. In later centuries they suffered persecution because of such unorthodox views and, like the Bektashis, the Melamia would eventually be suppressed.

Below: The prayer hall of the 13th-century convent of Bektashi dervishes, Haçi Bektash, Turkey.

CHAPTER TWELVE

Twilight in the West

Driven away in the Reconquista

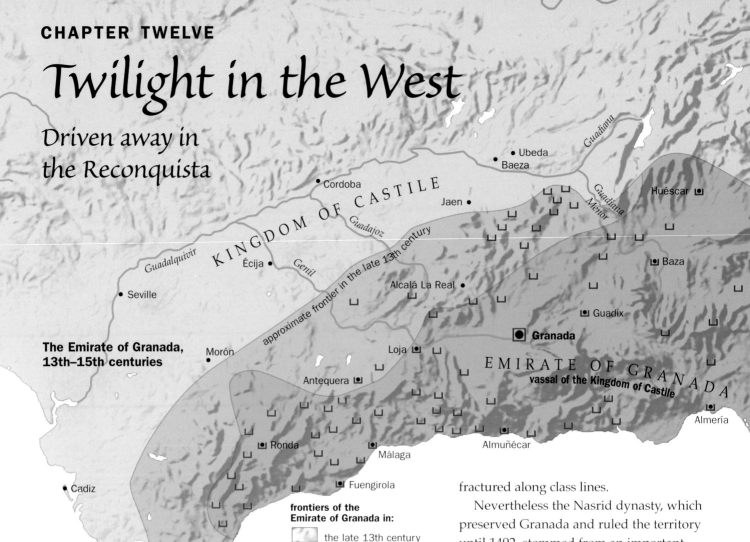

The Emirate of Granada, 13th–15th centuries

approximate frontier in the late 13th century

KINGDOM OF CASTILE

Cordoba

Jaen

Ubeda
Baeza

Huéscar

Baza

Alcalá La Real

Guadix

Granada

Écija

Genil

Guadajoz

Guadalquivir

Seville

Morón

Loja

EMIRATE OF GRANADA
vassal of the Kingdom of Castile

Antequera

Almería

Ronda

Málaga

Almuñécar

Cadiz

frontiers of the Emirate of Granada in:

the late 13th century

c.1480

major fortifications

Fuengirola

Algeciras
Gibraltar

The 13th century was a time of catastrophe for Iberian Islam. Muwahhid power collapsed, to be followed by a third *ta'ifa* period whose rulers proved powerless to stop the Christian advance. By the end of this century only Granada remained as an Islamic state, but even this small emirate could only survive by paying tribute to Castile, its hugely more powerful Spanish neighbor.

Al-Andalus had shown itself to be rich and highly cultured, but militarily weak, while its own indigenous aristocracy often preferred Spanish or Portuguese domination to that of the Muwahhidun. In terms of social organization, the new clan system was not as strong as the old tribal ties. Furthermore, the members of such clans were often scattered over much of the country rather than dominating a specific area. Wealth was also beginning to provide greater status than family lineage as Andalusian-Islamic society fractured along class lines.

Nevertheless the Nasrid dynasty, which preserved Granada and ruled the territory until 1492, stemmed from an important family of frontier warriors. At first these Nasrid rulers maintained their position by accepting Christian suzerainty and agreeing to supply troops in support of their Castilian overlords, but whereas the Nasrids subsequently reasserted their independence, other shadowy Islamic statelets like the Kingdom of Murcia did not and were soon absorbed.

Despite being an emphatically Islamic state, the Nasrid Emirate of Granada grew increasingly similar to Christian Spanish neighbors in many respects, and as a result had less in common with its North African fellow Muslims. At a popular level there was a substantial blurring of Muslim and Christian identities on both sides of the frontier. There were also lengthy periods of relative peace which led to mutual respect, even understanding, between the military elites of both sides.

This was strengthened by the frequent participation of Granadan troops as allies in various wars between the Christian kingdoms. It became common for individual soldiers to cross the frontier and change their

allegiance, sometimes more than once, and unofficial alliances were forged between supposedly opposing frontier clans. The Islamic and Christian aristocratic elites took part in each others' festivals, particularly those marking mid-summer, when both indulged in a distinctive form of light cavalry jousting using spears made of bamboo.

DIVIDED LOYALTIES

At another level, however, Granada developed a siege mentality that made religiously motivated warfare popular in some sections of society and encouraged the presence of enthusiastic volunteers from North Africa. Nevertheless, attitudes remained complex, with North African *ghazis* often being highly unpopular, while at a government level some Granadan rulers cultivated close relations with Christian Castile rather than Islamic Morocco.

Certain factors could not, however, be changed. Firstly there was a fundamental religious divide between Christian and Islamic states, and secondly Granada remained largely dependent on the rulers of North Africa for the wheat needed to feed their crowded population.

All sources confirm the strict discipline, frequent reviews of troops, and regular inspections of fortifications that typified the Granadan army. At such reviews the best soldiers would be rewarded, while the inadequate had their pay reduced. The main army bases were Granada, Málaga, Guadix, and Ronda; numerous smaller bases were spread along the frontiers and coast. The North African volunteers had their main headquarters in the coastal castle of Fuengirola.

In addition to strict discipline, Granadan soldiers were noted for their sobriety, frugality, and physical endurance. On campaign their morale was supported by religious figures, both orthodox and otherwise, plus a recognized corps of local guides, medics, armorers, and orators or poets to maintain morale.

In strategic terms Granadan warfare was dominated by passes through the surrounding mountain ranges. Raids tended to aim at economic targets such as orchards or mills, and both sides developed sophisticated early warning systems. In Granada, if an enemy raid was reported, local light troops tried to harass the foe as they advanced while the peasantry took refuge in fortifications. The enemy would be ambushed where possible and if a more determined resistance proved necessary, Granadan infantry would make use of natural obstacles, orchards, or irrigation ditches in an attempt to hamper the movement of enemy armored cavalry.

In 1394 one such raid led by the Master of the Crusading Order of Calatrava was routed by such Granadan frontier forces using crossbows, slings, javelins, and guns. The inclusion of firearms also shows that Granada was clearly attempting to keep up with the latest technological developments.

Above: Detail of a wall-painting of the early 14th century shows men of a Granadan army on the march. The painting is in the Torre de las Damas of the Alhambra, Granada.

Below: Interior of the Hamam public bath in Ronda, 12th–15th centuries.

Subjects of the Christian Kings

Most of the Islamic ruling and military elites of al-Andalus retreated to Granada or North Africa following the collapse of Islamic-Andalusian political power in the 13th century. The remaining communities became known as Mudejars.

Right: This Mudejar-style church tower in Terrer, Spain may possibly be a reused minaret from the previous mosque. The great minaret/church tower of Seville Cathedral is a notable Christian reuse.

Facing below: A 14th-century Mudejar-style decorated wooden ceiling in the Monastery of Santa Clara, formerly the Palace of Tordesillas.

The Mudejar Muslims who remained in the Iberian peninsula were renowned for being industrious and law abiding. Additionally, some Mudejar communities were famous for their skill in several important crafts or industries, ranging from ceramics to silk textiles. In the Andalusian countryside, their humbler country cousins remained the most hard-working peasant farmers.

Some of the cultural leadership remained, along with a substantial proportion of the ordinary Islamic population, and there was clearly greater continuity in the countryside than in the cities. On the other hand an Arab-speaking urban population remained in the suburbs around several great cities. Others were confined in ghettos by their new Christian rulers. From the point of view of these Christian kings, Islamic communities were a valuable asset, and in several cases were actually described as "royal treasures."

Mudejar art and architecture was a highly creative offshoot, or more accurately a continuation, of Islamic-Andalusian traditions which flourished within the greatly enlarged Christian kingdoms of Aragon, Navarre, Castile, and Portugal. It remained essentially true to the aesthetic ideals of western Islamic culture, with simple forms combined with abundant surface decoration. This can be seen in the decorative brickwork, stucco, wood carving, inlaid marquetry, tilework, and ceramic mosaics which decorate 14th and 15th century palaces built in Mudejar style. These were in turn largely made by Mudejar craftsmen for their Christian rulers.

FUSION OF CULTURES

At the same time, however, medieval Christian or Iberian Gothic influences inevitably percolated into many aspects of

The Alcazar of Seville, 13th century; largely rebuilt in 1364

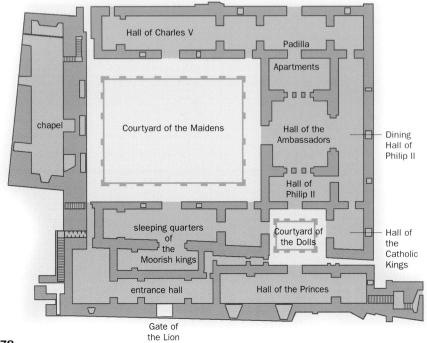

Hall of Charles V

Padilla

Apartments

chapel

Courtyard of the Maidens

Hall of the Ambassadors

Dining Hall of Philip II

Hall of Philip II

sleeping quarters of the Moorish kings

Courtyard of the Dolls

Hall of the Catholic Kings

entrance hall

Hall of the Princes

Gate of the Lion

Mudejar art and architecture. Some of the results are startling, such as the images of fully armored European knights and typical High Medieval heraldry incorporated into the otherwise typically "Moorish" decorations of the Palace of Tordesillas. Now called the Monastery of Santa Clara, it was built for King Alfonso XI about 1350, and even includes a typical Islamic *hamam* or communal bath house.

The most famous example of Mudejar architecture in Spain is, however, the Alcázar in Seville. The first Alcázar was built during the Muwahhidun period, but little of this remains. Nevertheless the Mudejar parts of the Alcázar somehow fail to create the sense of calm and serenity fundamental to true Islamic architecture. Instead the palace still betrays the brash aggressiveness of western European civilization, despite its abundant geometric and arabesque decoration, and its delicate Arabic inscriptions.

As Islamic minorities and "treasures" of the ruling kings, the Mudejar communities were entirely dependent upon these kings for their cultural and perhaps even physical survival. This probably accounted for the fact that several of them played a significant military role, especially in the technical fields. Some men who had served Christian kings earlier in their careers were subsequently recorded in the service of Granada or of other Islamic dynasties in North Africa.

There is also evidence that some Islamic Andalusian families of Arab origin had branches on both sides of the religious frontier in Spain. For example the most famous military writer and scholar in 14th century Granada was named Ibn Hudhayl, while a similarly named Hudhayl family provided Navarre with a Master of Crossbowmen and a Master of the King's Ordnances in Navarrese castles about the same time. This Master of the King's Ordnances was, in fact, involved in the early use of guns in Navarre.

In 14th- and early 15th-century Morocco the most elite bodyguard unit of the Marinid sultan appears to have been a small regiment of Andalusian refugees, some of whom had spent part of their lives as Mudejars under Christian rule in Spain. One such man was Ali al-Ishbili or "Ali from Seville," who was an engineer and specialist in siege warfare.

Above: The courtyard of the Alcazar Palace in Seville is a fine example of Mudejar architecture and adornment.

The Walled City of Fez

Fez in Morocco is one of the best preserved traditional cities in the Islamic world, uniquely divided into an economic/religious half and the older trade city. The customary way of life and forms of commerce thrive there to this day.

In the later medieval period the new Marinid ruling dynasty (1217–1465) made Fez its economic and political capital, and in 1276 they built a completely new city, Fez al-Jadid or "New Fez," next to the old city of Fez al-Bali. When the surrounding fortified walls of Fez al-Jadid had been completed, Marinid Sultan Ya'qub Abu Yusuf ordered that a large new Friday Mosque be built inside. This would serve as the main congregational mosque for the new city.

The cost of its building came from the revenues of the olive oil presses at Meknes, another large Moroccan city some distance to the west. These oil presses were probably *waqf* property. This meant that they had been given by their original owners, either private individuals or a ruling sultan, to be administered by a government department that was found in all Islamic states. The revenues of *waqf* property, whether the rents of houses, the profits of oil presses, or any such economic assets, were reserved for charitable purposes. These could in turn include the building or maintenance of religious buildings, the education of children, or support of the needy.

In Fez al-Jadid a special enclosure was erected in the new congregational mosque in 1280–1, to conceal the ruler from the ordinary people during prayers. At the same time new market streets were laid out from one city gate to another. A large *hamam* or public bath was similarly constructed. Finally the Marinid sultan ordered all his government ministers and senior officers to build their houses within the new city walls.

This entire process was a carefully regulated piece of town planning almost entirely controlled by the government. It was also documented in some detail, so that the anonymous author of a history called the *Dhakhirat al-Saniya* could write down the full story a generation later.

DISTRICTS AND PROFESSIONS

By the end of the medieval period, each group of craftsmen in the old city, Fez al-Bali, was concentrated in a specific area. Their

Below: The Old City of Fez in Morocco sprawls across a valley between its walls, as seen from the Marinid royal tombs.

location generally reflected two factors. The first was a matter of prestige, with high-status crafts like lawyers, booksellers, and papermakers (whom both businesses required) close to the main mosque. According to Leo Africanus, a North African convert from Islam to Christianity writing in the mid-16th century, there were 80 legal offices either against the wall of the main mosque or facing it. Thirty bookshops were situated a little further to the west.

The second factor that influenced the location of various professions in Fez, as in other Islamic cities, was access to water, and the amount of pollution which each trade tended to produce. For example, the noisy copper and brass merchants were not far from the main mosque, whereas the fruit sellers traded right outside its western door. In contrast the smelly dyers and millers were further down the stream that flowed through Fez al-Bali, while the butchers were at the very edge of town, where the now-polluted stream flowed out of the city.

Another very traditional aspect of medieval Islamic urban life was the role of citizens in defense of their own fortifications. This was as true of Fez as of most other Arab-Islamic cities. In the early 14th century the Moroccan chronicler Ibn Abi Zar described the military parades that such urban militias would hold: "The men from each *souk* [market] go out in a specific direction, each having a large bow and wearing their finest clothes. Each market has a flag which has its own distinctive sign and which bears a

design corresponding to each trade. Very early in the morning, when the sultan comes out [of his palace], these men form lines and march in front of him... until he goes to make his prayers. When he comes back the men of the markets return to their own homes."

The similarity between these craft-based urban militias and the guild-based militias of medieval Italian cities is remarkable, and must surely prove that there was some cultural exchange between them.

Above: Leather-dying vats in the Old City of Fez. The various crafts were all assigned their own sectors of the city by their Marinid rulers.

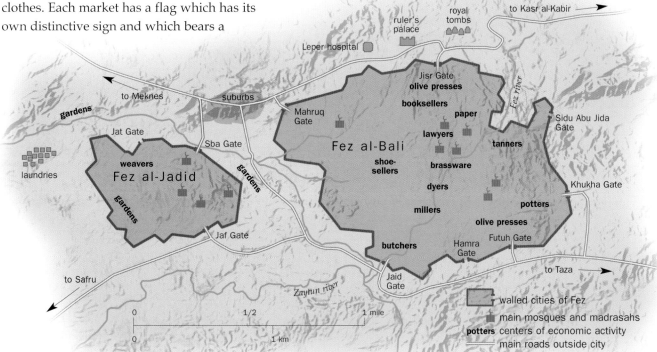

Fez in the 14th–15th centuries

to Kasr al-Kabir

royal tombs

ruler's palace

Leper hospital

Jisr Gate
olive presses

booksellers

to Meknes
suburbs

gardens

Mahruq Gate

paper

Sidu Abu Jida Gate

Jat Gate

lawyers

Fez river

Sba Gate

tanners

gardens

Fez al-Bali

weavers

shoe-sellers

brassware

laundries

Fez al-Jadid

dyers

Khukha Gate

gardens

millers

potters

olive presses

Jaf Gate

butchers

Hamra Gate

Futuh Gate

to Safru

Jaid Gate

to Taza

Zaytun river

0   1/2   1 mile

0   1 km

☐ walled cities of Fez
■ main mosques and madrasahs
potters centers of economic activity
— main roads outside city

Islam on the Defensive

Events took a different course in North Africa from that seen in the Iberian peninsula. The fall of the Muwahhidun was followed by a notable increase in Arab settlement of Morocco, while the north of the country went through another period of fragmentation.

The Marinid dynasty, which ruled most of Morocco after the Muwahhidun, was never as powerful as their predecessors. Further east the Tunisian island of Jerba was occupied by the Sicilians from 1284 to 1335, and the strategic port of Sabta (now Spanish-held Ceuta) fell to a Portuguese surprise attack in 1415. The Marinids were then unable to stop the Portuguese occupying other parts of northern Morocco.

Christian assaults did, however, prompt the development of local religious movements similar to the 11th- and 12th-century Murabitin, whose initial aim was to ransom captives enslaved by the Christians. They then developed into centers of local resistance. This process was also linked to a revival of *sufi* mysticism which led to the veneration of local saints called *marabuts* and the building of *zawia* religious centers, which again served as centers of resistance to Christian attack.

During the second half of the 15th century

Below: Minaret and wall of the abandoned counter-siege of the city of Mansoura, Algeria in 1303–6.

the Wattasids overthrew the last Marinids but were never so widely accepted. Local religious leaders dominated the far north and deep south of Morocco; those in the north claiming descent from the Idrisids, the first independent Islamic dynasty in Morocco, with those in the south joining forces to become the Sa'adian dynasty, which eventually overthrew the last feeble Wattasid ruler in 1549.

HALTING CHRISTIAN EXPANSION

By then there had been a steady influx of Andalusian refugees from Granada into Morocco, greatly strengthening the north's ability to defeat subsequent Christian invasions. Andalusians who settled in Morocco in the late 13th and 14th centuries retained their identity and were reinforced by these later waves of refugees. They continued to enjoy a privileged position, free of the provincial loyalties which divided the local Moroccan tribes.

While the Marinids dominated Morocco, the Hafsids dominated Tunisia and much of what is now Algeria. They had started as a detached fragment of the Muwahhid state as the latter fragmented. The Hafsids continued to maintain Muwahhidun traditions throughout their history.

The power of several Berber tribes in what are now Libya, Tunisia, and Algeria had, however, been seriously undermined by the arrival of the Arab Banu Hilal and Banu Sulaym tribes in the 11th century. The Arab tribes of North Africa also tended to be notably turbulent and difficult to govern.

Between the Hafsids of Tunisia and the Marinids of Morocco lay the territory of a third dynasty, the Ziyanids, based on the town of Tlemsen. Because of their vulnerable position these Ziyanids cultivated an alliance with the Christian kingdom of Aragon in Spain, since both feared the Marinids.

Crossbows became increasingly common in late medieval Morocco, and most crossbow-makers of 15th-century Fez were of Andalusian origin. They were also

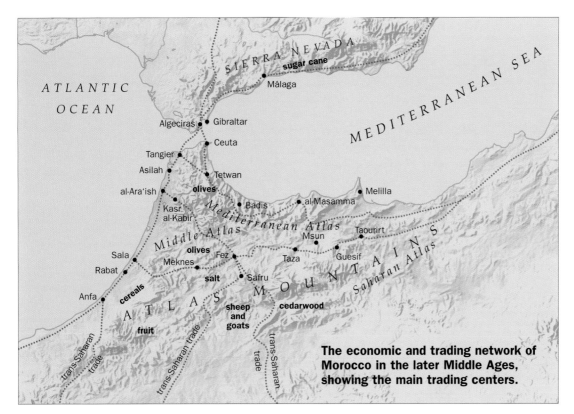

The economic and trading network of Morocco in the later Middle Ages, showing the main trading centers.

Below: The tower Xauen's fortifications stand above the town's market square in Morocco, set against a backdrop of the Atlas Mountains.

renowned for the manufacture of swords and war axes. Leo Africanus, in his highly detailed description of Fez, stated that the craftsmen who made leather scabbards worked in an area close to those making leather horse harnesses, whereas the craftsmen making other weapons were close to the butchers' area.

The 13th century saw a decline in North African naval power, although there was later a small revival in response to Christian piracy. Shipbuilding may also have slumped because in the 14th century Morocco purchased ships from as far away as Egypt. The Hafsids of Tunisia were in a slightly better position, since they had access to the forests of eastern Algeria.

From the late 14th century onward the Hafsid navy became more aggressive, attacking Christian pirate lairs in Sicily, Malta, and elsewhere. Some of these raids were officially sanctioned while others appear to have been individually and religiously motivated.

In 1428 a Portuguese observer provided an interesting description of such Hafsid vessels. Most were galleys of 25–30 rowing benches, although the Hafsid ruler also had seven "great galleys" capable of carrying a hundred horses. They were said to be even larger than the famous Venetian "great galleys." Unfortunately their rigging was not described, though other evidence suggests

that the traditional triangular lateen sail declined in importance from the late 13th century onward, to be progressively replaced by the square-rigged sails that were more suitable for bigger ships.

The Golden Evening

The Nasrid or Banu'l-Ahmar dynasty ruled the last independent bastion of Islamic civilization in the Iberian peninsula from 1232 to 1492. They were as dedicated to culture and the well-being of their people as they were to the defense of their frontiers.

Right: A section of the outer fortified wall of the Alhambra, seen from the Torre del Peinador.

Despite the Nasrid Emirate of Granada's vulnerable position and the overpopulation that resulted from a massive influx of refugees from conquered regions, it was remarkably prosperous in the 14th and 15th centuries. Public order also seems to have been far better than that seen on the Christian side of the frontier, and justice was administered strictly, even harshly. The poor and weak generally benefited from this system, whereas the turbulent Arab-Islamic

Above: Golden evening sunlight illuminates the Alhambra Palace against a background of the Sierra Nevada peaks.

aristocracy had a less stable existence.

The government of Granada established homes for the blind, infirm, or aged, and there were several kinds of hospital according to the physical or mental problems of those afflicted. The ruling emir reportedly visited such establishments to check on their effectiveness, his visits unannounced and without ceremony. Chroniclers also describe several Nasrid rulers as being very keen on education, creating numerous centers of learning where a great variety of subjects were taught.

Another important field of public works, whose results can still be seen in Granada and other towns which once formed part of the Nasrid emirate, was the provision of clean and adequate water supplies. This was, of course, in a very long established Islamic and Andalusian tradition. Fountains, public baths, aqueducts, and small canals criss-crossed town and country, especially in the densely cultivated area of market gardens and orchards which surrounded all Andalusian cities. This maintained the ancient fertility of the valleys and produced abundant crops.

However, much of the best agricultural land was planted with mulberry trees that produced food for silkworms, which in turn brought great wealth to Granada. The emirate rarely if ever seems to have been self-sufficient in food production, especially in grain for bread. Large ships brought vital supplies from Islamic states in North Africa. But once Nasrid naval power declined and the Muslims lost control of the seas between the Mediterranean coast of Andalusia and Morocco, Granada became extremely vulnerable to blockade by the Spanish.

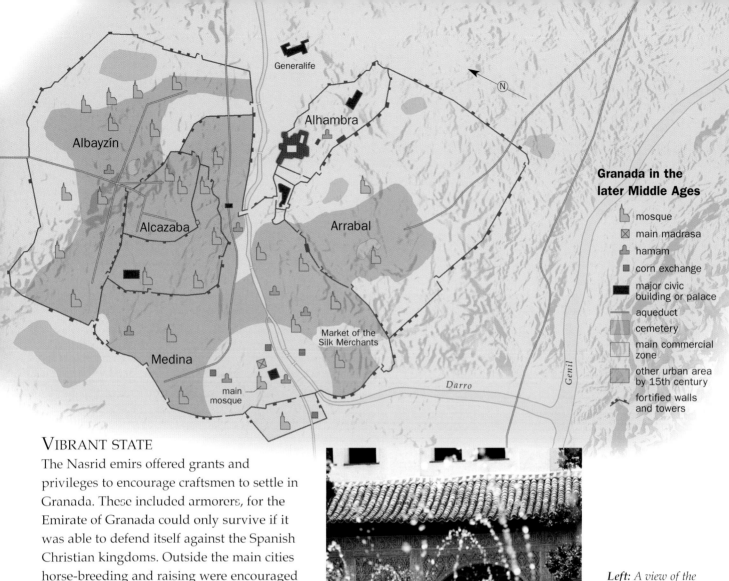

Granada in the
later Middle Ages

- Generalife
- Alhambra
- Albayzín
- Alcazaba
- Arrabal
- Medina
- Market of the Silk Merchants
- main mosque
- Darro
- Genil

mosque
main madrasa
hamam
corn exchange
major civic building or palace
aqueduct
cemetery
main commercial zone
other urban area by 15th century
fortified walls and towers

VIBRANT STATE

The Nasrid emirs offered grants and privileges to encourage craftsmen to settle in Granada. These included armorers, for the Emirate of Granada could only survive if it was able to defend itself against the Spanish Christian kingdoms. Outside the main cities horse-breeding and raising were encouraged for similar reasons. While the production of silk textiles became a major export for Granada, the mining of gold, silver, and other metals was expanded in the mountains.

In the mid-13th century work began on enlarging, strengthening, and beautifying the existing citadel of Granada. This would become the astonishing Alhambra Palace. Here, inside a massively powerful fortress, the traditional Islamic and Andalusian love of gardens and flowing water resulted in an oasis of tranquillity. This continues to amaze modern visitors, despite the changes that have been inflicted over subsequent centuries.

The Alhambra included residential quarters, mosques, baths, and public audience chambers. Its intricate decoration is largely of carved stucco and tiled mosaics, though it also includes several remarkable ceiling and wall-paintings. The former appear to have been created by visiting European artists or by men strongly influenced by European Gothic art, while the latter are entirely within an Islamic artistic

Left: A view of the Generalife water gardens, Granada.

tradition going back to the Abbasid and even Umayyad periods.

Other similar palaces were built elsewhere, including at Málaga, but virtually nothing of these survive. In contrast the astonishing Generalife Gardens on a hill overlooking the Alhambra do still exist. They were originally laid out in the early 14th century and consist of a series of gardens and pavilions fed by streams that run down the hillside.

The Fall of Granada

In 1492 the city of Granada fell to the combined armies of Queen Isabella of Castile and King Ferdinand of Aragon. This marked the end of a nine-year campaign, itself the culmination of a process of Christian conquest that history records, rather misleadingly, as the Reconquista.

The Granada campaign was not entirely one-sided, despite the overwhelming strength of the Christian armies. It was also interrupted by civil wars on the Islamic side, causing political weaknesses that Ferdinand and Isabella used to their advantage.

In 1479 the rival Spanish kingdoms of Castile and Aragon had been united under the rule of Isabella and Ferdinand who had married ten years earlier, before either came to the throne. In 1481 the army of Granada seized the frontier town of Zahara in reprisal for a series of Castilian raids. Other raids and counter-raids followed, the Castilians defeated outside Loja. A palace coup in Granada then replaced Emir Ali Abu'l-Hassan with his son Mohammed XII. He in turn was captured by the Castilians following an unsuccessful Granadan raid and Ali Abu'l-Hassan regained the throne, but the Castilians released his son in the

hope of dividing the loyalties of Granada.

This mixture of military and political maneuvering was typical of the campaign. Although the people of Granada fought hard, by 1485 the western part of the emirate had fallen to the Spaniards. In 1487 Málaga fell, followed two years later by the eastern half of the state. The Islamic Emirate of Granada was now reduced to the city of Granada itself plus some surrounding territory, the rugged Alpujarras mountains to the southeast, and a short length of coast which lacked large harbors.

The last chapter in the history of the last independent Islamic state in the Iberian peninsula was heroic but also tragic. The winter of 1490–91 was quiet, while Ferdinand and Isabella prepared for their final assault.

FINAL STAND

Protests from the Mamluk sultan of Egypt, contrasting the good treatment enjoyed by his Christian subjects with the persecution suffered by Muslims in Spain, were ignored. The sultan did not, however, feel capable of doing anything more, since the Mamluks had recently asked for Spanish naval

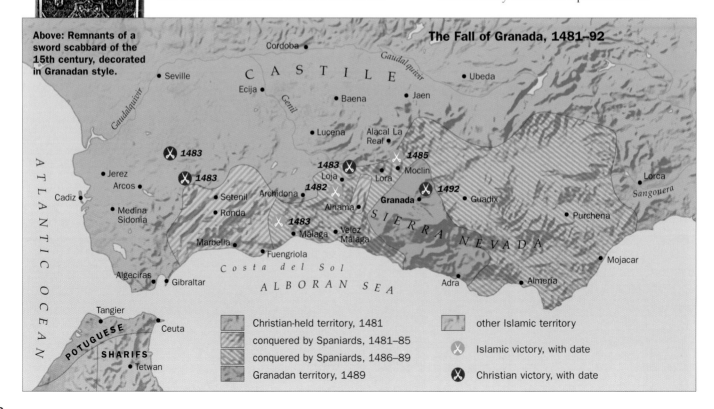

Above: Remnants of a sword scabbard of the 15th century, decorated in Granadan style.

The Fall of Granada, 1481–92

Legend:
- Christian-held territory, 1481
- conquered by Spaniards, 1481–85
- conquered by Spaniards, 1486–89
- Granadan territory, 1489
- other Islamic territory
- ⊗ Islamic victory, with date
- ⊗ Christian victory, with date

support against the Ottoman Turks. The Ottomans were preoccupied with their own campaigns in the Balkans. Mohammed XII's last appeal to the Wattasid ruler of Fez received no reply and the neighboring ruler of Tlemsen in western Algeria had already abandoned Granada in return for trade relations with Spain.

In April 1491 a huge Spanish army entered what remained of Granadan territory and established a camp south of the city. What followed was a protracted siege rather than a great battle. It was punctuated by more active moments and by a series of duels between the cavalry of both sides. These were so often lost by the Spanish champions that Ferdinand banned his knights from accepting further challenges.

The biggest clash came in June 1491 when Isabella requested to see the famous Alhambra Palace, if only from a distance. Ferdinand and a large force escorted her to the village of La Zubia, which had a good

Above and below left: Embroidered coat and helmet of Boabdil, last Moorish ruler of Granada. The name is a Spanish corruption of Abu Abdullah, son of Ali Abu'l Hassan. Proclaimed king in 1482, he was taken prisoner at Lucena in 1483, and only obtained his freedom by consenting to hold Granada in tribute to Ferdinand and Isabella.

Right: An artillery bastion added to the outer defenses of Granada in the late 15th century.

view, but the sight of so many Spanish banners prompted the Granadans to make a major sortie, even dragging some small cannon with them. This time, however, the Muslims were defeated.

Once the Spaniards had built a permanent city called Santa Fé as their siege camp, the fate of Granada was sealed. Furthermore Mohammed XII had now become very unpopular in Granada, especially after the people learned about his supposedly secret surrender negotiations with the enemy. Fear of an uprising in favor of continued resistance by the population of Granada caused the surrender date to be brought forward.

According to legend one of the greatest heroes of the siege, Musa Ibn Abu'l-Gazan, refused to accept the Spaniards' terms and instead rode out of Granada fully armed. He supposedly met a group of Spanish knights near the Genil and killed several before, desperately wounded, he threw himself into the river and disappeared. Sadly this is probably a legend, typical of heroic myths that grow after a terrible defeat to ease the pain of those who have lost.

Moors and Moriscos

Following the Christian conquest of Islamic Spain, Muslims in the country were increasingly marginalized. Most who would not convert to Christianity emigrated, many settling in Morocco.

Right: Orgiva in the Alpujarras mountains was the center of the last Mudejar uprising in Spain against Christian oppression.

Following the conquest of Granada, Mohammed XII, the last Islamic ruler—known as Boabdil to the Spaniards—was given the Alpujarras mountains in the east of what had been the Emirate of Granada. By this means the Castilians and Aragonese hoped that they would not have to conquer the Alpujarras' rugged terrain and fierce inhabitants. However, Boabdil seems to have been unable to accept his new and reduced status, so in 1492 or 1493 he left for Tlemsen in Morocco.

According to some sources Boabdil's wife died and was buried at Mondújar, but the *Life of Cardinal Mendoza* records that Boabdil's wife and children settled in Madrid, where they converted to Christianity. The end of Boabdil's life is similarly clouded, although it seems that he may have been killed at about 80 years of age, fighting for the ruler of Fez against Sharifian rebels at the battle of Abu 'Aqba in 1536.

According to the Spanish chronicler Màrmol; "with him [the ruler of Fez] was Muley [Ali] Abi Abdallah el Zogoibi, king that was of Granada.... In this battle el Zogoibi died, which made a mockery of Fortune, for death struck him as he was defending the kingdom of somebody else when he had not dared defend his own." Apparently some of his descendants were still living on charitable relief in Fez almost a hundred years later.

Other senior Islamic leaders similarly found life under Spanish rule intolerable. Among them was Mohammed XIII, called al-Zagal, who had been a rival ruler of Granada during the civil wars that had weakened the emirate before its final collapse. He sold his estates and left for Algeria in 1490, dying there four years later.

Another legendary account of his fate claims that, after emigrating to North Africa, al-Zagal was blinded by the ruler of Fez and spent the last years of his life as a wandering outcast, wearing a badge that read: "This is the hapless king of Andalusia."

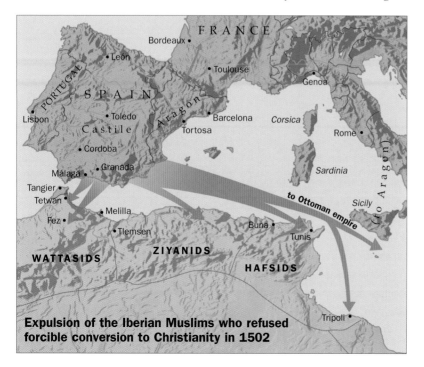

Expulsion of the Iberian Muslims who refused forcible conversion to Christianity in 1502

1405	1412	1415	1416	1437	1444	1453	1461
Tamerlane's empire collapses on his death	Ottomans under Sultan Mehmet I (the Restorer) retake Asia Minor	Portuguese take Sabta (Ceuta) and from there occupy northern Morocco	Venetians destroy a Turkish fleet under Muhammed I at Gallipoli	Ottoman doctor Sinoplu Mumin writes his *Zahire-i Muradiye* medical encyclopedia	Ottomans under Murad II defeat Christians at Varna, Bulgaria	Constantinople falls to the Ottomans under Mehmet II (the Conqueror)	With the loss of Trebizond to the Ottomans, the Byzantine empire ceases to exist

EMIGRATION ENCOURAGED

The previously powerful Banu'l-Sarraj family had moved into the Alpujarra mountains, but in March 1493 almost the whole family emigrated to North Africa, as did so many others. The Spanish ensured that free passage aboard ship was available for any Muslims to leave Andalusia in the three years following Granada's fall. Even later, the costs of such voyages were kept artificially low to encourage people to leave.

Some of those who left Spain found life so hard in North Africa that they returned. Among those who endured the difficulties and made a new life in Morocco was a Granadan military leader named Abd al-Hasan Ali al-Manzari. He arrived with a small number of followers to repopulate the town of Tetwan, which had been demolished by Portuguese invaders. It was rebuilt and became a major center for Andalusian refugees, as well as for resistance to Portuguese and Spanish invasion.

Refugees continued to leave what had been the Emirate of Granada during the early 16th century. These people spoke Spanish and often had knowledge of advanced European military techniques. Handgunners were especially welcomed and in Morocco they became part of a new Jaysh al-Nar or "Fire Army." Peaceful farmers were similarly encouraged to settle in the fertile regions of northern Morocco.

Those Muslims who remained generally had to live outside the walls of the main cities, as had been the case following the dramatic Christian conquests of the 13th century. Once again it tended to be the ordinary people and the poor who stayed, and at first the new Christian Archbishop of Granada tried to encourage conversion to Christianity by tactful means. He made a clear distinction between Islamic beliefs, which were not considered acceptable, and Moorish social customs, which were. He also prevented the Spanish Inquisition from operating in Granada.

Unfortunately, four years after the

conquest this policy was changed by Cardinal Cisneros, and the religious intolerance that was becoming characteristic of Spain now spread to Granada. This was followed by savage oppression, which in turn resulted in revolts, and in 1502 the Mudejars or Muslims of Castile and León were forced to convert to Christianity or leave the country. Even then the tragedy was not over.

The Moriscos or Moors who had converted to Christianity but retained various Arab-Andalusian social customs were declared to be false Christians, who were said to practice Islam in secret. Between 1609 and 1614 mass expulsion of these Moriscos finally brought the story of Andalusian Islam to an end. Elsewhere beyond the confines of western Europe, Islam would continue to spread and flourish to the modern day.

Above: A fragment of a wall-painting in the Church of Vera Cruz, Segovia, Spain depicts a converted Moor praying to the Virgin Mary.

1464	1475	1478	1487	1492	1499	c.1500	1502
With King Sunni Ali's expansion campaign, the Songhay empire begins	Ottomans conquer Crimea on the Black Sea coast	The Portuguese have control of the west coast of Africa	A Mamluk army manages to defeat Ottoman invaders in the frontier province of Cilicia	Fall of the Nasrid dynasty of Granada to the Christian Spaniards; end of the Reconquista	Turks defeat the Venetians at Lepanto, seizing Aegean and Ionian territories	Soba, the capital of Alwa, is taken by the Islamic Funj of Africa	Mudejars in Spain are forced to convert to Christianity or leave the country

Further reading

The following list only includes books in European languages, plus Turkish.

Ahmad, A., *A History of Islamic Sicily* (Edinburgh 1975).

Ahsan, M.M., *Social Life under the Abbasids, 170–289 AH, 786–902 AD* (London 1979).

Alexander, D. (ed.), *Furusiyya: Volume I, The Horse in the Art of the Near East* (Riyadh 1996).

Allan, J.W., *Persian Metal Technology 700-1300 AD* (London 1979).

Arberry, A.J. (ed.), *The Legacy of Persia* (Oxford 1953).

Baker, P.L., *Islamic Textiles* (London 1995).

Bianquis, T., *Damas et la Syrie sous la Domination Fatimide* (Damascus 1986).

Bosworth, C.E., *The New Islamic Dynasties* (Edinburgh 1996).

Brett, M., & W. Forman, *The Moors: Islam in the West* (London 1980).

Brice, W.C. (ed.), *An Historical Atlas of Islam* (Leiden 1981).

Campi, J.M., & F. Sabaté, *Atlas de la "Reconquista," La frontera peninsular entre los siglos VIII y XV* (Barcelona 1998).

Creswell, K.A.C., *A Short Account of Early Muslim Architecture* (London 1958).

Elbeheiry, S., *Les Institutions de l'Égypte au Temps des Ayyubides* (Lille 1972).

Elisséef, N., *Nur al-Din, un Grand Prince Musulman de Syria au Temps des Croisades* (Damascus 1967).

Ettinghausen, R., & O. Grabar, *The Art and Architecture of Islam 650–1250* (London 1987).

Facey, W. (ed.), *Oman, a seafaring nation* (Muscat 1979).

Fahmy, A.M., *Muslim Sea-Power in the Eastern Mediterranean from the Seventh to the Tenth Century AD* (Cairo 1966).

Frye, R.N., *The Golden Age of Persia: The Arabs in the East* (London 1993).

Gabrieli, F., *Muhammad and the Conquests of Islam* (London 1968).

Glubb., J., *Soldiers of Fortune, The Story of the Mamlukes* (New York 1973).

Grousset, R., *The Empire of the Steppes, a History of Central Asia* (New Brunswick 1970).

Grube, E.J., *The World of Islam* (London 1966).

Guthrie, S., *Arab Social Life in the Middle Ages* (London 1995).

Hassan, A.Y. al-, & D.R.Hill, *Islamic Technology, An illustrated history* (Cambridge 1986).

Hillenbrand, C., *The Crusades; Islamic Perspectives* (Edinburgh 1999).

Hourani, A.H., & S.M. Stern (eds.), *The Islamic City* (Oxford 1970).

Irwin, R., *The Arabian Nights, A Companion* (London 1994).

Irwin, R., *The Middle East in the Middle Ages: The early Mamluk Sultanate 1250-1382* (London 1986).

Jandora, J.W., *Militarism in Arab Society: An Historical and Bibliographical Sourcebook* (Westport 1997).

Koçu, R.E., *Yeniçeriler* (The Janissaries) (Istanbul 1964).

Kretschmar, M., *Pferd und Reiter im Orient* (Hildesheim 1980).

Lane, E.W., *Arabian Society in the Middle Ages* (London 1883, reprinted London 1971).

Lévi-Provençal, E., *Histoire de l'Espagne Musulmane*, three vols. (Paris 1950-67).

Lewis, B. (ed.), *The World of Islam* (London 1976).

Lings, M., *Muhammad, his life based on the earliest sources* (London 1983).

Lyons, M.C.,, & D.E.P. Jackson, *Saladin, The Politics of the Holy War* (Cambridge 1982).

Michell, G. (ed.), *Architecture of the Islamic World, its historical and social meaning* (London 1978).

Montgomery Watt, W., *The Majesty that was Islam* (London 1975).

Nasr, S.H., *Islamic Science, An Illustrated Study* (London 1976).

Nicolle, D., *Medieval Warfare Source Book, Volume 2: Christian Europe and its Neighbours* (London 1996).

Patton, D., *Badr al-Din Lu'lu, Atabeg of Mosul, 1211–1259* (Seattle 1991).

Pitcher, D.E., *An Historical Geography of the Ottoman Empire* (Leiden 1972).

Pryor, J.H., *Geography, Technology and War, Studies in the Maritime History of the Mediterranean 649-1571* (Cambridge 1988).

Roolvink, R., *Historical Atlas of the Muslim Peoples* (Amsterdam n.d.).

Salahi, A., *Muhammad, Man and Prophet* (Leicester 1995).

Saleh, K. al-, *Fabled Cities, Princes & Jinn from Arab Myths and Legends* (London 1985).

Salibi, K.S., *Syria under Islam, Empire on Trial 634–1097* (New York 1977).

Schacht, J., & C.E. Bosworth (eds.), *The Legacy of Islam* (Oxford 1974).

Shaw, S.J., *History of the Ottoman Empire and Modern Turkey, Volume 1: Empire of the Gazis: The rise and Decline of the Ottoman Empire, 1280–1808* (Cambridge 1976).

Sordo, E., *Moorish Spain* (London 1963).

Talbot Rice, D., *Islamic Art* (London 1965).

Talbot Rice, T., *The Seljuks in Asia Minor* (London 1961).

Valeev, F.K., & G.F. Valeeva-Sultanova, *Drevnee Iskusstvo Tatarstana* (The Old Art of Tatarstan) (Kazan 2002).

Museums

Austria
Vienna: Kunsthistorisches Museum; Nationalbibliothek.
Egypt
Cairo: Museum of Arab and Islamic Art; National Library.
France
Paris: Bibliothéque Nationale; Musée du Louvre.
Germany
Berlin: Museum für Islamische Kunst in the Staatliche Museum Dahlem; Islamische Museum on the Museum Insel.
Iran
Tehran: Islamic Museum in the grounds of the Archaeological Museum; Reza Abbasi Museum.
Iraq
Baghdad: National Archaeological Museum.
Israel
Jerusalem (Israeli occupied East Jerusalem): Rockefeller Museum.
Italy
Bologna: Museo Civico Medievale.
Milan: Biblioteca Ambrosiana.
Naples: Museo di Palazzo di Capidimonte.
Rome: Instituto di Studi sul Medeo Oriente, Museo; Biblioteca Apostolica Vaticana.
Liechtenstein
Vaduz: Furusiyya Art Foundation.
Russia
St. Petersburg: Oriental Institute Library; State Hermitage Museum.
Spain
Cordoba: Medina Azahara Site Museum.
Madrid: Museo Arqueológico Nacional; Museo del Ejército.
Syria
Damascus: National Museum.
Tunisia
Ruqada: Museum of Islamic Studies
Tunis: Bardo Museum.
Turkey
Ankara: Archaeological Museum.
Bodrum: Castle Museum.
Istanbul: Askeri Museum; Millet Library; Museum of Turkish and Islamic Art; Suleymaniye Library; Topkapi Library & Topkapi Museum.
Konya: Ince Minare Seljuk Museum; Karatay Medresse Ceramics Museum; Mevlana Museum.
UK
London: British Library; British Museum; Victoria & Albert Museum.
Oxford: Ashmolean Museum; Bodleian Library.
USA
Baltimore: Walters Art Gallery.
Boston: Fogg Art Museum; Museum of Fine Arts.
Cincinnati: Museum of Art.
Cleveland: Museum of Art.
Detroit: Art Institute.
New York: Brooklyn Museum; Metropolitan Museum of Art; Pierpont Morgan Library.
Washington: Freer Gallery of Art; Textiles Museum.

Index